Corporate Messiah

Corporate Messiah

The Hiring and Firing of Million-Dollar Managers

Patricia O'Toole

WILLIAM MORROW AND COMPANY, INC.

NEW YORK | 1984

Library of Congress Catalog Card Number: 83-83019

ISBN: 0-688-03110-2

Printed in the United States of America

3   4   5   6   7   8   9   10

BOOK DESIGN BY ELLEN LO GIUDICE

To Judith Daniels
A wonderful editor, and the one who
gave me my first big break

Contents

Chapter 1

Corporate Messiah

AN OPEN CHECKBOOK lay on the table between the two men. "Write in any salary you want," the older man said.

"You can't afford me," the younger man said.

"Go ahead. Put down anything you want."

Thinking it was all a game and that the older man would call it off when he tired of it, the younger man wrote in a figure: $1 million. Enough money so that even if he spent $1,000 a day, it would take almost three years to run through it. The older man didn't flinch, so the younger man kept the game alive. He made a list that included maids, chauffeurs, cars, apartments, country club memberships—frills worth an extra $250,000 a year. He stopped when he couldn't think of anything else he wanted.

"It's yours," the older man said.

The younger man was sorely tempted, but he held back. Not because he worried about taking advantage of the older man but because he feared that the two of them wouldn't be able to work together. The older man was Carl Rosen, the craggy, outspoken chairman of Puritan Fashions Corporation of New York. He promised to stay out of the younger man's way, pointing out that he was

9

going to retire soon. "I'm sixty-two years old," he had said. "I need you to run the business." But the younger man, president Warren Hirsh of Murjani International, was not sure the arrangement would work. As Hirsh saw it, the two of them would butt heads constantly. He didn't like being Number Two, and neither did Rosen. Rosen said he understood and invited Hirsh to spell out the authority he wanted in his contract. Then, urging Hirsh to think over the offer, he left.

There was a lot to think over. At forty-eight, Warren Hirsh was one of the sultans of Seventh Avenue, running a $200-million-a-year business he had built almost single-handedly. In 1977, he had been inspired to add status to that most proletarian of garments, the blue jean, by embroidering the hip pockets with the aristocratic scrawl of Gloria Vanderbilt. Overnight, thanks to television commercials run during the 1978 Academy Awards show, Vanderbilt jeans became a must-have for hundreds of thousands of women.

The Murjani family rewarded Hirsh with salaries of well over $500,000 a year but denied him the prize he really wanted: a piece of the business. In 1980, they told him they would like to make him a partner but couldn't because of the way the company was structured. Although Hirsh had no plans to leave Murjani, his disappointment made him weigh Carl Rosen's offer more carefully than he would have if Murjani had come through.

Rosen's courtship had begun on June 21, 1980, at a dinner in Hirsh's honor at the Waldorf-Astoria. Hirsh had been named man of the year by the Israeli Bond Committee, and Rosen had come to join in the tribute. At a cocktail party before the dinner, Rosen suggested that he and Hirsh get together for lunch. Two weeks later they did, at Le Cirque, a posh Manhattan restaurant high on Rosen's list of places to do business. It was in Hirsh's office after lunch that Rosen took out his checkbook.

Hirsh thought about Rosen's offer for several days. He was tempted, but an old memory nagged at him. Hirsh had worked for Rosen once before—so long ago Rosen had forgotten. But Hirsh vividly remembered an evening at the Eden Roc Hotel in Miami Beach. Rosen was throwing a party, and Hirsh arrived two hours late because of a meeting with a customer. Rosen took note of the junior salesman's tardiness and bellowed at him from across the room. An offended Hirsh marched up to his boss and replied in kind. Caught off-balance, Rosen had little choice but to throw an arm around Hirsh and stoutly declare that he liked a man who stood up to him.

Mulling over Rosen's million-dollar offer, Hirsh decided to put the memory aside. Whatever dangers he might face when he ventured into Carl Rosen's kingdom were preferable to the certainty that he would never own part of Murjani. He told Murjani he was leaving. They had a surprising response: If Hirsh would stay, a partnership might be worked out after all. Too late, Hirsh said. He, his secretary, his son, and his brother were going to Puritan.

That was a double blow to Murjani. Not only was the company losing its locomotive, but also Hirsh was defecting to the archrival. Puritan Fashions held the license to market Calvin Klein jeans, the line that posed the biggest threat to Gloria Vanderbilt's place as the best-selling status jean. The Klein jeans, selling at the rate of $65 million a year, lagged far behind Vanderbilt's yearly take of $200 million, but if anyone could narrow the gap, it was Warren Hirsh. In hiring the Israeli Bond Committee's man of the year, Carl Rosen had pulled off the fashion industry's coup of the year.

"Make no mistake about it," Rosen told *Women's Wear Daily* on July 21, the day he announced Hirsh's appointment as president. "The future of the company is in Warren's hands. At the proper time he will succeed me as chief executive officer."

Murjani lost no time in downplaying Hirsh's role in the company's success. A breath of fresh air was just what was needed, Murjani said. The company wasn't going to be a "one-man show" anymore.

TEN DAYS after Hirsh's appointment, Puritan reported its earnings for the second quarter of 1980. Profits were down 93.7 percent from the year before, but no one was particularly alarmed. It was all part of Rosen's corporate remodeling. He was putting an end to Puritan's history as a manufacturer of inexpensive dresses for what the rag trade called "the masses with fat asses." Henceforth, Rosen had decreed, Puritan would make nothing but clothes designed by the likes of Diane Von Furstenberg and Calvin Klein. With their higher price tags, the designer wear had the potential to turn Puritan into one of the most profitable operations on Seventh Avenue. The marketing audacity of Warren Hirsh, who had unabashedly tried to get Jacqueline Onassis to sign her name to Murjani's jeans before he settled for Gloria Vanderbilt, would speed up the transformation.

In his first weeks on the job, Hirsh tangled with Rosen from time to time, but the energetic new president felt secure in his position. "I took charge very quickly," he said. "Carl might not have liked certain things I was doing, but there wasn't much he could do about it because my authority was spelled out in my contract." Apart from the power it conferred, the contract would have done a baseball player proud—it guaranteed Hirsh $7.5 million over a five-year period.

But less than two months after Hirsh became president, five-year contract notwithstanding, *People* magazine detected intimations of mortality in Warren Hirsh's new career. Hirsh told *People* he would leave Puritan if Rosen "ruffled his feathers"—a remark suggesting that a little feather-ruffling had been going on. Indeed it had, and Hirsh wasn't just on the receiving end. A *New York Daily News* reporter had called to ask his opinion of the new Calvin Klein TV commercials that featured teenage siren Brooke Shields wearing jeans tighter than sausage skins. Hirsh told the reporter he wondered whether viewers would be offended by the south-of-the-waistline close-up of Miss Shields and by her sultry delivery of a line that could only be classified as a single entendre: "There's nothing that comes between me and my Calvins."

The day after the interview, while Hirsh was at a meeting away from the office, Rosen phoned to tell him to hightail it to Puritan. Hirsh said he'd be there in an hour and a half. Rosen told him he'd better come immediately because Calvin Klein and his business manager, Barry Schwartz, were furious about the story in the *Daily News*. Hirsh hadn't seen it yet. Rosen began reading it over the phone, starting with the headline: "Warren Hirsh to Drop Calvin Klein Commercials." That went far beyond the opinions Hirsh had ventured in his interview, and he tried to explain. Rosen didn't want explanations, he wanted Warren Hirsh in his office—right now—to face the wrath of Klein and Schwartz. "I don't work for them," Hirsh said. "I'll see you in an hour and a half."

Ninety minutes later, he arrived. "The meeting lasted thirty seconds," Hirsh recalls. "Calvin and Barry said they couldn't work with me. That was it."

As soon as Hirsh and Rosen were alone, Rosen expressed his concern over whether the problems could be worked out.

"I don't have any problems," Hirsh said. "I have a five-year contract."

Rosen did have a problem. Hirsh might have thought he didn't work for Calvin Klein, but he was wrong. Everyone at Puritan worked for Calvin. Calvin's jeans accounted for almost half of Puritan's revenues, and they had carried the company from a $6 million net loss in 1978 to a $6 million gain a year later. On top of that, Klein and Schwartz owned a sizable chunk of Puritan stock—about 4 percent. Rosen wasn't about to let anything come between him and his Calvin.

Klein has refused to discuss his ire but is said to have resented Hirsh's tampering with the image-making efforts of Calvin Klein Ltd. Intimately involved in the promotion of his products, Klein thought about his ads as intently as he thought about his clothes; both were the way they were because that's how he wanted them to be. He saw nothing tawdry in the combination of pubescence and sensuality. To him the commercials were things of beauty and conveyed a sense of female independence so strong that he and his colleagues referred to the Brooke Shields ad as "The Feminist."

The rift over the commercials wasn't the first dustup between Klein and Hirsh. A few weeks earlier, the two had had a disagreement over rock star Elton John. Before Hirsh left Murjani, John had been scheduled to give a concert in Central Park under Murjani's sponsorship. When Hirsh went to Puritan, Calvin Klein became the sponsor of the event. Hirsh took credit for the arrangements, but Klein insisted that Elton John's manager had contacted Klein, not Hirsh, about the switch. Such details are nothing but the flotsam of the cosmos, but Klein may have been concerned that this was just the beginning of Hirsh's interference.

Like Rosen, Klein hadn't anticipated any difficulties with the new Puritan president. Asked at a party for Hirsh whether he foresaw any friction between his own low-key style and the flash that was Hirsh's trademark, Klein had said, "I feel great, ecstatic. I'm not concerned at all. Certainly he's done a great job with the competition."

The problem lay in reaching an agreement on what constituted "a great job." To Klein, the phrase meant getting his jeans into as many stores as Gloria Vanderbilt was in. Murjani's marketing system was much superior to Puritan's, and Klein felt that a similar system for Puritan was the quickest road to big sales. But Hirsh's idea of doing a great job meant running the whole show, and marketing was part of that. "I didn't know how influential Calvin was at Puritan," Hirsh says. "I assumed he would have a major say in determining product. Since he's a terrific designer, I would have had great respect for the contributions he could make to developing our products. But I had no idea how much clout he had in the operation of the whole company."

In the end, Calvin's muscle counted more than Hirsh's contract. Only eight weeks after Hirsh had started his new job, a limousine pulled up to Puritan's headquarters at 1400 Broadway and waited while cartons full of Hirsh's belongings were brought down from his office. For two days Hirsh's lawyers haggled with Puritan's lawyers over the price for buying out his contract. They settled on the same figure Hirsh had written in Rosen's checkbook: $1 million.

A MILLION DOLLARS for eight weeks' work. To Hirsh that was a windfall and a way out of a job he now knew he shouldn't have taken. To Rosen, the whole affair was an expensive mistake at a time when Puritan couldn't afford it. The company's losses for the year would come to $3.4 million.

It would be easy to relegate Warren Hirsh's experience to the footnotes of business history. As a corporation, Puritan is insignificant enough that even though its stock is publicly traded, securities analysts don't bother to follow it. And since the fashion business is renowned for its egomania, what happened to Hirsh could be written off as the sort of thing that goes on in creative madhouses but not the "real" business world. But during the late 1970s and early 1980s, rapid hiring and firing at the top—along with million-dollar compensation contracts—spread to even the staidest of industries. Between 1976 and 1982, the annual firing and retirement rates of corporate presidents and chairmen more than doubled. From electronics to office equipment, from conglomerates to oil companies, from transportation to farm equipment—top executives in all these industries have been taken on or let go with unprecedented speed. And when they left, their replacements were much more likely to come from outside the company. Figures collected by Heidrick and Struggles, a Chicago-based executive recruiting firm, show that during the second half of the 1970s, outsiders filled about 40 percent more vacancies than they did in the first half.

Why had the revolving door begun to spin so fast? For American business, the late seventies and early eighties were the years of living dangerously. The old industrial economy began to disintegrate, but whatever would take its place—some sort of economy based on services and high technology—was not sufficiently developed to prevent the jolt. Across the country, blast furnaces went out, assembly lines stopped, factory gates were locked, and eleven million workers lost their jobs.

No sooner had corporate managements learned how to live with high interest rates and high inflation than they were forced to do business in an even more trying climate: one with high interest rates and almost no inflation. Financing growth with borrowed money had made sense when inflation helped revenues grow fast enough to offset the cost of borrowing. But when the balloon popped, corporations that had borrowed money at high rates were left with no easy way to repay the loans. As one observer summed it up, "Many companies failed to realize that when they authorized the issue of a 20-year bond with 16% coupons, they were promising their shareholders that they could raise their revenues by 16% every year for the next 20 years." The remedy—dumping the ventures financed with high-interest loans—was sometimes more painful than the ailment, so companies often decided to tough it out until the economy improved. Alas, the economy not only failed to cooperate, it kept deteriorating until it hit the lowest point in fifty years. By 1983, when things finally did begin to turn around, high debt costs had put many a venerable American corporation on the casualty list.

For twenty years or more, economists, futurists, and countless other -ists had talked about the coming of a global marketplace, so its blossoming in the late seventies was no great surprise. But hardly anyone foresaw the great wrench this development would cause in the United States. Overnight, the Japanese were manufacturing cheaper (and, many said, better) automobiles, televisions, steel, chemicals, and more. In less than a decade, Japanese cars rose from a mere 2 percent of the American market to more than 20 percent. More and more investment capital began flowing around the globe, to countries that could produce goods for less money than American industry could. Steel mills sprang up in South Korea and Brazil. High-tech manufacturers, including American ones, took their assembly operations to the cheap labor of Hong Kong and Taiwan. Even U.S. farmers, the most productive in the world, found themselves locked out of foreign markets by the agricultural policies of other nations, which subsidized their own farmers and made American crops too expensive.

U.S. preeminence in international affairs also exacerbated the position of American business in world markets. The arrival of the global marketplace meant that a single untoward political event could have multimillion-dollar repercussions for dozens of American businesses. After the 1980 Soviet invasion of Afghanistan, for example, NBC lost untold millions in advertising revenues because the United States decided not to participate in the Moscow Olympics, which NBC had planned to broadcast. The U.S. grain embargo intended to punish the Soviets for the invasion ended up hurting U.S. farmers and agricultural-equipment makers like International Harvester more than the Soviets, who simply did their grain shopping elsewhere. And the future of a $20 billion agreement between the U.S.S.R. and Occidental Petroleum was made so uncertain by U.S. economic sanctions that Occidental chairman Armand Hammer took to his jet and shuttled from one Eastern Bloc capital to another in the hope of salvaging the deal. For better or worse, the U.S. economy in the late seventies and early eighties became irrevocably woven into the world economy. Global interdependency was here to stay.

On a less cosmic scale, turnover at the top picked up speed because a generation of entrepreneurial titans reached retirement age. For men such as Hammer, William Paley of CBS, and Harold Geneen of ITT—builders of multibillion-dollar empires—it was time to step down. But with few exceptions, they could not bring themselves to hand over the scepter, and one crown prince after another was forced into exile.

The confusions and strains caused by the sudden collapse of the U.S. industrial economy, the equally sudden rise of the global market, inflation, recession, and high interest rates left many corporate managements feeling that the world was out of control. Not knowing how to adapt to an environment in which change was the only constant, most corporations focused their energies on increasing—or regaining—control over their businesses. For the most part, control meant control over numbers, especially the sacred bottom line. Management by the numbers became the strategy for survival, and numbers experts were running more corporations than ever before. Bottom lines were fattened by cutting costs, changing accounting procedures, and shifting assets to make the most of corporate tax laws—moves that added little productive value to the enterprise but did create the illusion of higher profits.

At many troubled companies, another illusion took hold: the belief that salvation lay in the hands of supremely capable executives, if only they could be found and hired. The quest for these corporate messiahs played itself out differently in different companies, but in simplified form, the reasoning went like this: "We've botched it and we need help. Only an outsider can set things right because all of us on the inside have had a hand in causing the problems. Since it will take an extraordinary leader to save us, we're going to have to pay an extraordinary amount to get him to take on this impossible task."

More often than not, the corporate messiah's task *did* prove impossible—but not because the company was beyond redemption. A bigger problem was that the million-dollar compensation contract used to lure a savior set up such unrealistically high hopes for a quick miracle that the savior usually was doomed from the start. As soon as he proved unable to walk on water, his days were numbered.

The situation is fraught with other perils as well. At the top, most executive searches are carried out in secret. Corporate boards want to conceal the fact that they are looking outside for a new president or chairman lest their competitors and Wall Street conclude that the present management is weak. In addition, there is often a need to conceal the search from their own senior executives, whom they have decided to pass over for the job.

On the other side of the transaction, the candidate wants to keep the matter confidential so his current employer won't find out he's considering another job. And although a corporation can guard its anonymity by using an executive search firm to delve discreetly into a candidate's background, the candidate is less well positioned to get the inside story on his corporate suitor. He has to be careful not to give himself away, and his best sources of information—other executives in the company—are usually off limits.

A company in need of a messiah is also a company in a hurry. Eager to find a hero, the search committee often puts more energy into persuading the candidate to take the job than into considering how well he will mesh with the company. Because of the need for secrecy, interviews and meetings typically take place away from the office, in restaurants or other social settings. If the candidate's professional credentials are in order, a little charm and goodwill on his part go a long way toward convincing the company there is no need to look farther.

The cost and complexity of a first-class search for a new president or chairman also reinforce the belief that the corporation really is getting a messiah. At large companies, the fee paid to the search firm runs to several hundred thousand dollars. Lawyers and compensation consultants are engaged at great expense to come up with contracts that candidates will find irresistible. A corporate director may be retained at a six-figure sum to oversee the search. Intelligence on the best and brightest is gathered through impressive webs of contacts. No stone is left unturned, no avenue unexplored. All of this plus the secrecy, the size of the messiah's paycheck, and the need for swift change create enormous expectations. As executive recruiter David S. Joys told *The New York Times Magazine*, "The thinking becomes, 'We've scoured the country.

We've chosen this guy from dozens. He must be Superman.' And when he isn't, things can go sour very quickly."

But that is getting ahead of the story. Before things go sour—and sometimes even afterward—the life of a corporate messiah can be very sweet. Very sweet indeed.

Chapter 2

Mad Money

Executive Compensation

WAS IT MADNESS to pay Warren Hirsh $1 million for eight weeks as president of Puritan Fashions? His lawyers would say it wasn't; Hirsh's contract entitled him to the money. Puritan's chairman, Carl Rosen, could plausibly argue that his plan to pay Hirsh a million dollars a year was a smart one: Hirsh's track record with Vanderbilt jeans gave Rosen every reason to expect that Hirsh would provide a hefty return on the investment.

But $1 million for eight weeks' work comes to $125,000 a week—seven and a half times more than the median annual income of the full-time American worker. United Auto Workers members on Detroit assembly lines, whose wages have been blamed for everything from inflation to the nation's inability to compete with carmakers in Japan, earn less in a year than Hirsh made in a single day.

Hirsh's experience catches the eye because it is so out of the ordinary, but the ranks of million-dollar managers in American business are not exactly thin. A 1983 *Forbes* magazine tally of 800 chief executives' pay, including their gains on company stock, showed that 114 of them earned at least $1 million in 1982; 18 of these earned more than $2 million. The top ten ran from $2.5 million for Harrington Drake of Dun & Bradstreet to $51.5 million for Frederick W. Smith of Federal Express.

Millionaires. In the popular mind they have always been entrepreneurs—robber barons such as Vanderbilt and Gould, and wheeler-dealers in the Howard Hughes mold. Although America's corporate chieftains have never lived in poverty, in the past they generally had to make do with substantially less than did successful entrepreneurs. The businesses they were entrusted to manage, after all, belonged not to them but to the company's shareholders. Since 1932, when Eugene Grace hauled in more than $1.6 million for a year's work, million-dollar managers have popped up here and there, but it wasn't until 1974 that executive paychecks began putting on weight.

The turning point came when Revlon hired Michel Bergerac as president, luring him away from his job as president of the European operations of International Telephone and Telegraph Corporation. Revlon before Bergerac had been ruled by its founder, Charles Revson, whose management style ran a short gamut from brutal to savage. He thought nothing of calling employees at home at two in the morning for long discussions, and it has been said that he "chewed up executives the way some people chew vitamins." One of Revson's convictions: "Creative people are like a wet towel. You wring them out and pick up another one." Vice-presidents quit or were sent packing so often that the revolving door never stopped.

Knowing that his days at Revlon could be numbered, Bergerac wrote himself a contract that would cushion any fall from grace: a guarantee of $325,000 a year for five years, generous stock options, and, best of all, a no-strings-attached bonus of $1.5 million simply for signing on. The total price tag came to $4.5 million. Under the terms of the deal, it was conceivable that Bergerac could have come to work at nine on Monday morning, been fired at ten, and walked out the door with the full $4.5 million.

It didn't work out that way. Revson, ill with cancer when he hired Bergerac, died in 1975. Bergerac still heads Revlon, and by 1982 his annual paycheck had swelled to $1,125,000.

In the years since Bergerac blazed the trail, the stakes of the executive pay game have risen higher and higher, and the game itself has grown increasingly complicated. The accounting firm of Peat, Marwick, Mitchell & Co. estimated that in 1980, the typical chief operating officer of a manufacturer with annual sales of $1.5 billion earned a base salary of $300,000, an annual bonus of $150,000 to $300,000 depending on the company's earnings, an assortment of stock options, a pension plan geared to provide 65 percent of the executive's salary and bonus during the last five years with the company, life insurance worth $900,000, a souped-up health insurance plan, and a bouquet of perquisites that usually includes a car, memberships in a luncheon club and a country club, and access to professional help with taxes and personal financial planning.

When the chief comes from another company (as Bergerac did and as most corporate messiahs do), he generally is given a bonus of at least a year's salary to make up for benefits lost in leaving his old firm. Sometimes, when taking the job involves great personal risk, this front-end bonus is significantly higher. Thomas H. Wyman came to CBS from Pillsbury in 1980 as the fifth CBS president in nine years. With Bergerac's precedent, Wyman landed a $1 million bonus for coming aboard.

Xerox president Archie R. McCardell also got $1.5 million just for signing with ailing International Harvester in 1977. In addition, the company loaned him $1.8 million so he could buy Harvester stock. The most attractive feature of the loan was that if he met certain profit goals over the next seven years, he wouldn't have to pay back a dime.

Are these executives worth what they're paid? Defenders of the system argue that they are, especially when a big slice of the pie is a reward for having increased the company's earnings. Compensation experts and executive recruiters say that $1 million dangled before a company president will drive him to do everything he can to see that the corporation meets financial goals like higher earnings and a better return on investment. "People work for money," declares one executive compensation specialist. "Money is the only tangible, objective measure of business achievement. Talk is cheap and titles often are meaningless, but cash compensation—in exchange for performance, not promises—can buy substantial incremental profits."

Until the U.S. auto industry began taking a beating from foreign car manufacturers, the generous bonuses paid by General Motors were often cited as proof that big incentives paid to executives produced bigger and bigger profits. The belief that only enormous paychecks had the power to generate strong corporate earnings was so sacrosanct that critics excoriated General Motors when it decided to help the government fight inflation by holding down executive raises in 1978. "Incentive will dwindle," *Barron's* said in an editorial. "Efficiency will suffer." Arguing that the move was "good for neither General Motors nor the country," *Barron's* darkly forecast that GM and fellow traitors like American Telephone & Telegraph Company would be "locked into paying their best people—if they stay—increasingly less than they're worth."

So it seems that million-dollar paychecks provide two incentives: They give executives a reason to perform and a reason to stay with their companies. At least one chief executive, chairman David J. Mahoney of Norton Simon Incorporated, would have the world believe that his annual compensation of well over a million dollars ($2,996,036 in 1982) is justified by the performance he turns in year after year. He once pointed out in an interview that after thirty years in the business world, his personal worth came to a mere $20 million, which he found rather pale next to the $50 million to $500 million amassed by eighty-three entrepreneurs he'd read about in *Fortune* a few years before.

The entrepreneurial argument is also invoked in defense of the $7.8 million that Mesa Petroleum of Amarillo, Texas, paid to T. Boone Pickens, Jr., in 1980. In 1979, shareholders granted Pickens an option to purchase 1.5 million shares of the company's common stock as what Mesa directors called "a special incentive" to persuade him "to remain active on a full-time basis . . . for an extended period." After the options were granted, Mesa's stock split two for one—twice—which left Pickens with the right to buy 6 million shares at $11.50 each instead of the original 1.5 million shares at $46 each. By the spring of 1981, the price of Mesa's stock had risen enough to make Pickens' options worth almost $180 million, or about $110 million more than he'd have to pay for them.

Two angry stockholders sued to nullify the options on the grounds that such compensation is excessive, but fans of Pickens say he's worth every penny. One securities analyst believes that "Mesa Petroleum is 100 percent Boone Pickens." Others point to the fact that Pickens was among the first to understand the potential of offshore drilling, and they cite his prescience in dumping the company's Canadian properties before Canada put stiff price controls on foreign natural gas producers. Finally, with Pickens at the reins, Mesa's earnings almost tripled between 1975 and 1980.

Although stockholder suits on executive compensation

issues are rare, and stockholder victories rarer still, the plaintiffs in the Mesa case actually won—sort of. In the fall of 1982, Pickens' options were reduced 20 percent from 6 million to 4.8 million shares, and when the price of Mesa's stock tumbled along with that of other oil and gas producers, the options yielded a paper profit of only $27 million—down considerably from their $110 million peak in the spring of 1981.

But with Pickens as with Mahoney, one message comes across loud and clear: Unless a corporation pays its chief executive handsomely, he'll head for greener pastures.

Those who question the appropriateness of paying any executive $1 million a year get a fascinating array of rationales. First is the scope of responsibility resting on a chief executive's shoulders—billions of dollars, thousands of employees. Another line of reasoning views chief executives as victims: They are to be compensated not only for performance but also for the heavy personal toll exacted by their duties. There is also the argument that a CEO's lofty station imposes the burden of having to maintain a princely life-style. As one chief executive told *Industry Week*, "you have to do certain things when you're the mayor of the town that you don't have to do when you're a garbage collector." (The assumption here is that chief executives live high above Park Avenue and buy Picassos not because they want to but because they have to.)

Then there's the "I know it sounds like a lot but it's really only ..." rationale. Thus the $3,348,000 paid to Exxon chief executive Clifton G. Garvin, Jr., in 1980 works out to only .00325 percent of the company's revenues for the year.

But the best explanation for million-dollar paychecks is the Wayne Newton argument: When Wayne Newton earns $9 million for 37 weeks onstage in Las Vagas, is it really so outrageous to pay James H. Evans of Union Pacific $2,835,731 for a good year's work? If Sugar Ray Leonard can get $13 million for a single fight—and if Gary Carter can earn $2.2 million a year for playing baseball— why shouldn't the head of a complex, multinational corporation fetch $1 million a year?

Why indeed? The only problem with comparing paychecks is that there are no grounds for comparison. When Barbara Walters signed her $1 million contract with ABC in 1976, a reporter asked Walter Cronkite if he thought she was worth it. Compared to what? Walter wanted to know. He thought that compared to a rock star she was, but compared to a really good schoolteacher she wasn't. Alexander Haig, as president of United Technologies Corporation in Hartford, Connecticut, earned $738,000 plus stock options in 1980. As U.S. Secretary of State—surely a position of greater responsibility—he earned $69,630 in 1981. Comparing worth even in the same general line of work is tricky. Why, for instance, should the writers of television movies earn so much more than the writers of magazine articles? Or pediatricians so much less than surgeons?

The answers have less to do with the relative merits of various pursuits than with what the traffic will bear. A banker who serves as a director of several corporations explains how chief executives use their muscle to get more money from the directors: "They ask for bonuses on the strength of having got some big piece of business. 'That's what we pay you for,' some director will grumble. Even though the other directors usually agree with this objection, the CEO always gets what he asks for. It's less trouble to give him the money than to look for a replacement who might not even do as good a job."

Directors unwittingly play another role in raising executive pay. "Companies tend to get directors from other companies that are larger, higher-paid organisms than their own, so when directors look at the pay of this group, it doesn't seem so large," says one expert on executive compensation. "This is a very real factor that has tended to ratchet pay upward during the last twenty years."

Ironically, compensation surveys, which show salary ranges for hundreds of positions in dozens of industries, have also become a tool to justify ever-fatter executive paychecks. "Let's say the survey shows that in a certain industry, a certain position pays anywhere from $25,000 to $75,000," the compensation expert says. "The average is $50,000, but everybody thinks he's worth more than average. His boss lets him have more because that raises his pay, too."

The defenders of fat paychecks often argue that without large rewards, no one would make the personal sacrifices that go with running a big corporation. When *Barron's* scolded General Motors for holding down executive pay, it predicted that the move would "relentlessly narrow" the gap between salaried executives and the hourly wage earner. Eventually, *Barron's* said, we'll have another Britain on our hands, with managers, doctors, and lawyers often earning "no more than what can be earned by a senior man on the shop floor."

Though it is difficult to believe that paying a man $2 million will make him work twice as hard as if he were paid only $1 million, there may be some truth in the *Barron's* argument. Because salaries for running Britain's massive state-owned industries are so low compared with executive salaries in the private sector, Britain has had a difficult time recruiting the top-drawer talent it needs if these industries are to be put back on their feet. "In practical terms," one British business observer has written, "adoption of a market standard in the State sector would probably mean paying salaries of £100,000–£150,000 a year [two to three times more than British law permits] to

the chairman of British Steel, British Leyland, Gas Council, Electricity Council and so on. Only in this way . . . will
it be possible to attract the right man for the job. . . . It is
idle to argue that people can still be found at current
levels of pay to fill vacancies in State industry. Someone
can always be found: the moral of the British Steel episode
is that someone who accepted a sub-market rate may well
be the wrong man."

On the chance that a more expensive executive might be
able to fix British Steel, Britain bent its pay rules to hire
Ian MacGregor, the retired chairman of Amax, an American metals and mining concern. MacGregor's salary was
still the state-prescribed £48,500, but the New York office
of Lazard Frères, the investment banking firm where Mac-
Gregor was a general partner, collected $1.2 million from
Britain for the loss of his services and may get up to $3.3
million if he meets certain goals.

For centuries, economists, labor theorists, and utopians
have struggled to devise fair standards for remunerating
various kinds of human toil. Ancient Greek armies solved
the problem tidily by paying rank-and-file soldiers one
stater of Cyzicus a month, their captains twice that, and
generals four times as much as the basic soldier's pay.
Management theorist Peter Drucker has suggested that
chief executives should earn no more than twenty-five
times the amount paid to the company's lowest-paid
worker. Using that standard and assuming that the worker
on a company's bottom rung earns minimum wage—about
$7,300 a year—a chief executive should earn no more than
$182,500. This is less than half the median salary and
bonus earned by the 798 chief executives in *Forbes'* 1982
compensation survey. Put another way, if Warner Communications chief Steven Ross's $22,554,410 met Druck-
er's criterion, each worker in the lowest reaches of the
company would have had to earn $902,176 for the year.

But the problems that arise when an executive earns a million or more of what S. J. Perelman called "those artistic pale green rugs issued by the Treasury Department" have less to do with abstractions such as fairness and propriety than with highly pragmatic matters like how much this largesse costs shareholders, and effects—intended and otherwise—that large executive salaries have on a company's earnings.

When an executive exercises an option to buy his company's stock for substantially less than market value, that can lower the value of all the shares outstanding. As one critic has pointed out, "This is no hypothetical problem for companies like General Dynamics, which recently had as much as 15 percent of its equity under option." In 1975, stock options allowed the chairman of General Dynamics to buy $4.2 million worth of the company's stock for half that amount.

Too often, the critics charge, pay at the top bears little relation to a company's performance. In a 1981 survey of executive compensation, *Business Week* noted that the average profit drop at companies where profits declined in 1980 was 24 percent, but total compensation for executives at these companies rose 6.5 percent. Even in 1983, after two long, hard years of recession, the salaries of most corporate chief executives continued to rise. *Business Week*'s 1983 survey of executive compensation for 1982 showed that salaries and bonuses rose 5.5 percent while corporate earnings fell by about the same amount. Although this was the lowest increase in more than a decade, and there were signs that 1983 would not bring many big salary increases, some companies tried to make up the difference by giving their top executives more generous stock options and by promising higher retirement benefits.

Hard times also forced General Motors executives to forgo bonuses in 1980 and 1981. To gain concessions from the United Auto Workers in 1982, GM promised that white-collar workers would share in the sacrifices, with cuts in benefits, holidays, and cost-of-living increases. Chairman Roger Smith, whose 1981 compensation of $489,000 didn't include cost-of-living adjustments, nevertheless volunteered to cut his pay along with everybody else—by $135 a month. "It would have been better for him to do absolutely nothing," scoffed UAW president Douglas Fraser. Once the UAW concessions—$2.5 billion worth—were gained, GM angered union members again by tactlessly announcing plans to plump up executive bonuses. The ensuing protest forced GM to back off, but this boneheaded move breathed new life into union members' old suspicions that GM managers cared about nothing but their own well-being.

So far no one has discovered a rational explanation for the size of the salaries paid to top executives, and one doesn't have to look far to find discrepancies between executive pay and corporate performance. In 1982, Union Carbide's earnings fell 52 percent, but the company's chairman got a raise of 21 percent. The chairman and president of Mobil were each given raises of about 35 percent during 1982, while corporate earnings dropped 43 percent. Of the twenty food-industry companies listed in the 1981 *Fortune* 500, Norton Simon, Inc. ranked eighteenth in return on equity, but its chairman, David Mahoney, had the biggest paycheck.

At Playboy Enterprises, even though millions of dollars went down the bunny hole when the company mismanaged casinos in Atlantic City and London, there was still enough lettuce left to make everybody feel good. For fiscal 1982, chairman and chief executive officer Hugh Hefner earned only $401,539, but the company continued to pick up the tab on his home improvements. Since buying a Los Angeles mansion for $1,050,000 in 1971, Playboy has spent $8,775,000 fixing it up—including $2,176,000 on Hef's office and personal quarters in the house. Sir John Treacher, who failed to rescue Playboy's British operations, nevertheless got $740,000 in salary and severance pay for fiscal 1982. President and chief operating officer Derick January Daniels, bumped out to make room for a promising young executive named Christie Hefner, was given severance pay of $476,000 to be paid at $13,222 a month.

A management consultant and an accountant who analyzed top executive pay at 148 companies in a wide range of industries found only a frail connection between pay and corporate profits. The survey also failed to turn up a significant link between executive pay and the rewards that stockholders received for the year. The researchers concluded that executives are well paid simply because they "tend to be good bargainers. . . . They are people who possess toughness and imagination and who are excellent politicians. In most cases they have used their political ability to rise through the ranks. . . . Once they get to the top, they continue to use this toughness, imagination, and political know-how to find ways to justify their huge salaries."

But even the most fair-minded attempts to reward executives based on the increases they bring to a company's earnings for the year can backfire in unexpected ways. With all eyes focused on the year's bottom line, the temptation is to defer expenditures that won't yield an immediate profit. Research and development, advertising, maintenance, investment in new technology, purchase of needed equipment—all can be cut back or put off in the interest of fattening the year's net earnings and hyping executive bonuses. "A good, smart executive can really milk a division to make himself look good, then move onto something better and leave someone else to mop up," says an experienced management consultant who has watched it happen.

A chief executive's emphasis on short-term results is

communicated down the line, and throughout the company, executives with bottom-line responsibilities find themselves under pressure to make decisions that will pay off sooner rather than later. As a result, says Professor Alfred Rappaport of Northwestern University's Graduate School of Management, "the attitude of many divisional managers can be summed up as: 'It's fine to talk about the long run, but I won't be here in the long run if I don't do something about the short run.'" Compounding the problem, Rappaport says, is the fact that bonuses usually escalate rapidly once earnings goals are met. In 1976, for example, the average top executive's salary rose 14.7 percent from 1975, but his bonus climbed 67.1 percent. Thus, by tying executive pay to annual earnings performance, companies put executives in a position where their personal interests often conflict with the interests of the corporation and its shareholders.

Consider what happened at a pharmaceutical company that had fallen behind its competitors: To regain its edge, it drew up a five-year plan that increased spending for research and development, advertising, and plant modernization. The executives charged with carrying out the plan agreed it was a good one, but the expenditures required had the effect of wiping out most of their bonuses. Such conflicts have to be resolved before executives can be expected to cooperate on long-term strategic changes, but a study by two compensation experts at the management consulting firm of McKinsey & Company contends that few corporations "consider the implications of a strategy shift on incentive pay."

Another set of conflicts arises because top executives play such a large role in determining their own pay. Although directors, lawyers, accountants, bankers, and others often participate in making decisions on paychecks for those at the top, one compensation expert (who is not alone in his views) says the question always on their minds is, "What does top management want?" He adds: "Consultants, accounting firms, lawyers, and others play a far more important role than is generally recognized . . . nevertheless, these specialists originate compensation plans as well as develop ideas submitted to them by their clients. Of course, they depend on senior executive approval for their consulting employment." In addition, he notes, even when directors come from outside the company, they could well be personal friends of the top officers, and they also tend to be sympathetic because they are frequently corporate officers themselves. As one director explains it, "It's a club, and the club takes care of its own."

Given all the flaws in the system for paying America's corporate presidents and chairmen, it is not surprising that the most ardent defenders of the status quo are the million-dollar executives themselves. But the ranks of reformers are growing, and a number of companies have taken the initiative in searching for alternative ways to reward their executives for long-term rather than short-term achievements. At Koppers Company, an executive bonus plan drawn up in the late seventies set goals for three years instead of one. Some companies are experimenting with rewards based on the corporation's performance in comparison with that of competitors over several years. A five-year plan at Phillips Petroleum, for example, will give executives stock or cash bonuses only if the company outperforms at least four of ten competitors in either earnings-per-share growth or average return on corporate assets. The better Phillips stacks up against the competition, the bigger the bonuses. But even these systems aren't perfect. Inflation can cause earnings to soar and, depending on the ups and downs on the dollar in world currency markets, a company's foreign dealings can add or subtract enormous sums from the bottom line. And as Archie

McCardell and International Harvester would find out the hard way, even the most carefully thought-out compensation scheme can't, in the end, provide for all contingencies.

Because of the endless variables, raw numbers simply don't tell enough about how a company's past performance might help it fare in the future. The next generation of refinements in executive compensation probably will pay top executives on the basis of how successful they are in achieving strategic goals such as larger market share and improved quality. And to remove the penalties that executives suffer when they decide to allocate money for replacing antiquated capital equipment or for research and development, some reformers have suggested that such expenses be considered apart from other aspects of the executive's performance.

Although these changes represent efforts to make the executive pay system fairer and more rational, they sidestep the troubling question of whether million-dollar executives are overpaid. Here and there, however, stockholders have begun to ask loud questions in public about the appropriateness of paychecks as long as phone numbers. Three Exxon shareholders, upset over chief executive Clifton Garvin's 1980 take of $3.3 million (including more than $2 million in stock gains), filed a resolution in the company's 1981 proxy statement that aimed to tighten the restrictions on future stock option plans. Among other things, the resolution called for a one-year limit on the options and sought to restrict the amount of options to one and a half times the executive's cash compensation. To the surprise of no one, Exxon's board of directors urged shareholders to vote against the proposal. "Competition for executive talent in our industry is intense," the board explained, "and it is important that Exxon's Incentive Program enhance the Corporation's ability to compete with others in attracting and retaining individuals of outstanding ability who are essential to the growth and earnings of the Corporation." The proposal, like the vast majority of shareholder proposals, was soundly defeated.

Whatever an executive might be worth *on* the job, shareholders have begun to protest the practice of paying enormous sums to those who have been fired. At the 1981 annual meeting of First Chicago Corporation, shareholders complained about the $781,349 given to chairman Robert Abboud when he got the ax the year before. Hefty severance payments to two other executives brought the total of First Chicago's good-bye money to more than $1 million for the year. One shareholder asked how the bank could justify this sort of charitableness for the fired Abboud when it was "so miserly" with pensions for retirees. As explained by chief executive Barry F. Sullivan (himself a "bonus baby," drawn to First Chicago by a compensation package that included a $1.5 million eight-year loan at 8 percent interest), the separation payments were "reasonable and appropriate" and "well within the customary range." More to the point, the bank *had* to pay off Abboud because it was part of his employment contract.

At RCA and one of its subsidiaries, NBC, the tab for four high-level departures during 1980 and 1981 came to $4.7 million: $1.25 million for RCA president Maurice Valente, on the job for less than six months; $1.25 million for RCA chairman Edgar Griffiths, who resigned under fire but was given a five-year consulting contract at $250,000 a year; $705,000 for Jane Cahill Pfeiffer after twenty months as chairman of NBC; and $1.5 million for deposed NBC president Fred Silverman, whose million-dollar-a-year contract still had eighteen months to go. RCA may have yet another hefty severance settlement to make. Its current chairman, Thornton Bradshaw, is widely regarded as a temporary chief because of his age—sixty-three when he took over in 1981. Nevertheless, Bradshaw was given a five-year contract guaranteeing him at least $938,500 a year.

At CBS, John D. Backe walked away with $2 million when his services as president were no longer required.

The size of these settlements has opened the eyes of executives farther down the ladder, and one executive recruiter estimates that 80 to 90 percent of executives earning $100,000 or more a year now have severance provisions in their contracts.

For one brief shining moment, annual meeting day, shareholder protests can draw attention to the unseemly bulges in executive wallets, but it is unlikely that such complaints will ever gather enough steam to change the system. As one authority on executive pay has pointed out, the individual stockholders of most large corporations number in the millions, with each one owning only a tiny portion of the shares outstanding. In addition, they are too spread out to be mobilized for action and are baffled by the complexities of compensation plans.

Those complexities are not accidental. One compensation expert believes that "many incentive plans, the way they are set up now, are giveaway devices by which companies can pay their officers more than stockholders would tolerate if the whole thing came as straightforward salary."

Even a matter as theoretically simple as a bonus has become part of the subterfuge. At the top, the time-honored notion of a bonus as a reward for outstanding performance has ceased to obtain. As soon as salary is agreed upon, the next order of business is to dicker over a guaranteed bonus. When Maurice Valente became president of RCA, for example, his salary was set at $400,000, and he was promised an annual bonus of at least $200,000. Why not just give him a salary of $600,000? A compensation consultant explains: "These arrangements allow corporate officers, when asked about their salaries, to give answers that are a good deal more palatable to the outside world. And they allow companies that calculate stock options and raises on the basis of salary to use a smaller figure as the base. So a 10 percent raise for someone with a $400,000 salary would be $20,000 less than for someone with a $600,000 salary." That second reason, of course, is pure hot air—the sort of elaborate rationale that compensation consultants are paid to devise to help their clients justify doing what they want to do. If a 10 percent raise on a $600,000 salary were really a problem, the percentage could simply be reduced.

But to dwell on salaries and bonuses is to miss the real action in executive compensation, since they amount to only a small portion of pay at the top. For the ten best-paid chief executives in *Forbes'* 1982 list, the combination of salary and bonus accounted for only one fifth of total compensation. The rest came from stock gains and fringe benefits, like the $173,000 in carrying costs that ITT pays on chairman Rand Araskog's New York apartment.

In all the creative obfuscation that goes into hiding executive compensation from shareholders and other interested parties, there is nothing quite as labyrinthine as the stock gain. Depending on which of the endless combinations and permutations find their way into a company's system for pay at the top, an executive might qualify for one or more of the following: *stock options,* which give an executive the right to buy a specified number of shares of company stock at a set price; *restricted stock,* which is awarded for having met certain objectives and usually requires an executive to stay with the company for a specific period and not sell the stock for a certain length of time; *performance shares* (also known as *performance units*), which are awarded based on success in meeting predetermined goals; *stock appreciation rights,* which are delayed bonuses, in cash or stock, tied to a future rise in the price of a company's stock. The basic idea behind all these stock benefits is to allow executives to acquire their shares for less than market value, which can lead to enormous personal gains. An executive with an option to buy 100,000 shares of his company's stock at even $2 a share less than the market price makes an instant $200,000 simply by exercising this option.

In the merger mania of 1981 and 1982, a number of corporations added "takeover protection" to their executives' compensation contracts. Two months before chemical giant DuPont bought Conoco, an international energy firm, Conoco directors gave nine top executives contracts that would pay off if they quit or were fired after Conoco was acquired by another company. Under the agreement, chairman Ralph Bailey would get $637,716 a year until 1989 if he decided not to play ball with DuPont. By 1983, more than fifteen hundred companies had adopted these "golden parachutes" to ease executive bailouts. One of the most golden came about during the 1982 corporate merger contest that pitted Bendix against Allied in the pursuit of Martin Marietta. While Bendix was trying to swallow Martin Marietta, Allied swallowed Bendix. In 1983, two top Bendix officers resigned after concluding they would play greatly reduced roles in managing the new company. Terms of their golden parachutes are complicated, but former Bendix chairman William Agee could collect as much as $4 million, and former Bendix president Alonzo McDonald could gain up to $2.2 million.

The rationale behind these cushy arrangements? When key managers are assured a soft landing, the theory goes, they can keep their eyes fixed on the corporate good rather than their own personal needs. Only if they are relieved of personal worries, it is said, can they concentrate on the tough decisions that need to be made in a takeover battle. These managers have good reason to worry. A 1983 study by an executive recruiting firm shows that almost 90 percent of the chief executive officers of acquired companies don't survive as top dog after the acquisition.

Rounding out the pay package are the perks. One recent list of possibilities included cars, parking, use of corporate aircraft, executive dining rooms (private ones adjacent to one's office, in some cases), physical fitness programs, availability of company hotel rooms or apartments, legal services, tax assistance, financial counseling, personal protection (usually reserved for executives in sensitive industries or foreign countries), travel expenses for one's spouse, business liability insurance (to cover damages that might be claimed by others because of the way an executive did his job), personal liability insurance, allowances for children's education, low- or no-interest loans, medical examinations (often at a facility near a posh resort), life insurance, kidnap and ransom insurance, and business travel accident insurance.

Compensation specialists say that one reason pay at the top is so complicated is that ever-changing tax laws have forced lawyers and accountants to go to ever greater lengths in an effort to keep executive paychecks away from the tax man. But the Securities and Exchange Commission, which prescribes the manner in which publicly owned corporations report their finances, has taken a more skeptical view of the hodgepodge. Until 1978, the lack of detailed rules on reporting compensation at the top allowed corporations to camouflage information in narrative discussions and footnotes, and only a Sherlock Holmes with an M.B.A. in finance could figure out just how much the nation's business leaders were being paid. Since then the SEC has revised the rules twice and now requires proxy statements to include separate tables showing basic compensation, options, stock appreciation rights, and pensions for the company's five highest-paid officers.

As much as the new rules help, there still might be a way for some executives to avoid baring their souls: They can refuse to become corporate officers. When Barry Diller was president of Paramount Pictures, he steered clear of becoming an officer of Gulf + Western, which owns Paramount, for precisely that reason. As he explained to *The New York Times*, "I don't think it's anyone's business what I make, and I don't want to be a target more than I'm a target already."

Another potential problem for shareholders wanting to know more about executive paychecks: The SEC may relax its rules for reporting noncash compensation such as stock options, apparently because the rules are burdensome and confusing. Burdensome and confusing they certainly are, but since the information they furnish is vital to stockholders, investors would be better served if the SEC would simplify the rules rather than drop them.

No one can say when, how, or if executive compensation will return from the stratosphere, but the procession of million-dollar managers is sure to get longer. As any millionaire will tell you, $1 million isn't what it used to be. Fifty years ago, when soreheads groused about the million-plus earned by Eugene Grace of Bethlehem Steel, $1 million bought five times what it buys today. Besides that, underneath the high-mindedness that condemns $1 million paychecks and asks, "How do they get away with it?" there lurks another question, equally pressing: "Where can I get in line?"

Chapter 3

Sowing and Reaping

Archie McCardell and International Harvester

In 1977, three years after Michel Bergerac became the first of the million-dollar bonus babies, a consultant to International Harvester came up with a compensation contract that upped the ante considerably. Besides a five-year term, a salary of $460,000, and a Bergerac-style sign-on bonus of $1.5 million, Harvester would offer a $1.8 million loan for the purchase of company stock. Best of all, if certain corporate performance goals were met, the loan would not have to be repaid.

The company had good reason for going to such lengths. Booz, Allen & Hamilton, a management consulting firm, had recommended that Harvester reorganize from top to bottom and bring in a new president from the outside. Since Harvester's lackluster performance for the past thirty years was no secret in the business world, the company was going to have to dangle an irresistible carrot to attract a high-caliber executive. The opportunity to borrow $1.8 million with the possibility of not having to pay it back became that carrot. Besides, Harvester figured it had nothing to lose. If the holder of the contract met the goals, $1.8 million would be a small price to pay. If he didn't, Harvester would get its money back.

The man carrying out the prescribed reorganization was Brooks McCormick, great-grandnephew of Cyrus. Since Cyrus's invention of the reaper in 1831, the company had grown into one of the world's largest manufacturers of trucks, agricultural equipment, and construction machinery, with gross sales of more than $5 billion a year. But it still wasn't as profitable as its two biggest rivals, Deere & Company and Caterpillar Tractor Company. Shortly after becoming president in 1971, Brooks had determined that if Harvester was ever going to catch up to the competition, it would need a corporate overhaul. As a McCormick, Brooks symbolized all the old ways of doing things, especially the deep traditions of paternalism and conservatism, but he was dead set on being the agent of change. He redrew the organization chart, replacing a tight, centralized authority structure with a looser order based on product groups, which made individual managers more accountable for their profits and losses. He began trying to identify operations that might be put up for sale, and he dared to look for ways to trim fat from the sacred cow: labor. Because of a long-standing management habit of knuckling under in minor union squabbles, Harvester's labor costs were the highest in the industry. Although corporate earnings improved dramatically under Brooks' leadership, Harvester still didn't measure up to the competition, and its debt continued to swell. So, early in 1977, perhaps feeling that an outsider would be able to move farther and faster than a McCormick could, Brooks put the solid-gold compensation contract in his pocket and went looking for help.

The man he wanted was a thousand miles away from Harvester's Chicago headquarters, serving as president and chief operating officer of Xerox, in Stamford, Connecticut. Archie R. McCardell, fifty-one, appealed to Brooks McCormick and his board of directors for at least two reasons. He was a fearless cost-cutter who had weeded eight thousand employees from the Xerox ranks in a single year, and before joining Xerox, he had worked for Ford, which faced many of the same manufacturing and labor problems that deviled Harvester.

The first contact was made by an executive recruiter who was assigned the delicate task of asking McCardell whether he would consider a new job—without telling him who wanted to know. McCardell said he wasn't interested. A few months later, the headhunter tried again, this time revealing that the suitor was International Harvester. McCardell declined once more. "I knew they had a long history of high costs and were seriously underfinanced," he says. "And I didn't want to go back into that kind of manufacturing." Undaunted, Harvester then dispatched a board member to call on McCardell. The headhunter paid another visit, this time bearing an invitation to have dinner with Brooks McCormick when McCardell went to Chicago that spring for Xerox's annual meeting. "That was hard to turn down," McCardell says.

So, it developed, was McCormick's job offer. In addition to the tantalizing compensation package, there was the prospect of becoming CEO within a year—an opportunity McCardell was not likely to have at Xerox.

As for Harvester's financial problems, "Brooks was pretty frank," McCardell says. In addition to high labor costs and management overstaffing, production inefficiencies and thin profit margins had left the company unable to afford the modernization it needed if it was ever going to run like a Deere. One of Harvester's plants, a truck factory in Fort Wayne, had been built before McCardell was born. More than half of Deere's plants were less than a decade old, and many others were being updated, which went a long way toward explaining why Deere's manufacturing costs were the lowest in the industry and why it earned twice as much per employee as Harvester did. There was no question that McCardell would have his work cut out for him at Harvester, but after several rounds of discussion, both he and McCormick thought he could do the job.

By the time McCardell came to work at Harvester at the end of August 1977, his compensation agreement had been tuned to a fare-thee-well. The work of Charles Bowen, retired chief of Booz, Allen and longtime guru to Harvester on executive and compensation matters, the contract was now as intricate as a symphony. On the subject of the loan, the contract basically said the $1.8 million would be forgiven if McCardell increased profitability to the average level of six Harvester rivals. At the time, Harvester lagged far behind, with profitability of 6.86 percent compared to 10.5 percent for the rest of the pack. The contract gave him seven years to close the gap but said forgiveness could come sooner than that if he met the goals early. The contract also hedged Harvester's bet in two significant ways. If one of the six competitors had a net loss for the year, it would be excluded from the calculations; that precaution would keep one loser from pulling the group average down to a level too easy for McCardell to reach. A Harvester board committee was also given authority to change the contract's objectives if it decided that McCardell's self-interest was leading him to make decisions damaging to the company—such as putting off modernization expenditures in order to boost earnings in the short run. No matter how you looked at it, the contract seemed like a great idea—brilliant, in fact. No one could have foreseen the disaster it would create.

McCardell spent his first Harvester days at meetings, listening to group presidents make their annual budget presentations. He had planned to do a lot of listening before he went into action, but he couldn't live with what he had heard so far. Not only were executives unable to answer the questions he asked, they seemed willing to sit passively by and accept projections that 1978's pretax earnings would not be as good as 1977's. McCardell stunned them all by rejecting their budget proposals.

How did he get away with an insult of that magnitude when he was still the new kid on the block? It wasn't so much that he was Brooks' fair-haired boy, or that Harvester executives realized the company could use a strong dose of salvation. His personality explains more than a little about his success in getting Harvester managers to go along with what he wanted to accomplish. Affable and approachable, he often works with his shoes off, shirt-sleeves rolled up, and vest unbuttoned. Cigars and Archie McCardell are never very far away from each other, which adds to his informality. His conversation is considerably less guarded than that of many top executives, and one effect of that at Harvester was to make managers feel more at ease in discussing business problems. "He is incredibly self-controlled, never loses his temper," said one Harvester executive. "If he disagrees with you, he is very patient, he just asks questions, makes suggestions, moves you over bit by bit. When you leave a meeting with him, you often realize that he's moved you around 180 degrees."

To make his managers think in terms of comparing Harvester's performance to that of its strongest competitors (rather than to the company's own performance in previous years), McCardell ordered up numbers that would tell him how the top four companies in the business had fared in the two best of their most recent five years. Then he asked managers to calculate what Harvester would have reaped had it measured up to this crowd. The answer was unnerving: Instead of a pretax profit of $300 million, Harvester should have hit $800 million. The company was running $500 million a year behind.

Determined to close that gap, McCardell set a cost-cutting goal of $100 million for the upcoming fiscal year, which would begin November 1. To get the ball rolling, he pared 150 employees from his own staff. Through a combination of early retirements, hiring freezes, and layoffs, Harvester reduced the payroll from 93,000 to 90,000. From the vantage point of 1983, when the national unemployment rate was well over 10 percent, putting 3,000 people out of work had more elements of tragedy than triumph, but back in 1978 it was a different story. McCardell was widely praised for calling a halt to the expansion of Harvester's unproductive bureaucracy. When the fiscal year-end rolled around, he'd beaten his $100 million goal by $40 million.

The $140 million didn't add much to the bottom line, however. Harvester's profit actually declined, falling to $187 million from $204 million the year before. Nor did the savings help McCardell make any headway toward the forgiveness of his loan. Harvester's profitability fell while that of the six competitors listed in McCardell's contract rose. Most of the "saved" $140 million went into accounting adjustments.

The cost-cutting would continue. It would get harder, too, and not just because there was less fat left to trim. The layoffs McCardell was making had not gone unnoticed by the thirty-five thousand United Auto Workers members in Harvester's factories. Nor did the UAW take kindly to the consultants sent by headquarters to look for ways to make the plants more efficient. Higher productivity per employee might add to corporate profits, but in many cases it also led to fewer jobs.

Relations between Harvester's management and the

UAW had borne strange fruit over the years. Paternalistic Harvester, proud of the fact that it had stood by its workers even in the worst of the Depression, also had a maternal side—rushing to smooth ruffled feathers whenever little scuffles arose. Nobody worried about who was right in these spats; the important thing was to get the assembly lines running again. Headquarters judged plant managers more on the basis of how much their plants produced than on the costs of production, which could always be blamed on the high price of UAW labor. Giving in on minor grievances may have been the fastest way to start tractors and trucks rolling off the lines again, but it didn't win management any friends. It simply made the union more demanding. Although the company hadn't had a major strike since 1958, there were a hundred small ones between 1968 and 1978.

By the time McCardell arrived, the UAW had won some extraordinary—and expensive—privileges. One was the right to apply for an unlimited number of job changes within a plant. Workers could put their names in not only for promotions but also for lateral and even downward moves. "At one plant with 5,000 employees, there were 30,000 transfers in a single year," McCardell says. "Many workers didn't make any transfers, but others were changing jobs ten times a year. Each transfer cost us $1,000, so that was a cost penalty of $30 million a year in just one plant."

Another union right: Overtime at Harvester was strictly voluntary. When a plant manager wanted to run a factory on weekends, he had to ask workers to volunteer for the extra time. On one occasion, two hundred workers were asked, and a hundred agreed to come; on the appointed day, only a dozen or so showed up. Midwestern plant managers who made the mistake of trying to set up overtime shifts during pheasant-hunting season were practically laughed out of town. Neither of these rights was part of the main UAW-Harvester contract but had gradually spread from plant to plant as a result of management's willingness to appease. Perhaps the most significant thing about both rights was that workers at Harvester's two sharpest competitors, Deere and Caterpillar, didn't have them.

The company's labor picture was further clouded by a union practice known as "pattern bargaining." The UAW's three-year auto industry contracts all expired on September 15. Instead of bargaining with all the companies concerned, the UAW picked one and presented its wish list with the idea that if an agreement was not reached, the union might call a strike. Whatever settlement was reached in the negotiations was then considered by the UAW to be the least it would accept from companies not yet bargained with—the pattern for the industry, in other words. In the agricultural equipment business, the major contracts all expired on October 1. The UAW employed the same tactic of picking a single company, then using the result to reach settlements with the rest. The main difference was that the union usually was able to approach its first agricultural equipment company with the auto industry settlements in hand. That started the bidding war at a higher level and led to wages and benefits worth more than those in the auto business.

There was little McCardell could do about pattern bargaining, but management pussyfooting with the union was another matter. In the spring of 1978, shortly after being named chief executive officer, he decided to show the union that his determination to cut costs would affect the rank and file, too. The showdown came at a components plant in Louisville, where the company and the UAW disagreed on the piecework rates to be paid to nine employees. For once Harvester didn't back down. UAW members in the plant retaliated with a five-week strike that eventually put 12,000 Harvester workers on the sidelines for lack of the parts made in Louisville. After the strike, McCardell called 159 plant managers to headquarters and asked them to take home the message that the union had not been singled out for a special attack in his cost-cutting plans. So Round One went to the UAW.

For Archie McCardell and International Harvester, the fiscal year that began on November 1, 1978, would be the best of times and the worst of times. On the positive side, McCardell set a cost-cutting goal of $240 million for the year and announced to securities analysts that he wouldn't stop squeezing until he had wrung out $500 million a year in operating expenses. Inventory systems were being centralized and computerized so the company would know what goods it had where, which would provide a better balance between the supply of production parts and the demand for them. Like the auto companies, Harvester needed thousands of kinds of parts to manufacture its products. Since excess widgets cost money to make and store, the potential for waste was enormous.

Looking for ways to sell operations peripheral to the company's main businesses, McCardell pursued the time-honored strategy for getting rid of excess baggage. Publicly, Harvester denied that it had plans to dispose of any operations. "Since we were only *developing* plans, we could make the denials in all honesty," McCardell explains. "Announcing plans would have only destroyed the value of what we were trying to sell."

The austerities paid handsome dividends to Harvester and McCardell. Earnings for the year ended October 31, 1979, soared to a record $370 million—twice what they'd been the year before. Even more impressive, Harvester's profitability squeaked past that of the six rivals listed in McCardell's contract. The contract allowed for early forgiveness of the $1.8 million loan in the event of "distinguished performance," and judging from the earnings statement, distinguished performance was exactly what McCardell had given.

There was just one monkey wrench in the works. The contract between Harvester and the UAW had expired October 1, and although the union agreed to a one-month extension to keep the assembly lines running while negotiations continued, the two sides were miles apart. The time had come, McCardell believed, for the company to stand firm on key issues, including voluntary overtime and unrestricted job transfers. If he didn't face up to these issues now, it would be three years before he had another chance. He couldn't see the point of handing Deere and Caterpillar that advantage yet again.

The union, of course, was loath to give back privileges it had come to view as inalienable rights. And besides protecting what it already had, it was insisting that any new Harvester plant also be a UAW plant. Negotiators went round and round to no avail. On November 1, 1979—the day after Harvester finished its record-breaking year—the UAW began one of the longest strikes in its history. When it was settled five and a half months later, in the spring of 1980, there were not exactly smiles all around. The hardship suffered by union members as they struggled to make ends meet on strike-fund checks of about $60 a week instead of take-home pay of $240 or more left a lasting bitterness.

Harvester's wallet took a beating, too, with estimated losses running from $200 million to $479 million, depending on who did the counting. McCardell leans toward the low estimates. "By the time the strike ended, the recession had begun, so we would have been reducing production anyway. And before the strike, sales were higher than usual because our dealers were building up their inventories in anticipation of the strike." The official bottom line, which accounted for neither the strike nor the recession but simply recorded what happened, showed a loss of $479 million for the first six months of Harvester's fiscal year. Debt jumped more than 40 percent to almost $2 billion, which lowered the company's credit rating and curtailed its borrowing power, and the stock dropped from $45 a share to $27.

Looking back on the strike, McCardell concedes that it lasted longer than he thought it would. If he had it to do over again, he says, "I wouldn't follow the conventional wisdom about CEOs staying away from the unions. I wouldn't delegate so much of this responsibility to human resources people. After the strike, I talked a lot to hourly employees, and I think that if I'd done it before, I would have had more understanding from the union. I don't think the strike would have been eliminated if I had done this, but maybe it would have been shorter." Still, he feels the company made important gains because of the strike. "We had identified six areas that represented about two-thirds of our cost penalty [as compared with competitors], and the changes we got reduced the penalty by two-thirds."

Two thirds of two thirds works out to about a half, which is the long way of saying the strike ended in a draw. Harvester succeeded in limiting job transfers at most plants, but an employee still could make six changes a year. Overtime was still largely voluntary. The UAW didn't win the right to represent workers in all new Harvester plants, although it did secure the promise of some preferential treatment at a factory being planned for Oklahoma.

In McCardell's view, the strike was a stalemate "if you looked only at the issues. If you looked at it in terms of the company's history—with management never getting anything from the union—it was quite an achievement to get half of what we asked for."

The business press, assessing who had won the strike,

concluded that the UAW had. There were reasons to think so at the time, especially if one judged by the damage to Harvester's balance sheet, which was more than a little ragged around the edges. But the UAW's victory was more apparent than real, since both sides emerged from the strike only to face a recession that would turn into the worst in fifty years—and would ravage the farm economy. The right to keep overtime voluntary wasn't going to mean much when there wasn't any overtime to be worked.

NOT LONG after the strike, and well before anyone understood how long the recession would drag on, Harvester's board committee on organization met to talk about how much of McCardell's $1.8 million loan they might forgive as a result of the company's spectacular earnings in 1979. As Carol Loomis reported in *Fortune*, legal counsel at the meeting told directors that since McCardell had turned in corporate earnings that met the goals spelled out in his contract, the board was "required to give him total forgiveness." Also in keeping with the contract, forgiveness would be spread out over five years, at the rate of $360,000 a year. Questioning the wisdom of the contract's conditions, Loomis noted that Harvester's 1979 earnings exceeded those of its six rivals only because of a fluke. The United Kingdom was handing out special tax credits to certain companies that year, and $95 million of Her Majesty's benevolence went to Massey-Ferguson—one of the competitors named in McCardell's contract. "Without the credit," Loomis explained, "Massey would have recorded a loss and been omitted from the calculation. The remaining five players would then have shown an average [profitability] ratio of 10.39%. *With* the tax credit, Massey realized a small profit and therefore got counted. It pulled down the average to 9.15%"—and put Harvester, with its 9.55 percent profitability for the year, out in front.

Fluke or no fluke, strike losses notwithstanding, and with debt well beyond the $2 billion mark, Harvester's directors were still persuaded that 1979's triumphs meant forgiveness was in order. When they announced their decision in the fall of 1980, they were greeted with jeers from Wall Street and other quarters. Many securities analysts gave McCardell high marks but thought the loan forgiveness should have been put on hold in view of Harvester's 1980 problems. Other critics pointed out that Chrysler's Lee Iacocca was seeing *his* troubled company through— and winning major concessions from the UAW—by working for $1 a year. Whether McCardell was entitled to forgiveness or not, it just didn't *look* good at a time when Harvester was reeling from the two-fisted blows of high interest rates on its massive debt and disappearing markets for its farm equipment.

THE SEVENTIES had begun a golden era for American farmers, with Washington urging them to grow more so the United States could become the breadbasket of the world. (It was a matter of pitting our "food weapon" against OPEC's "oil weapon," U.S. Secretary of Agriculture Earl Butz told farmers.) Easy credit enabled them to buy more land, and a slew of technological improvements raised productivity to the point where one farmer could feed seventy-eight people.

The eighties weren't going to be nearly as kind. Overproduction of every major commodity crop—wheat, soybeans, cotton, sugar, and corn—was driving prices well below production costs. In the summer of 1982, the bushel of wheat that cost $6.32 to produce sold for $3.41. Nor did the world seem all that eager to eat from the American breadbasket. For one thing, other countries had agricultural surpluses of their own. For another, when President Carter shut off grain sales to the Soviet Union in retaliation for the invasion of Afghanistan, America's reliability as a supplier was called into question. (And in the end, U.S. farmers suffered more than the Soviets, who simply bought their grain from other sources.) The Japanese, irritated by limits on how many U.S. soybeans they could import, took their trade to Brazil, even though they had to spend several hundred million dollars to get the Brazilian soybean business up and running. Yet another problem: The strength of the dollar made U.S. commodities among the most expensive on the world market.

On top of these troubles, farm costs were soaring. In the wake of the OPEC oil shocks of 1973 and 1974, prices of fuel, fertilizer, and agricultural chemicals doubled and redoubled. Farm equipment had grown vastly more sophisticated in the years since World War II—and vastly more expensive. In 1950, when wheat sold for $2 a bushel, a new combine cost $3,600. By 1982, the price of wheat hadn't even doubled but a new combine cost $50,000—up almost fourteen times. The cost of loans to buy farm equipment also shot through the roof, with the prime rate rising from 2.25 percent in 1950 to 16 percent in 1982. And those interest costs were punishing thousands of farmers who had taken out big loans to buy more land. Using the inflated paper value of the land they already owned as collateral for loans, many farmers had been able to borrow hundreds of thousands of dollars. But with crop prices so depressed, they often found their interest payments far outstripping their income. By 1982, they couldn't even solve their problem by selling land. The bubble had burst. Even prime midwestern acreage was going for as much as 33 percent less than in the late seventies. Overnight, the farm economy was turned upside down. The only truth that still held was Louis XIV's observation that "credit supports agriculture like a rope supports a hanged man."

Squeezed from all sides—by high production costs, low

crop prices, rising interest rates, and falling land values—
farmers had to cut back wherever they could. Like new-
car shoppers made faint by the 1982 average sticker price
of $9,300, farmers walked away from dealers' showrooms
determined to fix up their old rigs rather than borrow upward of $50,000 for new tractors and other gear. Silos
bulging with excess crops also forced them to trim production, which meant the farm equipment they already
owned would get less use and last longer.

Economies like these soon made themselves felt at companies such as International Harvester. Dealers were hit
first. In the boom year of 1979, selling a piece of equipment usually took five meetings between dealer and
farmer, one Harvester dealer recalled. By 1982 it took ten,
and the comparison shopping being done by farmers
forced competing dealers to keep shaving prices until they
made almost no profit. The high interest rates hurting
farmers also hurt dealers, who typically financed their inventories with borrowed money.

The chickens next began to roost in farm-equipment
factories, which had to stop making tractors, cornheads,
balers, moldboard plows, and the like until farmers started
buying again. At Harvester, after the 1980 fiscal year
ended in October with an operating loss of $375 million—
more than the company's record-setting earnings of the
year before—layoffs became a way of life. In the next year,
ten thousand blue-collar and two thousand white-collar
employees would lose their jobs. The salaries of thirty
thousand white-collar workers would be frozen, executive
paychecks would be cut 20 percent, and common stock
dividends would be eliminated. By 1983, Harvester would
have only forty-three thousand employees—less than half
the number on the payroll when McCardell took over.

The outlook in 1980 was as bleak as could be, but
McCardell remained an optimist. In fiscal 1981 he would

cut another $400 million from Harvester's costs, which would help the company weather the storm. And, perverse as it seems, the economic clouds even had some silver linings: Inventory reductions meant reduced interest expenses, and lower production meant lower costs for items such as materials, energy, and transportation. All in all, Harvester estimated, its costs for the fiscal year ending October 31, 1982, would be $650 million less than in fiscal 1981. The belt could be tightened only so many notches, of course, and cost-cutting can't entirely compensate for lost revenues. But it wasn't unreasonable for Harvester to view the recession as a time to whip the company into shape so it could make the most of the inevitable comeback.

The trouble was, the comeback was a lot farther off than anyone knew, and Harvester's debt was rapidly getting out of hand. In fiscal 1981 McCardell made at least five estimates of the company's earnings. At first he predicted Harvester would have an operating profit. Succeeding forecasts revealed losses, each one larger than the last, with a final estimate of $500 million worth of red ink. When the accountants finally closed the books on the year, the operating loss came to $635.7 million. McCardell nevertheless defends his forecasts and contends they came as no surprise to the bankers who were becoming increasingly involved in Harvester's affairs. "Before we made those forecasts, we'd ask the bankers what they thought interest rates were going to be," McCardell says. "Bankers were the biggest contributors to the assumptions on which those forecasts were based."

BY JUNE 1981, despite every cost-cutting trick in the book, Harvester's debt had risen sharply from the $2 billion level that had been causing worries at the end of the strike only a year before. Beyond the burning question of how Harvester would manage to repay this debt were other grave questions: With no cash to spare, how would the company continue to modernize its factories? If it didn't modernize, how would it ever catch up with its competitors? Now that the whole world knew about Harvester's woes, how could the company get more than fire-sale prices for the operations it had to sell to get the cash it needed to stay in business? Could the company hang on until farmers started buying tractors again?

In the summer of 1981, the story of International Harvester began unfolding as one of the priciest corporate cliff-hangers of all time. More than a few people asked who was to blame, and Archie McCardell emerged as the scapegoat of choice. His devotion to cost-cutting, which had made him a hero during his first two years on the job, was now seen as myopic. He should have concentrated on strategy, his old fans decided. Others faulted him for not cutting far enough fast enough. Still others, overlooking his years at Ford, insisted that his Xerox experience had left him ill equipped to handle the UAW. And there was the undying issue of his $1.8 million loan forgiveness. Twice the board of directors considered taking it back, but the complexities of the contract were such that there seemed to be no way to do it without costing the company even more money. The general impression was that Archie McCardell had gotten rich by mugging a cripple.

The bankers who were spending more and more of their time at Harvester cared less about who was to blame than about how to stop the bleeding. With almost $5 billion at stake, they couldn't afford to let Harvester die, but saving it was going to be a long haul. The company couldn't raise money by issuing new stock or bonds, since few investors would be stouthearted enough to bet on a company whose credit rating continued to drop. Bankruptcy was not a desirable option, either. Harvester valued its assets at $5.6 billion, but in all likelihood a piece-by-piece sell-off would yield only a fraction of that. Like Harvester, other makers of trucks and agricultural equipment had cut back production sharply because of the recession. They would have little interest in buying more manufacturing capacity, even at bargain-basement prices. By forcing Harvester into bankruptcy, lenders would probably recoup very little.

That left only one workable strategy: Revise loan agreements to allow Harvester to pay off its debts at lower interest rates over a longer period. (This was the game the world's biggest banks would be forced to play for even higher stakes a year later, when countries from Argentina to Zaïre found themselves unable to repay loans of hundreds of billions of dollars.) It took months for Harvester and its bankers to restructure $4.9 billion of Harvester's finances, and events of the period did little to ease bankers' anxieties. The company's $168 million operating loss for the quarter ended July 31, 1981, was larger than expected, working capital stood at an emaciated $350 million (down 75 percent in one year), and the outlook for the farm economy was even less promising than when the restructuring talks had begun. Little things kept going wrong, too. A deal to sell twenty-five hundred tractors to Mexico inexplicably fell through, leaving the company holding at least $50 million worth of tractors decked out with Spanish decals and metric-system gauges. The tractors were quickly converted for use by American farmers, but to get rid of them, Harvester had to offer them to dealers free of the interest charges usually paid while machinery is waiting to be sold. Another quirk of fate: The Army saw fit to give a $65 million contract for combat earthmovers to Paccar, one of Harvester's archrivals, even though Harvester had done the development work for the vehicles.

To raise cash and pull in its horns, Harvester began selling off everything extraneous to its truck and tractor operations: The Solar Turbines division, interests in an iron-ore mine and in a Japanese venture, its hydraulics business, and its off-highway hauler business. The construction division would also be sold—but for some $300 million less than book value. The company also ended operations in Spain. In two years, these sell-offs and other moves would reduce Harvester's assets from $5.6 billion to $3.7 billion.

McCardell kept swinging his cost-cutting ax, with more layoffs, plant closings, and inventory reductions of several hundred million dollars during the 1981 fiscal year. Following the trail blazed by Chrysler, he asked for concessions from suppliers, dealers, and the UAW. Suppliers and dealers, already stung by the recession, didn't have much to give. Like the banks, however, they stood to lose even more if Harvester went under. And they were told that if they didn't go along, Harvester would take its business to suppliers who would.

When Harvester told the UAW the company could well go bankrupt without union concessions of $100 million, the UAW thought it smelled a new plot to bust the union. McCardell's loan forgiveness (and a similar arrangement worth almost $1 million for Harvester president Warren Hayford) only reinforced the UAW's conviction that management was out to bleed the union man. Before agreeing to concede one nickel, the UAW said, it would wait to see what Harvester would do to trim waste in management. The union was particularly upset about what it called "outrageously high salaries" for McCardell and other senior executives. Although managerial paychecks were slashed 20 percent during 1981 while Harvester UAW members got average increases of $2,500, what stuck in the union's craw was the $480,000 a year McCardell was earning even after the management pay cuts. Stockholders would voice similar complaints at the company's 1982 annual meeting: "Twenty percent of $500,000, $600,000, that's not a big hurt for you," one shareholder told Harvester's top executives. "You're not looking out for the stockholders, you're not looking at the product, you're looking out for yourselves."

The union's animosity was about to be exacerbated. In January 1982, only a few weeks after Harvester told the UAW the concessions were a matter of life and death, bonuses of $6 million were handed out to managers. Fuming, UAW official Stephen Yokich said he was "very concerned that the company simply didn't understand the statements we made . . . regarding equality of sacrifice."

Why, in the middle of delicate negotiations with its touchiest allies, would Harvester make a move guaranteed to rile them? McCardell finds the bonuses easy to defend. "They were for middle-management people, not top executives, and they amounted to only about 20 percent of what a normal bonus would have been. These employees had done a superb job of reducing inventories by $500 million. As far as I'm concerned, the company survived that year because of what these people achieved. We had been taking money away from salaried employees [through pay cuts and pay freezes] while union workers were getting pay increases. We would have been breaking faith with these managers if we hadn't given those bonuses."

Fairness, it seems, is in the eye of the beholder. But however justifiable the management bonuses may have been, Harvester's timing was off. Coming on the heels of the plea for union concessions, the bonuses just didn't *look* good—any more than McCardell's loan forgiveness had looked good after the losses caused by the strike and the deepening recession. Harvester had to buy peace with the UAW by promising to put $6 million in the union's supplemental unemployment benefits fund.

Still the rift was not healed. In addition to its obsession with management waste, the union began demanding job security in exchange for the wage and benefit concessions

Harvester wanted. With a third of its thirty thousand Harvester members laid off indefinitely (a word that was coming to mean "permanently" at factories throughout the industrial Midwest), the UAW wanted guarantees for those who were still on the job. It also wanted the right of "traveling seniority," which would enable workers laid off at one plant to move to another and keep their seniority. And to save jobs, it wanted to limit "outsourcing," the practice of buying parts from other manufacturers instead of making them in-house.

The wrangling that began in November didn't come to an end until five months later. At the end of April 1982, the UAW gave up $200 million by agreeing to forgo annual pay increases of 3 percent along with certain holidays and other fringes, and by suspending cost-of-living adjustments until "adequate profitability" again smiled on International Harvester. Harvester pledged "equality of sacrifice" throughout the company and promised the UAW a share of any pretax profits during 1983 and 1984. It also agreed to let the UAW renegotiate the concessions if pretax profits from continuing operations topped $300 million for two quarters in a row—a highly unlikely event. Assorted other promises included sixty days' notice of any new outsourcing plans and, when possible, six months' notice of plant closings.

PLANT CLOSINGS were becoming a real sore spot for everyone at Harvester, thanks to a media circus touched off by Harvester's decision to shut one of its three North American truck factories. The plant in Chatham, Ontario, was quickly ruled out because without a Canadian factory, Harvester would have to pay import duties on goods it wanted to sell in Canada. That left the factory in Fort Wayne and the one in Springfield, Ohio. In January 1982, before Harvester decided that one of the plants would definitely have to go, Springfield city officials and business leaders, worried about the ill health of their town's largest employer, flew to Chicago to find out how they could help the company. Harvester suggested they figure out a way to buy the Springfield plant and lease it back to the company, which would give Harvester a badly needed cash transfusion. "They said they couldn't make any guarantee about what they would do, but they promised not to take any action until at least the end of March," says Larry Krukewitt, director of the Springfield Area Chamber of Commerce. "At first it appeared that both plants would be kept open, but by mid-March they told us they would have to close one. They would decide on the basis of which community came up with the best financial assistance."

Overnight, Harvester's decision to close one of the two plants was transformed into a corporate version of the shoot-out at the O.K. Corral, with Springfield and Fort Wayne facing off for a fight to the death. It didn't matter that the two cities didn't see each other as enemies, or that Harvester was bending over backward to stave off a bidding war. What captured the public imagination was the contest. There would be a winner and a loser, and whoever lost would lose big because Harvester was the major employer in both communities. Coming at the deepest point of a recession that had taken hundreds of thousands of jobs away from midwestern factory workers, the contest was a powerful symbol of industrial failure: two buzzards fighting over a corpse. Unable to resist the drama, the television networks parked their cameras in both cities and waited for a loser.

But, says Krukewitt, "the enemy was never Fort Wayne. It was the multi-million-dollar size of the deal we were trying to put together. We didn't know whether we could get enough money to give Harvester the help it needed."

Springfield offered Harvester $20 million worth of aid,

and Fort Wayne matched that. Springfield came up with another $10 million. Fort Wayne found another $11 million. In the end the contest that wasn't a contest was decided by the one difference that did exist: The Springfield plant, built in 1966, was one of the largest, most efficient truck factories in the world. The Fort Wayne plant was a 1923 relic. Harvester chose to consolidate its U.S. truck manufacturing operations in Springfield.

The elimination of four thousand jobs was a blow to Fort Wayne, but not everyone there was convinced that Springfield's victory was all it was cracked up to be. "Quite a few business people made the remark that if International Harvester goes bankrupt, Fort Wayne might be better off as a result of having lost out to Springfield," says Fred Baughman, coordinator of Fort Wayne's economic development commission. The age of the plant would have made it extremely hard to sell, leaving Fort Wayne hard pressed to repay the millions it planned to borrow.

Springfield was better fixed. Having paid only $28 million for a plant valued at eight times that, Springfield stood a good chance of recovering its investment even if Harvester went out of business. "Whether the trucks rolling off the line have IH or ABC stamped on them is immaterial," Krukewitt says. "We now have control of our destiny because we've got title to the plant. Other firms have already shown interest in the plant, so if Harvester stops making trucks there, we would probably have a buyer. That will enable us to keep those jobs in Springfield."

EARLY IN 1982, at about the same time Springfield and Fort Wayne learned that only one of the truck factories would survive, nervous bankers began to lean harder on International Harvester. When the banks had begun restructuring Harvester's debt the summer before, the idea had been to buy time so the company could hang on until the economy recovered. But no one foresaw how long that would take. Harvester's losses for the quarter ended January 31, 1982 came to almost $300 million, which was more than the company expected, and the demand for trucks and tractors continued to shrink. If things didn't improve soon—and it looked as though they wouldn't— Harvester's net worth would soon fall below the level specified in the debt agreement.

Long before this, one of Harvester's two hundred lenders, the First National Bank of Commerce of New Orleans, had decided that enough was enough. Unwilling to go along with the debt restructuring, it demanded—and eventually got—repayment of a $3.5 million loan. But with no hope of collecting their debts unless the company survived, Harvester's big bankers were forced to take a different tack. They sent their "workout specialists" (also known as "goons" and "undertakers") to push for more cost-cutting. At the end of April, just four months after the debt restructuring had been signed and sealed, Harvester had to ask bankers for more breathing room. To avoid being in default of the debt agreements, it requested that its minimum net worth requirement be lowered. And it asked permission for a bigger ratio of debt to net worth. Bankers had little choice but to go along.

While Harvester executives struggled to keep bankers happy and to convince UAW that concessions were desperately needed, McCardell was waging a struggle of his own with the company's board of directors. The subject: the loan forgiveness in his compensation contract. Although the UAW and shareholders attacked the company's largesse in the matter and generally looked on McCardell as a stick-up artist, the fact was that the loan forgiveness was having an untoward effect on McCardell's personal exchequer. The $1.8 million was being paid to him in five yearly installments of $360,000. The combination of having to forfeit half of that in taxes, his 20 percent pay cut, and the disintegrating value of the stock he had bought with the loan meant that he was losing money. "That was going to keep on happening for three more years, until the forgiveness was over," McCardell says. "There was no way I could protect myself because the contract prevented me from selling the shares without board approval." So McCardell wanted the loan forgiveness rescinded as badly as the UAW did.

He and Harvester's directors wisely decided to keep these matters private. "Both the company and McCardell had lost all credibility as far as compensation was concerned," McCardell says. "There was no way anybody would believe I was actually losing money every day I came to work. When the contract was drawn up, nobody foresaw how quickly the forgiveness would be earned out—or how quickly the company's profits would deteriorate after that. That compensation package was an absolute disaster to me and to the company from a public relations point of view. If you tried to think up a worse scenario, you couldn't do it."

In late April, when Harvester and its bankers were putting the finishing touches on the revised loan covenants and when management had reached a tentative agreement with the UAW on concessions worth $200 million, directors proposed a drastic solution to McCardell's problem: If he resigned, the company could write a termination agreement that would put a stop to his losses. In essence, the agreement would give him a severance payment of $600,000 and let him keep his sixty thousand shares. There would be no more loan forgiveness beyond the $720,000 he had already received (two of the five annual installments of $360,000 each). McCardell thought it over for an hour and decided to accept the offer. "We had finally finished laying out our long-term strategy, and I had reviewed it with our bankers and directors," he says. "The union concessions had been worked out. I felt I could walk away from the company with a clean conscience because I had done everything I could do."

On Sunday afternoon, May 2, Harvester announced McCardell's resignation. The news release gave no explanation, focusing instead on the new management team. Analysts and bankers filled the information void with their own theories. McCardell had been ousted, analysts said, because he refused to take a smaller role now that the bankers were tightening their grip. Bankers denied that they had pressed for McCardell's dismissal and said his leaving wouldn't solve Harvester's most immediate problem, which was the high cost of its debt. Still others contended that Harvester's continuing losses demanded a change of leadership to restore confidence in the company. Nobody guessed that Archie McCardell, the biggest "bonus baby" of them all, had resigned because he couldn't afford to stay. On Monday morning, after his first good night's sleep in two years, he sold the sixty thousand shares he'd bought at $30 for $5.

It would be both an oversimplification and an understatement to say that International Harvester failed in its attempt to buy a savior with a multimillion-dollar compensation package. As McCardell points out, the contract was a disaster. But the company's massive debt and the severely depressed markets for its products mask a genuine achievement of McCardell's tenure: Without the hundreds of millions of dollars he slashed from the company's yearly operating costs, it is doubtful that International Harvester would have been able to withstand the pounding it would take while it waited—and waited—for better times.

Chapter 4

High-Tech Dreams

Roy Ash and AM
International

IN THE MIDDLE OF 1976, when a stranger phoned with a
business challenge, Roy Ash was in a receptive mood. For
the last year and a half, since the events that came to be
known as Watergate had brought his Washington days to
an end, Ash had stayed on the sidelines and tended his
personal investments. He was meeting his goal of outper-
forming the Dow Jones Industrial Average, but it was a
humdrum life for someone who had spent more than half
his fifty-seven years at the top.

As a young man, Ash had talked his way into Harvard's
Graduate School of Business, even though he didn't have
an undergraduate degree. Perhaps to show Harvard it was
right to have taken a chance on him, he finished first in his
class. After World War II, he joined the aircraft manufacturing empire of Howard Hughes in Southern California
and fast-tracked into the assistant comptrollership. That's

where he was in 1953 when he and his boss, Charles
Thornton, left for reasons that have never been unani-
mously agreed upon. According to one story, Thornton
and Ash were sent packing after it was discovered that the
accounting department had attempted to bilk the U.S. Air
Force out of $43 million. But as Thornton told the story, he
quit because Howard Hughes refused to give him the authority he needed to function as assistant general manager.
Once out the door, Thornton and Ash started their own
company and borrowed $1.5 million to buy another, from
a man named Charles Litton. Thus was born Litton Industries. The small manufacturer of parts for the budding
electronics industry then went on an acquisition binge the
likes of which had rarely been seen. In four years, tiny Litton bought seventeen companies and reached the $100
million mark in sales. By 1967, Litton was ensconced in a
flashy Beverly Hills edifice that looked like a cross between
Mount Vernon and a honeymoon hotel. Annual net earnings of $83 million came from—among dozens of other
things—shipbuilding, cash registers, medical equipment,
missile guidance systems, and contracts for developing underdeveloped countries.

Ash served as president of Litton until 1972, when his
friend Richard Nixon asked him to become director of the
new Office of Management and Budget (OMB). Ash was
just the man for the job. OMB had been his suggestion,
made when he chaired President Nixon's advisory council
on executive organization. Ash had also been a big contrib-
utor to Nixon's presidential campaigns in 1968 and 1972.
In 1968, *The Congressional Record* noted, he and other
directors of Litton gave more to the Republican cause than
did the management of any other defense, aerospace, or
nuclear company with extensive federal contracts.

And 1972 was a good year to be leaving Litton. Sales for
the year still outstripped the $2 billion-plus that had

brought the company its record net earnings of more than $80 million in the late sixties, but profits had just about disappeared. For 1972, the black ink was a scant $1 million, with Litton staying out of the red only by including as assets some of the claims it had filed against the Navy in a dispute over late delivery of five amphibious assault ships. The fight with the Navy and a sense on Wall Street that the Litton conglomerate had grown into an ungovernable giant sent the company's stock plunging from its all-time high of $120 to $12.

Democratic members of Congress who opposed the appointment of Roy Ash as director of OMB made much of Litton's troubles. Citing delays and cost overruns on attack helicopters as well as problems in building new destroyers, Senator William Proxmire of Wisconsin accused Litton of running "two of the most highly inefficient and mismanaged military procurement operations in recent times." Representative Les Aspin of Wisconsin raised similar objections, dragged the Hughes Aircraft accounting skeleton out of the closet, and volunteered an observation that would furnish an invaluable clue to understanding the later business adventures of Roy Ash: In the face of adversity, Aspin said, "Litton always seems to have an 'everything's coming up roses' public attitude."

It took a series of strenuous hearings to overcome the congressional opposition, but eventually Ash won his appointment. He stayed at OMB until 1974, when Watergate drove the Nixon brigade from Washington. Although Ash had no part in the scandal, he offered his resignation to President Ford, as did many other Nixon appointees. The resignation accepted, he went home to an estate once owned by W. C. Fields in the Bel Air section of Los Angeles.

The stranger bursting in upon his boredom a year and a half later offered a challenge of a sort Ash had not yet tackled: the chance to resuscitate a corporation that had failed to keep up with technological change. The patient in question was Addressograph-Multigraph Corporation of Cleveland, whose inconsistent performance in the first half of the seventies gave an ugly sawtooth mien to its earnings charts. Founded in the 1890s by an inventor who hit on the idea of mechanizing mailing lists by embossing names and addresses on metal plates, the Addressograph Company had joined forces in 1930 with the American Multigraph Company, a maker of duplicating equipment. Once an aggressive innovator, Addressograph-Multigraph introduced offset duplicators in the 1930s that dominated the market for forty years. But the company's catatonia in the face of the high-tech developments that thrust IBM, Xerox, and others into the electronic vanguard led Wall Street to dub the company "Addressogrief-Multigrief."

The caller who wanted to discuss the company with Ash was John Birkelund, president of New Court Securities, the New York manager of investments for the Rothschild family. Although Birkelund did not represent Addressograph in any official capacity, he thought he might stand to gain by acting on his knowledge that some of Addressograph's directors yearned for a change in leadership.

It was a classic opportunity for a corporate messiah—a company wandering in the wilderness, driven out of Eden by forces it did not understand, longing for the Promised Land but not knowing how to find it. Sizing up the situation, a typical corporate messiah would have asked for a huge sign-on bonus, like the $1.5 million Michel Bergerac got for walking into the jaws of Charlie Revson. Or a monumental severance clause, like the one that left Warren Hirsh swimming in money after his two months at Puritan Fashions. But Roy Ash was after bigger fish. He told Birkelund he wanted to consider Addressograph-Multigraph as an investment possibility. If he liked what he saw, he would buy a big chunk of stock, and, if the directors agreed, he would take over as chairman and try to make his investment pay off.

After his five and a half months as president of RCA, Maurice Valente said he never would have gone there if he'd known how venomous the politics were. And Warren Hirsh regretted that he didn't have a clearer picture of Puritan Fashions, where whatever Calvin wanted, Calvin got. Ash's investigation of Addressograph was likewise incomplete—but for different reasons. With his extensive business connections, he probably could have found out practically anything about practically any corporation. But as a potential stockholder, he would have run afoul of the SEC if he had made a decision to buy Addressograph stock on the basis of information not available to the public. To avoid these problems, Ash studied Addressograph's annual reports, proxy statements, and other public documents, and he quickly concluded that the company could make "an interesting investment." Although the stock was selling for $9 a share, the company's assets came to twice that. To Ash, that meant that even if Addressograph proved beyond redemption and had to be sold off piece by piece, he would double his money.

Not that he expected the company to go belly up. As someone who had grown up with the electronics industry, he thought he knew enough to transform Addressograph-Multigraph from what he calls a "clanking gears, spinning wheels" company into a high-tech thoroughbred that could run neck-and-neck with IBM, Xerox, and the rest of the office-equipment herd. Another advantage: the company's size, which he describes as "large enough to do something with but not so huge that it would take a long time to change." Best of all, the company had more than $40 million in cash on hand, which would help with the corporate remodeling he had in mind.

So, with $1.35 million of his own money plus $1.35 million borrowed from Addressograph-Multigraph, Ash bought three hundred thousand shares of the company's stock and headed off to Cleveland to become chairman. During the next year or so, buoyed by investors' belief that Ash could deliver the company from lassitude, Addressograph stock climbed 55 percent. Ash's $2.7 million was now worth $4.2 million. Birkelund made out all right, too, earning a $150,000 finder's fee and a seat on the Addressograph board. Convinced he knew a good man when he saw one, Birkelund had his firm buy three hundred thousand shares, just like Ash. Everything was coming up roses.

Thanks largely to Ash's willingness to put his own money on the line, he began his new job with a degree of credibility unusually high for a corporate messiah. Unlike Valente at RCA, Ash wasn't being second-guessed by doubting Thomases or tattled on by some envious Judas who wanted his job. From the day Ash arrived—sans entourage—it seemed he would bear out one of Machiavelli's most astute observations in *The Prince:* "For the actions of a new prince are much more closely scrutinized than those of an established one, and when they are seen to be intelligent and effective, they may win over more men and create stronger bonds of obligation than have been felt to the old line."

Seen to be intelligent and effective, Machiavelli said. There is no question about Roy Ash's intelligence. Known as a brilliant conceptualizer with intense powers of concentration, he is also a grand talker—provocative, unpredictable, disarming. In a confession guaranteed to win the heart of anyone who writes for a living, he tells interviewers that he went to Addressograph-Multigraph so he could get out of "the really hard work" of finishing a book on the executive abilities of U.S. Presidents. Despite his troubles at Addressograph, Litton, and Hughes, he remains a favorite of the business press, perhaps because the aphorisms and analogies that come so easily to him provide refreshing relief from the gray-flannel mode of expression favored by executives. Ash is at his best when the talk is on lofty planes far from the mess of everyday life. "An entrepreneur," he says, "tends to bite off a little more than he can chew, hoping he'll quickly learn how to chew it." Or, "At a sufficiently high level of abstraction, all businesses are the same." Or, "The objective is to find the right balance between order and disorder, between rigor mortis and anarchy."

As for Roy Ash's effectiveness, time would tell. The point, as Machiavelli would say, was that in spite of Litton, in spite of Hughes, in spite of the congressional dogfight over his OMB appointment, when Ash came to Addressograph-Multigraph, he was *seen* as effective. For any new corporate messiah, that is enough.

With no apocalypse pending at the company, the task was not so much salvation as purification—a washing away of the sins of staid bureaucracy. Addressograph, for all its vices, had a saving grace: cash on hand of $42 million. That gave Ash considerable leeway to acquire promising new high-tech companies and, he says, "to introduce change at a rate that wasn't catastrophic." In his first days on the job, Ash told Addressograph employees to keep doing what they were doing and he would catch up with them. But he also let it be known that change was in the wind. At his first board of directors meeting, the new chairman broke with tradition by sitting at the side of the table instead of at the head. That may not seem like much, but the old seating arrangement reflected a pecking order made inviolable by the chairs themselves, which were adjusted for the heights of their occupants. Ash also shook up the status quo by going off to Minneapolis to check into a customer complaint. "Word of my trip spread through the company's entire U.S. sales organization in twenty-four hours," he says. "Every salesman and every sales manager began to think that maybe something was going on."

Something was. After a few weeks of asking questions and making notes on yellow tablets, Ash decided that Addressograph-Multigraph needed nothing less than a new culture. "The company had settled into a low, bureaucratic drone," he says. "They were doing what they'd done in the past rather than finding the future. They had made a few forays into promising new areas, but these were ancillary, toe-in-the-water efforts instead of mainstream ones. The whole structure was presided over by the people who'd come up through one product line—duplicating equipment. Even though good new ideas had been suggested from time to time, the people who made the suggestions didn't dominate the culture. They were up against a majority that was apprehensive about its ability to handle new and unfamiliar kinds of products. So the little forces for change were gobbled up by the big elements for stability."

Ash knew that the transformation he had in mind could not be accomplished overnight, and like many a reformer, he understood the importance of getting the symbols of change in place as soon as he could. Accordingly, he rechristened the company AM International and announced that it would move from Cleveland to Los Angeles. "I was trying to change the balance between order and disorder," he explains. "There was too much order, too little openness to change. Cleveland had had its great days in an earlier technological revolution, but after 1940, new things began to take place elsewhere. A company's setting has a significant bearing on its culture, sometimes even too much." The "too much" had a highly specific impact on AM: The high-tech executives Ash wanted to hire—from Litton and other California companies—didn't want to move to Cleveland. Los Angeles held another attraction, too: AM's new headquarters were just around the corner from the chairman's home in Bel Air.

(Ash is not the only CEO who has succeeded in moving a major corporation to his own neighborhood. In 1971, after Greyhound Corporation of Chicago acquired Armour & Co. of Chicago, Greyhound chairman Gerald Trautman decided he'd rather run the company from Phoenix, where he had lived since 1965. Two other top Greyhound executives also had personal interests in Arizona. So a consulting firm was hired to analyze the ramifications of relocating and reached the unsurprising conclusion that Phoenix was just the place for Greyhound. "You could read anything into that . . . study you wanted," a former Greyhound executive told *The Wall Street Journal.* A director added, "The public reason for the move was that it would help in combining Greyhound and Armour to move to a neutral site, and privately that it would lead to the resignation of people we really didn't want anyway.")

By 1983, the subject of corporate culture even made the best-seller list (*In Search of Excellence* by Thomas J. Peters and Robert H. Waterman, Jr.), but back in 1976, when Ash was restyling AM, it was heady new stuff. With it he managed to enchant management theorists, business observers, and Wall Street securities analysts. But back on earth, far from such abstractions, numbers told more about the real life of AM than words ever would. As Ash went around the company with his yellow tablets and his bottomless curiosity, he discovered to his horror that no one had ever thought to ask basic financial questions about AM's individual products. "We didn't know what it cost us to make any of our products, we just had one big pot of aggregate costs," he says. "We didn't even know which products gave us profits. Some people thought they knew, but when we began creating useful data about each product, we found that in some cases we'd been paying salesmen high commissions to sell products that actually lost money."

Not all the surprises turned up by Ash's financial investigation were unpleasant. The supplies and services that supported AM's equipment accounted for more sales and profits than anyone had realized, and AM's offset printing equipment was not nearly as threatened by electronic copying machines as the company had feared. These unexpected strengths may have actually hindered efforts to bring about radical change, however. As Terrence Deal and Allan Kennedy note in their book *Corporate Cultures,* the greater the threat from the outside and the better the threat is understood, "the greater the likelihood that a culture can be successfully turned in another direction." One big reason Lee Iacocca has accomplished so much at Chrysler is that unlike his predecessors, he was able to convince Chrysler's employees, suppliers, bankers, and ultimately Congress of the seriousness of myriad threats from the outside. But Ash's conclusions did not jibe with those of Deal and Kennedy. As Ash saw it, the profits generated by these older operations could be put to work buying the new technologies that would carry AM into the future. Duplicating machines might be destined for what is euphemistically known as a "mature market" (one that is not growing), but AM's grip on the duplicator field made the equipment a reliable source of money for years to come.

But the old way of putting all the money in one cookie jar was going to have to go, and not just because of the analytical shortcomings it created. The corporate transformation Ash had in mind would require a different sort of bookkeeping—and shake AM's culture to the roots. All old relationships were to be sundered, replaced by new bonds flowing from an entirely different form of organization. The shift, as revolutionary as if the leader of a socialist country decreed that henceforth the nation would be fascist, was from an organization based on tasks to one based on products. No longer would one sales department manage all of the corporation's sales efforts. From now on, each product line—duplicators, addressing machines, and so on—would be a separate division with its own sales department, service department, and so on.

Ash had two reasons for tearing up the old organization chart. "The first was to put some responsibility into the system at levels below the top," he explains. "With one sales organization in charge of all the company's products, it was hard to know who was responsible when something went wrong. Somehow, the system was always to blame. Unless you place responsibilities with individuals and give out rewards or penalties for individual performance, people aren't motivated." Perhaps even more important, turning AM into a Litton-style portfolio of companies would make it easier for Ash to sell off operations that didn't fit his high-tech dreams.

Once Ash began remaking AM in his own image, the revolving door began to spin with dizzying speed. By 1978, with his old Litton colleague James Mellor as hatchet man, Ash had cut AM's work force 6.5 percent by abolishing its international division and slicing the headquarters staff in half. It also shut its research and development unit, which may seem a peculiar move for a company longing to catapult itself into the technological vanguard. "R&D was important to us," Ash explains, "but the R&D people at AM were committed to mechanical products instead of electronic ones. You can't put one electronics guy in with a hundred mechanical guys and expect much to happen in electronics."

The heads continued to roll, and in short order Ash had replaced 80 percent of the company's management. AM's largest division, Multigraphics, went through four presidents in two years. By the end of 1981 that number was up to six, and more than thirty executives had held the seven top posts below the Multigraphics presidency. In Ash's view, this change in the ratio of order to disorder was just what the company needed. "Disorder can be unproductive when there's a protracted struggle for control and power, as there was at Hughes Aircraft," he says. "That wasn't the case at AM. We had the power from the day we walked in. Even though we weren't in the majority, we set the agenda, and we needed the people to match our goals. Substantial internal change is good as long as it's aligned with the organization's goals."

Not everyone shares this optimistic view of rapid turnover. "New executives usually bring in other new people, and if enough of this goes on, no one knows how the business runs," says Richard Gould, an organizational psychologist and executive with extensive experience in human resources. "Things almost always slow down when there's a new executive on the job. The learning curve can last up to a year." When executive turbulence is widespread in a company, Gould adds, it can have serious repercussions far down the line. "It scares the hell out of people. With this fear comes safety behavior, survival behavior. People start pulling back to protect themselves instead of thinking about the business."

The performance at AM's Multigraphics division seems to bear out Gould's observations on what can go wrong when a business is run by too many raw recruits. Multigraphics lost its position as Number One in one of AM's most important markets—mechanical duplicators priced between $10,000 and $20,000.

Nevertheless, when Roy Ash talked, Wall Street listened. After all, he had bet $2.7 million of his own money on AM. He wasn't about to let that slip away, was he? So the $14 million loss AM reported for the year ended July 31, 1977, was widely regarded as a sign that everything was coming up roses—proof that Ash was trimming the fat and getting AM into shape for the great race to automate the nation's offices. Summing up the year's achievements for a *Forbes* reporter, Ash said, "We had all our problems taken care of in just slightly less than one year's earnings." Even more impressive evidence that Ash was on the right track emerged the following year, when AM vaulted into the black with earnings of $21 million on sales of $667 million.

The master plan—to ditch money-losing product lines and fund high-tech acquisitions with proceeds from the winners—had a logic that appeared unassailable. And Ash's boundless optimism about his new adventure was, if not unassailable, at least immensely appealing. Here was a man with a vision, a strategy, and a big personal stake in making his efforts pay off.

But no one seems to have asked, until it was too late, whether the strategy could support the vision. With its research and development unit boarded up, AM had to buy new technology rather than grow its own. Although acquisitions presented no problem for a fearless conglomerateur like Roy Ash, running the new companies was not nearly as easy as buying them. The AM strategy began to go awry as early as 1978, with the $18 million purchase of Jacquard Systems, a maker of word processors and small computers. Jacquard's annual sales were only $2 million, but its products had won rave reviews in the technical press. Ash wanted to take the ball and run with it. Treating Jacquard like a favorite son, he pulled out the checkbook and underwrote bigger marketing efforts, more manufacturing capacity, and a revamped distribution system. But no amount of money could speed the solution of the serious technical problems Jacquard was having with a new word processor, and the intensity of the push to turn Jacquard into an AM star caused many executives to quit, which had the same ill effect on performance at Jacquard that it had at Multigraphics. As one computer industry analyst told *Business Week,* "The turnover was so high that the replacements didn't have anybody left to ask where to start looking for the answers to the problems." Ash's open-checkbook policy in the face of these problems quickly turned Jacquard into a financial black hole. Even though sales shot up to $40 million by 1980, Jacquard had consumed $60 million of AM's cash and was losing $20 million a year. There went the cash hoard of more than $40 million that Ash had had when he started his reign at AM.

If Jacquard had been AM's only acquisition, perhaps the company would have been able to get itself out from under the storm clouds piling up overhead. But by April 1979, Ash had made six acquisitions, including the $4.8 million purchase of a company called Infortext. A supplier of electronic record-keeping systems to monitor the use of office duplicators and copiers, Infortext was a company whose products were beamed at a market that failed to materialize. Despite ubiquitous complaints about employees who put Xerox copiers to personal use, few employers were willing to buy the AM gadget that would help end the abuse. Unfortunately, AM pumped $20 million into Infortext before reaching this conclusion.

Still, Ash saw no reason for despair. In early October 1979, predicting a loss for the quarter that would end October 31, Ash insisted that AM was "going over the peak right now" in development costs for new products. It was another way of saying that everything was coming up roses. And the following summer, despite Jacquard's expensive problems and Multigraphics' falling market share, Ash declared that AM's troubles were now safely consigned to the past.

But anyone who had looked at numbers other than the bottom line would have known that AM's real troubles were just about to begin. Revenues had risen since Ash had taken over, but net earnings in 1979 were no higher than they'd been before he came. More significant, 99 percent of those earnings came from AM's old businesses, not from the Ash acquisitions. When the company's third quarter ended on April 30, 1980, interest payments had tripled in one year. Almost two thirds of the $4.8 million profit for the quarter came not from product sales but from currency translation gains and the sale of rental contracts on some of AM's equipment.

But the biggest threat to the high-tech visions of Roy Ash was the surprising shortage of cash in AM's till. As of April 30, 1980, it was down to $2.8 million—nickels and dimes compared to the $56 million AM had had on hand three years earlier. From the start, the plan had been to plow the profits from AM's old product lines into promising new ventures. But the crumbling market share of an old mainstay like Multigraphics made it harder and harder to replace the cash flowing into new operations like Jacquard. And without large amounts of cash, there was no way to stay in the electronics office equipment game, where aggressive (that is, costly) marketing is *de rigueur.*

Ash, however, was more convinced than ever that his roses would soon be in bloom. Speaking to shareholders toward the end of 1980, he admitted that the company had made mistakes and was "probably a couple of quarters behind . . . earlier schedules." But, he said, "Our expectation is to more than offset the consequences of those mistakes by greater accomplishments."

Wall Street wasn't so sure. Analysts once enthralled by Ash and his big dreams were starting to feel put out. Four months before the shareholders meeting, Ash and other AM executives had led analysts to expect strong earnings gains for the quarter ending October 31. Then the quarter ended with a $9 million loss—on top of an unexpected loss of $1.5 million for the fiscal year that had ended the previous July 31. The loss for the year was attributed to sloppy bookkeeping at Jacquard and Multigraphics, discovered at the last minute by AM's auditors. Ash was no happier than anybody else about the discovery, but he believed he had solved the problem by firing his chief financial officer.

By late 1980, reality had wrestled Ash's dream to the ground. AM's short-term borrowings stood at $141 million—almost triple their level fifteen months before. Interest expense outstripped operating income two to one, and long-term debt had actually begun to exceed shareholders' equity. Understanding the seriousness of such numbers, Ash quickly applied tourniquets to stanch the flow of red ink: AM omitted its quarterly dividend on common stock, it began bulldogging customers who were late paying their bills, and it started reducing inventories, which had been edging upward. Finally, since he held to the conviction that it was only a matter of time before his high-tech gamble paid off, he wanted to issue new stock or bonds to buy AM a little staying power.

With losses and debts raining down on AM, the idea of raising money through a stock or bond issue seemed positively quixotic to many AM-watchers. Who could possibly be persuaded to invest in a company that had traded its deep sleep for such troubled dreams? Among those most disillusioned by Ash's failure to deliver the widely advertised cultural transformation was none other than director John Birkelund, the go-between who had brought Ash to AM. Concerned about the fate of his firm's investment in AM, Birkelund began to plot a palace revolt in the fall of 1980. The question of how to raise new financing for AM gave the insurrectionists the issue they needed to launch a coup against Ash.

The ace up Birkelund's sleeve was that he knew who could be persuaded to invest in AM's troubles. The in-

terested party was Madison Fund, Inc., then in the process
of changing itself from a mutual fund to a nondiversified
investment company, which meant it would no longer
have to invest its money in as many companies as publicly
owned mutual funds are required to do. Now free to buy
large stakes in a few companies, Madison was attracted to
AM for the same reason Ash had been: The company's
stock was selling for less than book value. Beyond that,
however, Ash and Madison had no common ground. Ash
was hellbent on high-tech, and Madison thought AM had
better shore up the house of cards by getting back to
basics. Madison was willing to put up $25.6 million to buy
1,475,000 new shares of AM (a 14 percent stake), but only
on the condition that Ash be forced out.

Ash, with his 3 percent share of AM, was no longer in a
position to fend off the rebels. The death of one of his most
powerful allies, an Addressograph-Multigraph heir who
controlled 9 percent of AM's stock, had left those holdings
in the hands of someone who had no faith in the rosy future that Ash had been promising for almost four years.
"There's quite a difference between knowing you have 12
percent of a company in your pocket and looking down at
nobody who owns more than 1 percent, and then finding
that you have 3 percent and are looking up at people who
represent 20 percent," Ash says.

The Ash regime ended on February 20, 1981, at a special board of directors meeting held at the Links Club in
New York. "The issue was power and control, not how the
company was doing," Ash insists. "February 20 was a day
to count noses as to who had the power and control."
When he saw that his defense of his tenure at AM was not
persuading any directors to change their votes, he resigned
and left the meeting. Before the meeting adjourned, the
board moved swiftly through an agenda that had been
planned for weeks. It approved the Madison Fund invest-

ment and appointed a new chairman and chief executive, Richard B. Black of Maremont Corporation, a Chicago manufacturer of auto parts. He had been lined up by John Birkelund, the same man who had recruited Ash.

Ash kept to himself whatever shock he might have felt. Convinced that the company's shaky performance played little if any role in his downfall, he maintained that AM's glory was just around the corner. "The last three years were spent in taking the company back from oblivion and giving it a future," he told *The New York Times* after the coup. "Now we're close to the harvest." To underscore his conviction, he announced that he would keep his three hundred thousand shares. Ironically, the payoff was almost immediate. On the news of Ash's firing, AM shares jumped $2.875 in one day, allowing Ash to reap a paper profit of $842,500 on his own demise. For once, everything *was* coming up roses.

Chapter 5

Low-Tech Realities

Richard Black and
AM International (Again)

LIKE ASH, Richard Black had looked at the public records of AM's finances and saw an opportunity he didn't want to resist. "From the financial data, it appeared that the company had only been breaking even for the past four or five years," Black says. "Inventories and receivables had ballooned over the last few quarters, and some products appeared to have problems, but from the outside all these problems looked manageable. It seemed to me that cutting the short-term debt and getting the inventories and receivables down to the company's more traditional levels would quickly help get the problems under control." Once before, at Maremont, Black had presided over a turnaround and increased sales from $50 million to $330 million in nine years. He had every reason to think his marketing and financial know-how would work at AM. He was also encouraged by Madison Fund's willingness to buy more than $25 million worth of AM stock. So, on the day Ash left, Black took over and bought 300,000 shares of AM for $3.3 million. He paid cash for half, and AM made him a low-interest loan for the rest. AM also agreed to pay him a salary of $300,000 plus a bonus tied to increases in the company's earnings per share.

It didn't take long for Black to find out that AM's finances were not what they appeared to be. In the discussions he had had with outside directors before taking the job, no one had told him of the substantial weaknesses in the company's internal financial controls. And when he showed up for his first day of work, loss figures for the quarter just ended were waiting for him on his desk.

That was only the curtain-raiser. Six weeks into the job and greatly concerned about the accuracy of AM's books, Black brought in a new accounting firm to do a special review of business and accounting practices. Unearthed in the weeks that followed were scores of mistakes, weak financial controls, obfuscations, and—by the company's own admission—"apparent intentional overstatements." The damages added up to a staggering $203 million. "I have never seen such a mess in my life," Black says. Among the specifics: significantly overstated sales, inventories that either did not exist or had not been for sale for several years, and insufficient reserves for product warranty claims. A few hints of the irregularities surfaced in 1983, when the SEC charged the company with concealing its financial problems and illegally inflating its revenues. By the SEC's estimate, improper accounting procedures added at least $23 million to pretax earnings during 1980 and 1981. Among other things, the SEC said AM's Multigraphics division rented equipment to a customer for a three-month trial but recorded the transaction as a sale.

All the details, and the explanations, will not be known for several years, as more than a dozen lawsuits against AM and several of its principals work their way through the courts. The problems were so widespread and had been going on for so long that the new management and its auditors could not even figure out how to conform to the standard accounting practice of making appropriate adjustments to earlier financial statements. There was nothing to do but swallow the whole $203 million write-down in one gulp.

After reviewing AM's operations, Black concluded that AM should go back to the businesses it knew best. Less than a month after coming to AM, he put up for sale several of Ash's high-tech acquisitions. "Every one of them was losing money and out of control," he says. At the top of the list were Jacquard and Infortext, which together had lost almost $150 million for AM between 1979 and 1981. Five other divisions were also on the block. The new AM would consist of only three groups: Varityper, which manufactures machinery for phototypesetting; Bruning, an engineering supplies business; and Multigraphics, a maker of offset printing equipment. None of these businesses had the alluring growth prospects of high-tech, but all were capable of growing at a steady 4 percent a year.

Black also moved AM's main offices to Chicago, giving the company its third headquarters city in four years. "Ninety percent of the company's employees were located east of the Mississippi," he says. "Multigraphics and Bruning, two of its biggest divisions, were in Chicago. Every time I wanted to reach a manager, he was on an airplane, flying between headquarters in Los Angeles and operations in the Midwest. People at headquarters were completely out of touch with what was happening in the divisions." He denies that the move was a way to thin the AM ranks. "No matter how the new management tried to let people go, it was going to be expensive because the golden hand-shakes went almost all the way down to the janitors." Ash's own severance settlement was fairly modest: $175,000 (equal to his salary had he stayed on until the end of the current year of his employment contract) plus a retirement benefit of $50,000 a year. His protégé James Mellor, forced to resign after Ash left, received a settlement of $295,000. The tab for the rest of the changing of the guard—severance bonuses for old AM officers and relocation bonuses for new ones—came to almost $200,000 for the year.

In the five months between Black's election as chairman and AM's fiscal year-end on July 31, 1981, the company's net worth dropped from $260 million to almost zero. The stock price also plunged, making Black's shares worth substantially less than the $3.3 million he had invested. Madison Fund suffered along with Black, and in October it declined to exercise an option to buy more AM stock. It also began publicly complaining that its $25 million investment had been made on the basis of misleading information.

There seemed to be no end to the bad news that Black had to report. Not long after he predicted that the company would lose $175 million for the year, he had to revise his forecast to an even gloomier $250 million. In late October, AM defaulted on more than $100 million of its $250 million in debt and had to strike a new bargain with its bankers in the United States, Canada, and Great Britain. Black's revised loss forecast for the year was just about on target—the final figure was $245 million, followed immediately by a loss of $19 million for the first quarter of the next fiscal year. In January, to stretch its resources as far as possible, the company cut wages by 8 percent and laid off 850 employees. Even after all this belt-tightening, AM was hanging by a thread. With little left to sell and corporate spending already pared to the bone, AM was now in the unenviable position of having to convince its bankers to tide it over until the remaining businesses generated enough income to begin making a dent in the company's bills.

Although Black was convinced that AM was now headed in the right direction, the withering of his $3.3 million investment was a source of considerable consternation to him. In less than a year, the stock had fallen from $11 a share to $4, reducing the net worth of his investment by more than $2 million. Believing that he had been led to invest in AM by what he calls "misrepresentations" in the company's financial statements, he decided to try to recoup his losses by suing. And because the statute of limitations on some of his claims was one year from the date he purchased the stock, the suit had to be filed sooner rather than later. He discussed the lawsuit with AM's directors, who urged him to stay on as chairman. He tried to do that—briefly—but in his double role as CEO and disaffected shareholder, he found himself faced with an insoluble conflict between his personal interests and the interests of the corporation. There was no choice but to resign.

Several months before, Madison Fund had also decided to sue, charging that the financial statements it had used to evaluate AM as an investment possibility "were materially and massively false and misleading." Especially upsetting to the fund was AM's lack of "resources to carry forward the development and marketing of some of its new products that had potential." The cast of defendants in this and the long line of other suits varied from case to case but typically included AM, Ash, director John Birkelund (who brought both Ash and Black to the company), several other present and former officers and directors, and Price Waterhouse, the company's auditors until Black dismissed them after the special review by another accounting firm.

When Black left, AM was entrusted to the care of Joe B.

Freeman, Jr., who had come to the company with Black to serve as chief financial officer. In late March 1982, AM announced that its second quarter, ended January 30, had brought yet another loss, this time of $17.6 million. The new loss touched off a new debt default, and by mid-April, AM was forced to declare bankruptcy. Total liabilities ran to more than $500 million.

To Ash, the rapid collapse of AM during Black's tenure proves that the retreat from high tech was a misbegotten strategy. Arguing that his own four and a half years at the helm strengthened AM, Ash says the new regime's decision to focus on old lines of business came when the payoff for the high-tech thrust was just around the corner. He admits he didn't expect all the new ventures to pan out, but he is convinced his efforts, had they been continued, would soon have yielded more black ink than red. "The new management didn't have the high-tech background or the confidence you need to bet on the future," Ash says. "They made tailpipes and mufflers."

The criticism irks Black. "I doubt that either Ash or any of his top management have had the experience I have in successful commercial design of computer software and operation of computer equipment," he says. "I have nothing against high-tech. And I don't think it's bad to acquire new businesses. But the end result isn't to buy them, it's to manage them so they make a profit. It's like getting married. The marriage is an event, but it's the living together afterward that's the hard part. The previous management talked about the company as high-tech, but it wasn't. In the copier business, they were trying to use technology from the fifties to compete against Xerox, IBM, and a dozen Japanese companies. Their electronic cash registers were to be used in businesses like McDonald's and Burger King, but the AM registers could record only a limited number of items. This was at a time when those potential customers were expanding the items they offered. Infortext was a disaster. Its sales were $2.5 million a year and so were its losses. It made a product to count photocopies, but the product didn't work and was priced too high. Infortext was carried on the books at $12 million when I arrived, but when it was sold several months later all it brought was a couple hundred thousand dollars. With Jacquard, they might have had a chance but they blew it. They started a large sales force and marketing efforts with no product, and they wasted $150 million. Looking at the new businesses the previous management had gone into, I could see no evidence of improvement, only deterioration. AM wasn't high tech. It was more like a turkey farm."

Chapter 6

The Long Good-bye

Aging Entrepreneurs and the Quest for the Chosen Son

OF ALL THE KINDS of managerial change at the top, probably none leaves new corporate presidents on thinner ice than the circumstances arising when the boss is a highly successful entrepreneur approaching retirement age. Potential successors often find themselves in a no-win situation: If they perform too well, the old man may feel in danger of being eclipsed; if they stumble, they may be judged unworthy to inherit the crown.

It is easy to understand the old entrepreneur's unwillingness to let go. What heir, no matter how skilled as an executive, could possibly care as much about an enterprise as the person who gave birth to it, nursed it, saw it through hard times, and made it succeed? Stepping down has other painful implications as well, since it forces the entrepreneur to accept that he is neither indispensable nor immortal. At Edwin Land's Polaroid, it was considered in poor taste to discuss who might succeed the venerable inventor, even after he turned seventy. "To talk about a successor is to acknowledge that Land himself will die," explained one of the company's managers. "That is not spoken of at Polaroid."

But in refusing to face the succession issue (or refusing to give potential successors the elbow room they need to prepare for the top job), entrepreneurs often end up sabotaging the company they have worked so hard to create. At Polaroid, after the company's instant cameras found their way into millions of homes, some executives thought it was time to branch out into new markets, exploring industrial and professional applications for instant photography. Land didn't see it that way, so the company continued to concentrate on selling to the masses. Earnings slid, and so did the value of the company's stock. Polaroid sold for more than $100 a share in the early seventies, but it had sunk to $20 by the time Land finally relinquished the chairmanship in 1982, at the age of seventy-three. Polaroid then began trying to reverse its fortunes by pushing into the industrial markets that were off limits when Land ran the company.

Although the problem Polaroid faced has plagued companies in many industries, U.S. airlines seem to have had more than their share of succession troubles. In the early days, American, Eastern, United, Pan Am, and Delta were run by pioneers of aviation, such as Eddie Rickenbacker and Juan Trippe. Strong-willed men with definite ideas, they refused to groom successors as they began to get old. Consequently, at all these airlines except Delta, the executives who eventually did take over didn't have the necessary experience. When they ran into turbulence, they left, which led to even more disarray. Delta escaped this fate only because its strong leader, C. E. Woolman, had a heart attack in his late sixties. Little by little, Delta's top executives began to assume Woolman's duties, creating a strong management team in the process. When Woolman died, the team was well equipped to carry on and turned Delta into the most profitable of the country's major airlines.

Despite the damage that powerful, inflexible older entrepreneurs can do to their companies by refusing to step down, many boards of directors do little but accede to the chief's wishes. Even when corporate policy imposes some restrictions on the CEO's reign, such as mandatory retirement age, the directors (many of whom were chosen by the old man) can vote to exempt him from the rules. Unlike the successions of Popes and U.S. Presidents, which take place in accordance with explicit procedures, succession in companies dominated by elderly entrepreneurs is usually disorderly and often chaotic.

As human beings, we are to be congratulated for having progressed beyond the days when primitive tribes put their kings to death before they showed signs of illness or senility. The Shilluk of the White Nile, for instance, informed the elderly king of his doom by spreading a white cloth over him as he slept. Soon afterward, he and a young virgin were sealed up in a hut without food or water, left to die of suffocation and hunger. Barbaric as such practices were, however, they sprang from an impressive rationale: Since the success of the year's harvest was thought to depend on the vigor of the king, a king with declining powers would bring failed crops—and starvation—to the tribe. In a corporation, alas, the leader actually does have a great deal of control over the tribal fortunes. An aging entrepreneur no longer suited to the CEO's tasks (because of failing powers or because the organization has grown too large for one-man rule) may indeed cause the sort of damage that aroused the fear of primitive peoples.

Consider the case of Armand Hammer, chairman of Occidental Petroleum Corporation. "I'm the chief executive," he announced shortly after his eighty-second birthday, "and I intend to remain here as long as God will permit me."

God has permitted Armand Hammer many things, and anyone gauche enough to suggest that immortality is not among them should be reminded of the astonishing events of 1976. Hammer, then seventy-eight, was on trial for making and concealing $54,000 worth of illegal contributions to the 1972 reelection campaign of President Nixon. Seriously ill during the trial, Hammer came to his sentencing in a wheelchair. The judge, perhaps feeling that Hammer was not long for this world, let him off with a $3,000 fine and a year's probation. As soon as the trial was over, Hammer's ailments disappeared. Cynics raised their eyebrows, but seven cardiologists—including three hired by the prosecution—had attested to the seriousness of Hammer's condition.

Now in his mid-eighties, Hammer still runs Occidental Petroleum as if his immortality were a matter of corporate policy. The company has had five presidents since 1970, three of them since 1979, and all but one seem to have thought they were being groomed to succeed Hammer when the time came. Maybe they were. The trouble is, the time never comes. And once Hammer's infatuation with his new presidents wears off, he can't resist the charm of new faces. It is a kind of philandering, complete with generous payoffs to salve hurt feelings when the romance is over.

According to one school, these high-level seductions and betrayals are nothing more than a harmless eccentricity. "So what if you pay a million dollars to get rid of somebody?" asks an eminent New York management consultant. "At large corporations, a million dollars is a drop in the bucket, a mistake hardly worth mentioning." In Occidental's case, however, the mistake is worth mentioning not only because it has been made again and again but also because of its effect on the price of the company's stock. In 1980, when Hammer got himself yet another president, Occidental stock sold for only three times earnings while the stocks of other oil companies were selling for six. The reason, securities analysts say, is that the octogenarian chairman's refusal to settle on a successor leaves unanswered too many key questions about the company's long-term plans. Since no one has the slightest idea of what the Hammerless Occidental will be, the stock is a risky buy.

But Hammer's critics have never had much luck in getting him to listen, much less to modify his behavior. At Occidental's annual meetings, which are held on Hammer's birthday, shareholders who express disagreeable views are routinely shouted down by the chairman. Snapshots from the 1980 meeting: Hammer yelling at shareholders who criticized the company's chemical waste disposal procedures, a church group being thrown out of the meeting room, and the birthday boy hollering at one woman shareholder, "I don't care what your opinion is right now. Go back to Buffalo." The performance was repeated in 1982, when shareholders tried to discuss some of the proposals in the proxy statement. Although the votes had already been counted and Hammer knew that the shareholder proposals had been defeated, he gracelessly cut them off.

In fairness to Hammer, it should be pointed out that ungrateful shareholders are a novelty to him. When he acquired control of the Los Angeles company in the mid-1950s, it had three employees and a net worth of about $30,000. Nearly sixty years old and a multimillionaire from a string of entrepreneurial ventures that included everything from Russian art and Angus bulls to pharmaceuticals and beer barrels, Hammer was hoping the company would be a good tax shelter. It didn't work out that way. Less than a decade later, Occidental's market value had climbed to $100 million, and by 1983 the $15 billion company ranked near the top of the *Fortune* 500 Industrials. Needless to say, two decades of spectacular growth had made Occidental's longtime shareholders rich and happy. They came to annual meetings to celebrate, share Hammer's birthday cake, and wish him many happy returns. The handful who came to criticize were spoilsports to be hooted down, as Jane Fonda was when she used the Academy Awards ceremony to give her opinions on Vietnam.

Whatever Occidental Petroleum will be after Hammer, it certainly won't be what it is now. Hammer's relationships with the mighty stretch back to the twenties and give him a stature more like that of a head of state than of a corporate CEO. In the course of a year he is likely to meet with a dozen presidents and prime ministers, the Pope, and an assortment of cabinet ministers. He is the sort of person who gets invited to intimate parties for Britain's Queen Mother. His relations with the Soviet Union have been warm since the days of Lenin, when Hammer, fresh out of the Columbia University Medical School, went to the Urals to help fight an outbreak of typhus. He had another errand as well. His father's pharmaceutical business, which the boy had run while going to medical school, had shipped pharmaceuticals to the new nation on credit. Young Hammer was supposed to settle the accounts. As he tells it, it was during this trip that his business career was thrust upon him: "I saw the horror of famine in the Urals and realized people could be saved by importing American grain. I put at risk a million dollars, for which I was reimbursed with Russian goods salable in the United States."

Such is Hammer's standing among leaders of the Eastern Bloc nations that when the Soviets invaded Afghanistan in 1980, he launched his own personal peace initiative, jetting off in his Boeing 727 to visit Leonid Brezhnev, the president of Pakistan, the head of the U.S. Senate Foreign Relations Committee, the U.S. Secretary of State, the British Foreign Secretary, and the Secretary General of the United Nations. Like Hammer's youthful mercy mission, this shuttle diplomacy had an eminently practical aim: The U.S. embargo on Soviet trade was hindering Occidental's extensive corporate dealings with the Soviets.

Hammer tried his hand at foreign affairs again in 1982, when he proposed that Occidental build a pipeline to carry liquefied coal from Siberia to Moscow. Since this proposal came at a time when the United States was neck-deep in an international dispute over a natural-gas pipeline between the Soviet Union and Western Europe, Reagan administration officials were a bit cross. But there wasn't much they could do about it, and they were eventually forced to back down on their threats to impose trade sanctions on Western European companies who continued to supply the Soviets with materials for the natural-gas pipeline.

Armand Hammer is the larger-than-life stuff of which jet-set novels are made: fearless, despotic, defiant, insatiable, cunning. When the federal government blamed the toxic waste problems at Love Canal on Hooker Chemical (an Occidental subsidiary that was not acquired until years after the wastes were buried), Hammer tried to buy his way out of the controversy by stepping up his contributions to cancer research. When Hammer wanted to diversify Occidental by buying Iowa Beef Processors, he used his Soviet connections to make the deal attractive to everybody. The Soviets would get state-of-the-art packing plants to alleviate their continuing meat shortages, and Americans would expand the foreign market for their beef. Claiming that he needs absolute power to make the on-the-spot decisions that keep the company competitive in the international oil market, he prides himself on the fact that he alone makes deals for Occidental. *"L'état c'est moi,"* said Louis XIV. Armand Hammer can say the same of Occidental Petroleum. Hammer's life makes colorful reading, and a Sidney Sheldon or a Harold Robbins would have no trouble writing an ending for the story. The empire would be in ashes, the tycoon undone by his illusions of omnipotence.

But those who want to know what will really happen to Occidental after Armand Hammer are going to have to wait. The ongoing succession planning done by companies like Exxon and General Electric, where the smooth transition from one chief executive to the next is viewed as crucial to continuity and growth, seems to mean nothing to Hammer. His presidents are sidekicks, and often he hires them the same way he fires them: on the spur of the moment. In 1980, for example, as soon as Hammer heard that First Chicago Corporation had fired chief executive A. Robert Abboud, Hammer phoned him and told him not to do anything until they talked. The talk quickly led to an offer of a $400,000 salary and the Occidental presidency. The man then in the job, Zoltan Merszei, who had arrived to much fanfare only a year before, would go back to his first Oxy title, vice-chairman.

What had Merszei done wrong? Nothing. When Merszei came to Occidental from Dow Chemical, Hammer described him as "the best acquisition I ever made." Merszei was also one of the most expensive. His base salary of $280,000 would be supplemented with an incentive bonus of $112,000, stock options, and an $800,000 sign-on bonus.

The contract guaranteed him at least $280,000 a year for five years. Merszei was expected to earn his keep as vice-chairman of Occidental and chief executive of Hooker by putting Hooker in order. Not only did the subsidiary have environmental troubles at Love Canal and elsewhere, its profits had nosedived despite the hundreds of millions of dollars Occidental was spending to modernize Hooker plants. Merszei rolled up his sleeves and went to work, spending much of his time at Hooker's main office in Houston. Believing that the bureaucracy there had put on too much weight, he immediately ordered a hiring freeze. People knew he meant business. They had already heard about the time he moved Dow Europe's headquarters from Zurich to Horgen, Switzerland. He purposely ordered a building too small for the staff, and he situated it in a place where zoning laws forbade expansion.

Only three months into revamping Hooker, Merszei's responsibilities suddenly changed. Hammer asked Joseph Baird, the company's president for six years, to resign. Merszei would still run Hooker, but he would also be Occidental's president.

Baird's sins against Hammer were easier to comprehend than Merszei's would be a year later when the presidential baton would pass yet again. Even though Baird had used his banker's expertise to clean up Occidental's balance sheet and improve the company's image with the investment community, earnings had been wildly erratic. Operations at Occidental's European refineries became so hopeless that the company had no choice but to close them and take a $122 million write-off. And when Baird took a leaf from ITT to tighten financial controls and reporting systems, the formality of the new procedures irritated the freewheeling Hammer. The last straw was Baird's 1978 attempt to acquire Mead, a Dayton-based paper-products manufacturer that did not want to be acquired. The eye-for-an-eye battle between the two companies created unfavorable publicity for Occidental and touched off assorted federal investigations of the company. Occidental lost its $8 million fight, and Baird lost his job. Mistakes and all, however, Baird was kissed off with a consulting contract estimated to be worth more than his $300,000-a-year paycheck.

Although Baird had lasted six years, he was still the third Occidental president to be bounced since 1970, so Merszei must have known that presidents are as important to Armand Hammer as bus drivers are to school principals. Accordingly, Merszei kept his ebullient self-confidence to himself and seldom missed a public opportunity to assert Hammer's primacy. After allowing to a *Business Week* reporter that he and Hammer were a lot alike, Merszei cited one main difference: "Dr. Hammer is more diverse in his interests and is a far more fascinating guy. Even smart guys like me can learn a tremendous amount from him." And when Hammer and Merszei did their first dog-and-pony show for securities analysts, *The Wall Street Journal* noted that Merszei let the limelight fall on Hammer.

Even if Merszei had been inclined to grandstand, there wouldn't have been much time. Despite the improvements Baird had made in Occidental's balance sheet, debt was twice as large as equity. Hooker's product line needed to be broadened to get away from its dependence on low-margin generic chemicals such as chlorine and caustic soda, which is used in a variety of chemical manufacturing and petroleum refining processes. Occidental's Island Creek Coal Company subsidiary also needed attention as it attempted to bounce back from a long coal strike.

Hammer had a full plate too, largely because of growing uncertainties over the prospects of the company's controversial ammonia deal with the Soviets. Hailed in 1973 as the largest trade agreement ever reached, the $20 billion, twenty-year pact called for Oxy to build fertilizer plants in the Soviet Union, then exchange Occidental-made superphosphoric acid for Soviet-produced agricultural chemicals such as ammonia, urea, and potash. But U.S. ammonia producers were beginning to wrap themselves in the flag and complain that the influx of "Communist" ammonia was driving prices down. And in 1980, when Washington responded to Moscow's invasion of Afghanistan by imposing a partial embargo on U.S. agricultural trade with the Soviet Union, the Soviets had a few complaints of their own. For one thing, they wanted more money for their ammonia—almost twice as much as Occidental felt it could get U.S. wholesalers to pay. In addition, construction of an ammonia pipeline had fallen behind schedule, and several of the plants built as part of the deal weren't functioning properly. Miffed with Occidental and hampered by the U.S. embargo, the Soviets had begun looking to other countries for supplies of superphosphoric acid. With the lifting of the embargo in the spring of 1981, Occidental and the Soviet Union resumed doing business together, but the big deals that Hammer loves to make with his Iron Curtain connections leave the company's fortunes vulnerable to East-West tensions.

On a Friday afternoon in August 1980, in the middle of Occidental's Soviet ammonia crisis, Armand Hammer delivered a thunderbolt to Zoltan Merszei. A special meeting of the board of directors would convene in an hour, and Hammer wanted Merszei to know about the main item on the agenda. Occidental was about to get a new president—A. Robert Abboud, fifty-one, the recently deposed chief executive officer of First Chicago Corporation.

Merszei was stunned. Was Hammer unhappy with his performance? Not in the least. Did Hammer want him to leave? Not at all. Hammer wanted him to stay on as head of Hooker and as vice-chairman with responsibility for Occidental's strategic planning.

It was clear that the chairman's mind was made up, so Merszei didn't argue. But he did ask the board if he was still a potential successor to Hammer. The board told him he was. Later, talking to reporters, Merszei admitted that he had been sidetracked by the management change, but he confidently made a prediction: "Sooner or later it will become obvious that I am the right man to succeed Dr. Hammer. I will never be content just running Hooker."

As for Abboud, the financial community could not understand what Hammer saw in him. He had no experience in the energy field, and his sandpaper personality had caused more than two hundred executives to quit during his eight-year reign at First Chicago. He was so disliked by his employees there that after he was fired, gleeful chants of "Ding-dong, the witch is gone" were heard in the hallways. On learning of Abboud's appointment, one Los Angeles banker said Occidental "has gone out of its corporate mind," and at least one securities analyst crossed the company off his list of stocks to buy.

Abboud kept out of the line of fire and tried to demonstrate that he knew his place. When asked what he would be doing at Occidental, he said, "My job is to do whatever the doctor wants done." Asked for his views on whether he would succeed Hammer, he shot back a line guaranteed to please the chairman: "Any notion that Armand Hammer is mortal should be discarded immediately."

For a while after Abboud came to Occidental, speculation centered on what would happen to Merszei. Was he, despite the board's assurance, out of the running for the chairman's job? The answer seems to be just what it always was: As long as Hammer is alive, there will be no clear line of succession. But whatever dreams Merszei might have had of turning Hooker Chemical into another Dow will not come to fruition. Hooker, perhaps to dissociate itself from the nasty business of Love Canal, has changed its name to Occidental Chemical Company, and bit by bit its operations are being sold off.

Abboud's future is equally unclear. If Hammer is enchanted by anyone, it is his old friend David H. Murdock, a California financier who is as devoted to avoiding publicity as Hammer is to attracting it. Murdock has made his fortune by buying sizable chunks of companies whose stock are selling for less than their assets are worth. Among his holdings in 1981 was a 19 percent stake in one of the nation's most profitable meatpackers, Iowa Beef Processors of Dakota City, Nebraska. When Murdock learned that Occidental was looking to get into the food business because of Hammer's conviction that the 1990s will be plagued by food shortages, he arranged introductions to the management of Iowa Beef. Hammer was delighted, Iowa Beef was delighted, and the $800 million merger that soon followed turned Murdock into Occidental's largest individual shareholder.

After the Iowa Beef deal, Murdock joined the Occidental board of directors. He has played an active role in company affairs, and for once the company seems to have a long-term strategy. The old days of an Occidental with three hundred subsidiaries spanning the globe have given way to a focus on food and oil.

But this sharper definition does not mean that Hammer has abandoned his grandiose visions of Occidental's future. In 1982 he presided over one of the largest of the large mergers made in the past few years, with Cities Service Co. of Tulsa. In one stroke, thanks to the vast U.S. oil reserves of Cities Service, Hammer drastically reduced Occidental's dependence on reserves in foreign countries, and he moved Occidental a giant step toward its new goals. As well conceived as the merger may have been, however, its $4 billion price tag has left Occidental scrambling to pay its bills. By the end of 1982, the company's long-term debt had topped $5 billion, and the annual cost of carrying that debt reached a staggering $400 million. Earnings for 1982 plummeted to $0.69 a share from $7.77 in 1981.

To dig itself out of this hole, Occidental has sold assets right and left—minerals, coal, plastics, supertankers, a pipeline, and an office building. The strategy may work, but as DuPont discovered when it found itself in similar straits after spending $7 billion to acquire Conoco, buyers can drive tough bargains when they know the fix a company is in.

Where all these changes leave the contenders for Hammer's job is anybody's guess. Just as before the merger, chemical operations are high on the list of items to be sold, which means Zoltan Merszei has the unsettling task of selling his responsibilities out from under himself. Hacking away at Occidental's debt will take all of Abboud's considerable banking expertise, but it is doubtful that he harbors any illusions about the ultimate reward for doing this job well. The intriguing dark horse and the center of speculation is Murdock, who controls 4 percent of Occidental's stock. At the beginning of 1983, Occidental's stock was selling for $50 a share less than its assets were worth. Even with the company's massive debt and the long slump in energy prices caused by the worldwide recession, Murdock might decide that owning more of Occidental—and running it—are opportunities too good to pass up. The only certainty in all these uncertainties is that Occidental Petroleum will have no new chairman until Armand Hammer changes his mind about living forever.

IF ARMAND HAMMER illustrates what can go wrong when a superannuated chief executive won't think about succession, then William Paley of CBS shows the problems that can arise when an aging entrepreneur won't *stop* thinking about it. Although Paley finally handed over the reins in 1983, at the age of eighty-one, it took him five presidents and almost twenty years to let go.

Roundly criticized for his peremptory dismissals of executives, Paley remains convinced that he always had the company's best interests at heart. After all, a television network isn't just any old ball-bearing company, it is an exceptional business—a public trust. Fair and balanced news reporting, which Paley claims to have invented for broadcasting when radio was in its infancy, was a responsibility he took very seriously. He wanted to leave CBS in the care of someone he believed would feel the same deep personal obligation to honor the trust.

The CBS chairman's thoughts turned to succession after World War II, as it became clear that television would bring enormous growth to CBS. Until then Paley had run the whole show, overseeing everything from programming to ad sales to corporate finance, as if the company were the same small sixteen-station network he had bought in 1928. But in 1946, Paley ceded the title of president and chief operating officer to Frank Stanton, his right-hand man for several years. Five years later, with television's future assured, CBS redrew its organization chart and set up six autonomous divisions. The six became eight, eight grew to ten, and in the mid-1960s Paley decided he didn't want his eggs in that many baskets. So in 1966 the company was remodeled again, this time divided into only two groups—broadcasting and nonbroadcasting.

At the same time, the board of directors asked Paley to continue as chairman beyond his upcoming sixty-fifth birthday, despite the company's policy of mandatory retirement at that age. That policy had been instituted by Frank Stanton, and if he ever believed it would help him accede to the chairmanship, he must have been sorely disappointed by Paley's decision to stay on. Ironically, of all the heirs apparent who would be discarded by Paley, Stanton was the one best suited to become the guardian of the public trust. By Paley's own admission, Stanton had the high standards and sense of style the chairman thought necessary, and he was an eloquent spokesman on the role of broadcasting in a free society, a matter of crucial importance to Paley. Beyond Stanton's professional idealism, which had won him the title of "statesman of broadcasting," he was a skilled manager, adept in maintaining good relations between CBS and its affiliated stations during a complicated period of growth and technological change. "And yet," Paley wrote of Stanton in his autobiography, "a strong personal friendship never developed between us. Our bond was business and it never seemed to go beyond that. We shared no outside activity. We never grew close. In fact, as the years went on, we seemed to grow further and further apart."

Speaking to securities analysts and the business press, chief executives never tire of saying that corporate decision-making is a highly rational process, driven by a concern for achieving desired results. Numbers figure heavily in major decisions, and the picture one gets is that a corporation is a smooth, well-oiled machine. One phrase crops up again and again: "There are no surprises around here." The implication seems to be that no matter what happens, the machine will keep right on humming because all the contingencies have been so carefully thought out. But in searching for explanations of many succession decisions, especially those made by entrepreneurs who have built a company from the ground up, one must look far and wide to find cases where logic has been pressed into service. The best explanation for why Stanton wasn't good enough to succeed Paley is no explanation at all: Stanton simply lacked a certain ineffable something. The handy thing about this *je ne sais quoi* factor (which would do in several more presidents) is that it lies outside the realm of rational discussion. How can you argue with a man who says the candidate in question won't do because he lacks "I don't know what"?

Whatever disappointment Stanton felt at being passed

over for the spot of chief executive he kept to himself. He signed a new five-year contract to stay on as president, and he and Paley began looking for another crown prince. Their first thought was to choose an insider, but when that didn't work, they engaged an executive search firm to look outside CBS. In 1971, after ruling out several candidates in preliminary interviews, Stanton presented Paley with Charles T. Ireland, Jr., who had been working for Harold Geneen at ITT. Paley thought CBS could benefit from Ireland's expertise in diversification and his experience in a corporation renowned for rigorous financial controls. And since Ireland was just over fifty, he was young enough to lead CBS for many years—provided he worked out. The board approved Ireland's appointment as president in September 1971. Stanton moved up to vice-chairman, with primary responsibility for teaching Ireland what he needed to know to stand on his own as president when Stanton retired in 1973. But six months after Ireland started at CBS, he had a heart attack. He recovered only to suffer a second one, which was fatal.

In a matter of weeks, Paley and Stanton settled on a new president—Arthur Taylor, the chief financial officer of International Paper. It was a controversial choice. Not only did Taylor know nothing about broadcasting, which irritated CBS executives, he was just thirty-seven—hardly a seasoned executive. But Paley thought he saw in Taylor a hard-charging, exceptionally bright young man with the financial acumen CBS needed. On top of that, Taylor was articulate and cultivated, much like Paley himself. Taylor had majored in Renaissance history at Brown University and played clarinet with the New Jersey Symphony.

From the start Taylor worked his financial magic, and Wall Street cheered the trim shape he gave to CBS. He arranged the sale of the New York Yankees, who hadn't won a pennant (or made any money) since Paley had acquired them several years earlier, after they'd won five pennants in a row. Taylor also cut budgets and began requiring executives to fill out long reports justifying their expenses. And to prove himself a worthy heir to the "statesman of broadcasting" mantle, Taylor initiated the Family Viewing Policy. After reading the surgeon general's 1972 report on the harm that television violence does to children, Taylor promised that CBS would not schedule shows "inappropriate to general family viewing" before nine at night.

On the face of it, the Family Viewing Policy was an initiative in the tradition of the high-minded pragmatism established by Paley and Stanton: Act in the public interest and do it soon, so you can do it your way before the Federal Communications Commission makes you do it theirs. But in laying down the law about family viewing, Taylor did not realize he was desecrating holy ground. CBS had been Number One in prime time for two decades, and the people most responsible for that were the programmers. Believing themselves possessed of conscience and taste, they did not take kindly to Taylor's suggestion that their excellence left room for improvement. Besides that, they could not understand why Taylor wanted to add such a big unknown to the network's winning formula.

Convinced that right was on his side, Taylor began to get a holier-than-thou reputation like the one that dogged Jane Cahill Pfeiffer when she served as chairman of NBC. "Pompous" was a favorite word used to describe Taylor. "Missionary" and "zealot" also crept into the conversations of resentful programmers. When NBC and ABC quickly followed CBS's lead on family viewing, programmers could no longer complain that the policy put the network at a competitive disadvantage. But the combination of family viewing, the crimp that Taylor had put in expense accounts, and the austerities he demanded deeply offended the CBS programmers, who were widely conceded to be the best in the business. In 1975, one of the most important of them, Fred Silverman, allowed himself to be wooed away by ABC. Not long afterward, CBS Network president Robert D. Wood resigned, and several other key executives soon followed him out the door. Then the unthinkable happened: CBS lost first place in prime time. Paley decided his fair-haired boy would have to go.

On the morning of October 13, 1976, Paley called Taylor into his office. Two CBS board members were also there. Paley explained his dissatisfaction and asked Taylor to resign immediately. The board of directors was scheduled to hold a regular meeting that morning, and Paley wanted the firing and hiring taken care of at the meeting.

Taylor was shocked. Also on the agenda for the meeting were CBS's earnings, which continued to break all records. Earnings had doubled in the four years Taylor had been president, and CBS was sitting on a nest egg of $400 million in cash. Except for the ratings slip, Taylor's was a record to be proud of, but it would have been pointless to argue with Paley. The chairman had the whole board behind him. Once he decided Taylor was not measuring up, Paley had explained his position to outside directors, and they agreed to let Taylor go as soon as a successor could be found. Now the successor was in the boardroom, being voted into office, and Arthur Taylor was cleaning out his desk. On Wall Street, news of Taylor's departure caused CBS stock to drop almost $3 a share during the next two days.

Written contracts complete with hefty severance clauses were not yet commonplace when Taylor was asked to resign, but he was well paid for his humiliation—$250,000 in 1977 and 1978.

"Just a case of bad chemistry," one CBS executive said when asked why Taylor had been sacked. It was another way of saying that Taylor lacked a certain *je ne sais quoi*.

Paley, who had just turned seventy-five, now pinned his

hopes on forty-four-year-old John Backe, the head of CBS's publishing group. Between 1973 and 1976, while many publishers complained about hard times, Backe had brought higher sales and profits to CBS's book and magazine operations. Paley admired Backe's managerial ability, integrity, and sensitivity to people. Here was a man, Paley wrote in his autobiography, who was "not only an outstanding business executive but also a good 'generalist' . . . who could apply his experience, acumen and common sense in a multiplicity of business affairs." After working with Backe for almost three years, Paley concluded: "I seem to be working as hard as ever, but now with a feeling of pleasure and comfort because my successor is in place."

But at the time of Backe's appointment, a successor was the last thing on Paley's mind. He wanted not to surrender control but to get it back so he could personally remove the stain of last place from the CBS prime-time escutcheon. He "thought he would plunge himself in and . . . be the savior," said Jack Schneider, a longtime CBS executive and once a contender for the corporate president's job. The budget for program development was doubled, and the network commissioned forty series pilots to the tune of almost $500,000 each. Paley's former standards of taste and style went out the window. In his drive to reclaim first place, Paley began demanding that CBS create shows like ABC's *Charlie's Angels*, which never would have gotten through the front door at the old first-place CBS. But this time his programming flair failed him. Despite the $32 million CBS poured into development, seven of its new shows bombed, sending the network's ratings down even farther and making life at CBS extraordinarily trying. "You don't know Paley until you know him when the Nielsens are down," one CBS executive said. Paley hounded his TV executives day and night, tracking them down at home and in restaurants.

On the defensive about these failures, network president

Robert Wussler told *The New York Times* that ABC had taken the lead by putting "junk" and "comic book stuff" on the air. The critics were quick to point out that CBS was playing the same game. Its low-rated *Wonder Woman* was both "comic book stuff" and an ABC reject. Wussler also tried to argue that Number One was not necessarily the most profitable place for a network to be. If first place could be bought only by blowing a lot of cash, the costs might outweigh the benefits, Wussler said. But in television, Number One is probably worth whatever it costs because big advertisers tend to buy commercial time first on the shows with the largest audiences. Local stations also command higher ad rates when their network is on top, so they were more than a little unnerved by Wussler's readiness to settle for less. In October 1977, Wussler found himself out of a job.

It was also hinted that Backe's job was on the line, but the new president adroitly picked his way through the brambles. He understood, as one ex-CBS executive later put it, that Paley had only two interests in life: what the ratings were and how to make them better. Backe was content to stay in the background and let Paley's programming brilliance lead the network out of the doldrums. For the first few months after Taylor was fired, Backe kept to himself, and when he finally granted an interview to *Broadcasting* magazine, he said he planned to be "inward-looking"—concerned primarily with CBS employees and shareholders. True to his word, he won the hearts of programmers by quickly dismantling Arthur Taylor's Family Viewing Policy, replacing it with a commitment to "self-regulation." He also set up a CBS School of Management, which would help CBS employees move up in the company by putting more emphasis on promoting from within. Colleagues praised his low-key style and his focus on solving problems rather than looking for scapegoats.

While Paley concentrated on programming, Backe moved ahead with CBS's diversification plans. In 1977 he bought Fawcett Books, a paperback publisher, and in 1978 he acquired Gabriel Industries, a toy manufacturer. The company's earnings continued to rise, and in 1978 the network regained first place. It seemed that lowering the common denominator was what it took to win the prime-time ratings race, and now CBS had proved it could descend to even greater depths than ABC had. *Dallas* and *Dukes of Hazzard* became pillars of the new success at CBS.

With all these triumphs, the climate at CBS was more hospitable than it had been in a long time, but there was one storm brewing: cable television, which agitated network executives and network television stations because they had no way of predicting how many viewers would be lured away by the dizzying array of movies, sports events, and special-interest programs being promised by the new technology. Some of the old guard hedged their bets by making their own cable plans, but the many who developed a siege mentality did not like hearing network executives wax enthusiastic about opportunities presented by this new era of "video abundance." In truth, there *was* reason to be disturbed, since the numbers being collected clearly showed that networks were losing audiences to cable. Between 1977 and 1981, the networks' share of TV viewers would drop from 91 to 83 percent, and CBS itself predicted that the share would drop to 70 percent by 1990.

Backe was all for leading the charge into cable so that CBS would be ready to capitalize on whatever opportunities arose. Paley too understood the possibilities and even gave his blessing to a CBS cable channel devoted to drama and music. (As one CBS executive explained, Paley loved the idea of a highbrow cable operation because it gave him the "programming to fill the vacuum that the people in his social set talk about.") But Paley began to worry that Backe's gung-ho approach was too threatening to the affiliate stations. Early in 1980, according to one account, Backe and Paley had a knock-down, drag-out fight over how CBS's multibillion-dollar investment in cable would be described in the annual report. Shortly after the dispute, Paley decided to order—unbeknownst to Backe—an "assessment" of Backe's performance as president. Paley was beginning to feel that even though Backe might be the right man to head CBS now, that didn't necessarily mean he was the right man for the future. Not wanting to subject himself to the heat he had had to take when he abruptly dismissed Arthur Taylor, Paley convinced the executive committee, which he chaired, to do the "assessment."

But on April 25, before this star chamber could deliver the judgment the chairman wanted, Backe found out what was going on. Furious, he threatened to resign unless the executive committee gave him a vote of confidence. He also confronted Paley, who tried to get him to withdraw the ultimatum.

Paley insisted the executive committee had not ruled against Backe. "It was an open question," Paley told a reporter. "He came to me and I told him the whole truth. That an assessment was being made. It's a prudent thing for a company to do from time to time, particularly when there's some change in the offing." Citing his age and the consequent need to have a successor in place, Paley said he had to be "a realist . . . and think of what might happen."

Two weeks later, in California, Backe appeared at the annual CBS affiliates meeting as if nothing had happened. Early on the morning of May 7 he left the Bel-Air Hotel in Los Angeles, boarded a CBS jet, and headed back to New York. He went straight to the office, and at six o'clock he resigned.

At first Paley professed to regret Backe's departure,

pointing out that when the assessment issue arose, he had done everything he could think of to get Backe "on the track" again. In a memo to CBS officers, Paley even went so far as to pretend that Backe had resigned because he had found something better to do. "We understand his decision to pursue another course," Paley wrote, as if Backe had been under no pressure at all. Later, when Wall Street asked how investors could have confidence in a company where management comings and goings seemed to be determined by caprice, Paley was forced to take the defensive. He characterized Backe's reaction to the assessment as "abnormal," and he said he felt a "Harvard Business School degree might be more essential at a company like General Electric than at CBS." That was a below-the-belt swipe, since Backe had an M.B.A. (though not from Harvard) and had spent a good part of his career at General Electric. When a reporter reminded Paley of the praise he had lavished on Backe only a year earlier, in his autobiography, Paley said, "I think he changed." Perhaps Backe had lost his *je ne sais quoi.*

This time no new president was waiting in the wings, but Paley did allow that neither Backe nor Taylor had lived up to the standards set by Frank Stanton. "Frank was terrific," he said soon after Backe quit. It must have been small comfort for Stanton to learn that Paley now considered him the best man for the job. Seven years past retirement age, Stanton was no longer in the running. Paley was still confident that he could fill the presidency with no trouble at all, despite the speed of the revolving door at CBS. His reason? "It's one of the best opportunities in the country," he said.

He was right—sort of. Less than three weeks after Backe quit, Paley announced that CBS had found another president, fifty-year-old Thomas H. Wyman, vice-chairman of Pillsbury. But this time, to cushion any possible fall,

CBS had to give its new president $1 million just for signing on. The company also promised Wyman a salary of at least $300,000 a year for three years. And, if CBS bounced him, he would walk away with two years' pay.

The contract signed, Wyman became CBS's fifth president in nine years. No one thought to ask Jimmy the Greek for odds on Wyman's survival, but he had at least two aces in his pocket. One was his success in working with autocratic older men. He had come up through the ranks at Polaroid, where the dominating presence was inventor-entrepreneur Edwin Land. And Wyman had worked smoothly with William Spoor, Pillsbury's toughest cookie. "He's got a lot of experience working with people who are eccentric," one of Wyman's colleagues said of him. "You might say he's got a master's degree in it." Wyman's chances of survival also were aided by the hardening conviction among CBS board members that firing presidents (or goading them into resigning) was no longer an option for the company.

"I have a successor in place," Paley told *Fortune* magazine after Wyman had been at CBS for two years. "Someone might say those are famous last words, but this time it's for real." A few weeks later, on the eve of his eighty-first birthday, he gave the penultimate proof that he meant what he said. He announced that Wyman would succeed him as chairman after the company's annual meeting in the spring of 1983. But Paley would stay on as a member of the board of directors, chairman of the board's executive committee, and a consultant. He would also keep his 7 percent of the company's stock and his elegant suite on the thirty-fifth floor of CBS's headquarters.

There is no way to judge what shape CBS would be in today if it had had one or two presidents instead of five during the past decade. And it is possible to argue that whatever the disruptions caused by presidential arrivals and departures, Paley himself provided sufficient continuity. But there is no denying that the company has lurched from one direction to another, with each new president veering sharply from his predecessor's plans. Taylor wanted to streamline CBS by selling the money-losing operations. Backe went down the acquisition road and pushed for an all-out involvement in cable. Wyman has sold one of Backe's pet acquisitions, Fawcett Books, and when CBS's cultural cable channel was discontinued after it proved a dismal financial failure, Wyman announced that CBS would approach cable with caution. Telling an audience of TV executives just what they wanted to hear, he declared, "Network television will remain overwhelmingly popular whether the public has the choice of 12, 24, 48 or 200 channels to watch."

Broadcasting continues to be the mainstay of CBS, accounting for almost half its annual revenues of $4 billion. Wyman's job will be to sustain that success and either dump or make more profitable the company's troubled ventures, which include records, parts of its publishing group, motion pictures, and musical instruments. According to one estimate, CBS operations producing a full $1 billion in revenues add almost nothing to the bottom line.

ANOTHER CONTENDER for the world record in the category of "Most Presidents Consumed by an Aging Chairman" is GAF Corporation. Six GAF presidents have come and gone in the past twenty years or so, the last three in fewer than four years.

The drum major at the head of this brisk parade is Jesse Werner, who began ruling GAF in the 1960s. By 1982, when he was sixty-five, the company had one of the worst financial performance records of any major U.S. corporation. In *Forbes* magazine's 1982 "Report on American Industry," GAF's profitability took 1,004th place out of the

1,023 corporations listed. Seventeen years after the company's stock was first sold to the public in 1965, "the shares are selling for about one-third of their original offering price," *Forbes* noted, adding that except for dividends, "the original investors have lost perhaps 90 percent of their investment, adjusted for inflation."

Nevertheless, Werner seemed to feel he didn't need any help running GAF. In 1981, after his sixth president left, Werner decided that presidents were more trouble than they were worth. Henceforth the company would be run by an office of the chairman, consisting of Werner, the vice-chairman, and several senior vice-presidents.

The board of directors couldn't have been nicer about the hard times Werner had been through. Instead of using his age as a pretext for letting him go, directors in 1982 signed him up for another five years—at more than $400,000 a year. Why would the board do such a thing? It could hardly have been expected to do otherwise, since six of its ten members were strong Werner loyalists. Two were GAF managers, one was a retired GAF executive, and three outside directors had close business ties to Werner: One was a GAF banker, another was a GAF contractor, and the third was chairman of a corporation on whose board Werner sits.

With all potential successors out of the way, Werner could move ahead with his plans to improve the flow of black ink at GAF. In a corporate version of robbing Peter to pay Paul, he sold half the company's businesses and used the proceeds to support the other half. By 1983, Werner had whittled GAF to half its former size.

Werner loyalists may have been content with his performance, but at least one large shareholder was not. Samuel J. Heyman, a Connecticut shopping-center developer, resented the idea that the proceeds from Werner's sell-offs were plowed back into GAF while stockholders shared none of the gains. In a 1983 battle that dragged on for months, Heyman and his band of dissidents, against enormous odds, rallied the votes to oust Werner. Unresolved after the coup was the issue of Werner's seven-figure employment contract, which runs until 1986.

HAROLD GENEEN of ITT did not go through crown princes the way Paley, Hammer, and Werner did but, like a number of strong-willed executives in recent years, he was unable to leave the company in the hands of his first successor. His achievements as chairman and chief executive officer of ITT are undeniable. When he joined the company in 1959, it had annual revenues of $766 million. By the end of 1977, when the time came to hand over the reins to his successor, revenues had increased more than twentyfold, to $16.7 billion. With operations in 80 countries, ITT was just about as international as a corporation could get, and the 275 companies Geneen acquired during his tenure made ITT one of the world's most diversified conglomerates. In addition to running foreign telephone companies and manufacturing telecommunications equipment, ITT was hosting travelers in its Sheraton hotels, selling insurance through The Hartford, dabbling in oil and gas, publishing books, and baking Twinkies and Wonder Bread. The drive to diversify sprang from Geneen's hunch that the company's foreign telephone and telegraph businesses were vulnerable to rising tides of nationalism and socialism in Third World countries. Fearing that unfriendly governments would expropriate these communications networks, Geneen sought to put ITT's eggs in hundreds of baskets so that when the shocks came, they could be readily absorbed. His intuition paid off. In the 1970s, several countries did nationalize ITT subsidiaries, and the settlements were decidedly parsimonious.

Geneen's fans love to point out that he is a high-school dropout, and for one of the most unusual reasons on record. At age sixteen he had decided he wanted to devote himself to accounting. Thus began a lifelong passion for figures that would earn him a reputation as the numbers man to end all numbers men. Numbers—and his tight control of them—became the glue that held the ITT empire together. To make the control as fail-safe as possible, Geneen devised an internal reporting system that requires the controller of each subsidiary to report to both the president of the subsidiary and the corporate controller at ITT headquarters in New York. The beauty of the system is that it keeps subsidiary presidents from rearranging the numbers to make things look better than they are.

Geneen's detractors say his obsession with tight controls made ITT a living hell for managers of subsidiaries. Everything they did was dissected by Geneen's massive headquarters staff who, according to one account, "could advance their own careers by finding problems and perhaps exaggerating their importance." In drawing up business plans and setting growth targets, line managers had to go head-to-head with product managers, who represented corporate headquarters. Tension between the two was inevitable. Product managers wanted more growth, more profitability, more everything, and line managers wanted less ambitious goals since they were the ones charged with bringing in the sheaves. When a line manager and a product manager could not agree on the subsidiary's goals—which some observers say happened once every too often—the dispute had to be arbitrated by the office of the president.

Then there was the ordeal known as the monthly management meeting. For three days—twelve- and fifteen-hour days, not the nine-to-five variety—150 or so managers sat around a single large table at ITT's Park Avenue headquarters and sweated bullets while Geneen grilled one after another on the minutiae of subsidiary operations. European managers got the same monthly treatment at the company's office in Brussels. Geneen, who reportedly traveled with seventeen briefcases crammed with the company's latest financial data, had a command of the numbers that was dazzlingly broad and deep. Not a single operating unit escaped his notice. A master of the withering question, Geneen demanded answers that were not opinions but what he called "unshakable facts"—preferably in numerical form.

A company joke explained that the G in Geneen was soft, as in "Jesus." That G may have been the only soft thing about Harold Geneen. To anyone who dared suggest that the mushy spots in ITT's performance might signal that it was time to start trimming the conglomerate, Geneen retorted that ITT didn't sell its problems, it solved them. In his mind, any manager worthy of the name would be able to turn a troubled company around. There wasn't even any mystery about it. You set yourself a goal—like the 10 percent growth in annual earnings per share that was his standard for years—and you march toward the goal quarter by quarter. "If you make your quarters, you'll make your year," he told managers again and again. Like chairman Edgar Griffiths of RCA and dozens of other chief executives who held sway in the days before the success of the Japanese turned American business upside down, Geneen believed that if you took care of the short term, the long term would take care of itself.

From the time Geneen took over in 1959 until the early 1970s, the Geneen Machine was a corporate marvel. The chairman's commitment to increasing earnings per share at a 10-percent-a-year clip made ITT's stock a Wall Street darling, and low-interest rates allowed ITT to buy any company that seemed like a good idea at the time. The fastest way for a corporation to grow is to acquire other companies, and nobody did that better than Harold Geneen. With sharp management and tight financial controls, new subsidiaries were whipped into shape and helped to plump the bottom line.

There was an occasional odd hitch, however. Like the accusations about ITT's involvement in Chile's 1970 presidential election. The company was said to have contributed $350,000 to the opponent of leftist candidate Salvador Allende. Years of congressional investigations into the matter yielded ambiguous results. At ITT's annual meeting in 1976, Geneen told shareholders that no one was sure if ITT had actually spent the money in the Chilean election, but if it had, it had done so legally. Besides, he said, making the contribution "would have only been for the purpose of seeking to preserve a major investment . . . amounting to $153 million for the stockholders." The investment was in the Chilean phone company. Never mind that ITT, if it did in fact make the contribution, was trying to subvert a democratic election in a foreign country. And never mind that if a foreign company pulled the same stunt in the United States, red-white-and-blue-blooded capitalists across the land would cry "Foul!" at the top of their lungs.

In 1972, ITT was accused of trying to influence a Justice Department antitrust decision by promising to contribute $400,000 to President Nixon's reelection campaign. The Justice Department forced ITT to sell several subsidiaries but allowed it to keep The Hartford Insurance Group. No one paid much attention to the decision until columnist Jack Anderson discovered that an ITT lobbyist named Dita Beard had written a confidential memo implying that Geneen got that settlement by making the campaign pledge. At the bottom of the memo Beard wrote a little note: "Please destroy this, huh?" What happened next is recounted in *Everybody's Business,* an almanac of American industry:

The day after Anderson's column appeared, ITT's Washington office was in a frenzy, as workers madly put their files through the paper shredder. Dita Beard disappeared to a Denver hospital, where she was visited secretly by E. Howard Hunt, of the infamous White House "plumbers." Wearing an ill-fitting red wig borrowed from the CIA and disguising his voice through a voice modifier, Hunt instructed her to denounce the memo as a fake (it wasn't). Eventually located by the FBI, Beard was questioned in her hospital room by a panel of senators sitting on the confirmation of Richard Kleindienst, who had supervised the settlement of the ITT-Hartford case. (Kleindienst pleaded guilty to a misdemeanor arising out of his testimony about the case.)

When novelists spin yarns like that, they are accused of stooping to cheap thrills.

Problems with such unusual contributions—politely described by congressional investigators as "questionable payments"—have continued to dog ITT. In 1982, a report filed in federal court by a special review committee of ITT directors tallied $13.9 million in questionable payments made between 1971 and 1975 and another $5.7 million in "possibly" questionable payments made since then. It is not clear what distinguishes questionable from possibly questionable payments. Even more mysterious than the payments themselves is how a company that prides itself on the strictness of its financial controls could let almost $20 million escape the eagle eyes of the controller's staff at corporate headquarters.

By the mid-1970s, the world in which Harold Geneen had stitched together his multinational conglomerate had changed. Low-interest rates no longer existed, and ITT's stock fell out of favor on Wall Street. Both of those happenings made growth by acquisition exceedingly difficult. It was easier to pay back money borrowed at 6 percent than money borrowed at 10 or 12 percent, and companies could be acquired for fewer ITT shares when the stock price was $50 than when it was $30. ITT now had its finger in so many pies that critics began calling it "International This & That." Securities analysts complained that the complexity of ITT made it impossible for them to get a handle on the company's performance. Diversification, considered the smart strategy of the 1960s, was losing popularity as analysts began paying less attention to earnings growth and more to profitability concepts such as return on equity and return on investment. "Bigger is better" was giving way to squeezing the most out of what you had.

Geneen was not insensitive to these changes. As a numbers man he couldn't be, because the numbers for 1974 and 1975 were down for the first time in more than a decade. Clearly something was amiss. To find out what, he turned to Lyman C. Hamilton, Jr., his chief financial officer and treasurer. Eugene E. Jennings, a psychologist, consultant, and professor of management at Michigan State University, has warned chief executives against their natural tendency to surround themselves with clones, and by this standard, the match between Geneen and Hamilton was a laudable one. Geneen was a builder, Hamilton a consolidator. Geneen ruled with an iron hand, Hamilton was pure velvet. Geneen was a furious talker, Hamilton a thoughtful listener. Geneen was nearing retirement age, Hamilton was in his late forties. The two were even physical opposites—Geneen short and bald, Hamilton a tall gentleman with the magisterial white hair that Central Casting reserves for business executives and U.S. Supreme Court justices.

An alumnus of the World Bank, where he rose to the rank of senior investment officer, Hamilton joined ITT in 1962. In 1974, when it became apparent that not even ITT's worldwide diversification could cushion it from the effects of a growing recession, Hamilton devised a strategy that became known as "zero incremental debt." It was an unfelicitous way of saying that ITT wasn't going to increase its borrowings. Properties and securities were sold, plant additions were put on hold, and by the end of 1975, ITT's debt had not only *not* increased, it had actually dropped by $385 million. Earnings were sliding—13 percent in 1974 and another 12 percent in 1975—but the balance sheet had a healthier glow than it had had in a long time.

Wall Street liked Hamilton because he had a way of making the company comprehensible. Instead of bragging about ITT's 280 profit centers, which boggled the minds of everyone but the encyclopedic Harold Geneen, Hamilton saw ITT as a simple beast with a few vital organs: telecommunications, financial services, natural resources, and a handful of other businesses, ranging from auto parts and aerospace/defense systems to consumer products and services. For his stellar performance in shoring up ITT's financial pilings, Hamilton in 1976 was anointed executive vice president.

And so began the guessing game of when Geneen would step down and who would succeed him when he did. Although Geneen turned sixty-five, ITT's mandatory retirement age, in 1975, directors extended his contract for another two years. The directors were glad to have him, but Geneen had his own reasons for wanting to stick around: He didn't want to leave until ITT bounced back from the jolts of 1974 and 1975. As one observer put it at the time, "[N]obody expects Geneen to pull out until he can go in something akin to a blaze of glory."

The *cognoscenti* watching the ITT succession bet on either Hamilton or another newcomer to the office of the president, a West Point graduate named Rand V. Araskog, who had come up through ITT's defense and aerospace businesses. Both were indefatigable up-and-comers, and since neither had been part of the office of the president until 1976, neither bore even the slightest taint of guilt by association in the scandals involving Chile and Nixon's re-election campaign. But not even the smartest of the bettors foresaw that in fairly short order, both Hamilton and Araskog would succeed Geneen.

The guessing game seemed to be over in February 1977, when the company announced that Hamilton would become president and chief executive officer on January 1, 1978. Geneen would stay on as chairman. At the time, it was presumed that the choice of Hamilton over Araskog suited Geneen as well as it suited the directors, but by June, Geneen was decidedly tepid about the crown prince. "Don't worry about Lyman Hamilton," he said. "He's okay." *Okay?* Was anyone ever damned with fainter praise? Geneen also pointed out that Hamilton was "backed up by a great team" and that he himself would be around to make sure Hamilton did a good job.

In Geneen's promise to keep an eye on things lay the seeds of Hamilton's undoing. Almost from the start, Geneen sent certain board members lengthy memos criticizing the new chief executive's performance. What disturbed Geneen most was Hamilton's plan to sell off parts of ITT. Since Geneen had acquired almost every one of ITT's subsidiaries, there was no way Hamilton could travel the divestiture route without offending the old man, but he might have made his efforts more palatable by seeking a consensus rather than acting alone. Nevertheless, whatever Geneen's misgivings, the board appeared to give Hamilton a vote of confidence in August 1978 when it told Geneen to stop meddling in the daily operations of the company.

Hamilton also brought drastic changes to the tone of the dreaded management meetings. Outside ITT, it was rumored that Hamilton had sawed the massive meeting table in half, leaving the part he no longer needed at one end of the room as a reminder that times had changed. Although there was no truth to the rumor, the change in style was unmistakable. Fewer people were required to attend the meetings, they lasted one day instead of three, and Hamilton presided over them in a low-key, temperate manner. All of it grated on Geneen's nerves. "I sit in meetings, and sure, I have to hold myself back from jumping and screaming," Geneen admitted to a reporter. But he also claimed to understand that his role was to support Hamilton, not oppose him.

In the end, however, Geneen couldn't bring himself to do that. The financial community praised Hamilton for reducing ITT's debt and improving its bond rating, but what Geneen noticed was that Hamilton had done it with the money he'd made by selling six companies. After giving his life's blood to building one of the biggest conglomerates in the world, Geneen was not about to sit idly by while somebody took it apart just to pay a few bills to please the nervous Nellies on Wall Street. There is disagreement about which of Hamilton's sins actually sent him to the guillotine, but one school contends it was his plans to sell the company's consumer-electronics businesses in Europe. At a regular monthly meeting with the ITT board's compensation committee on July 11, 1979—only a year and a half after Hamilton moved into the chief executive position— he was asked to resign.

The request came as a complete surprise to ITT management and to Hamilton himself, who thought that he had control of the board. As Hamilton reportedly told one securities analyst after the firing, "I thought my assignment was to run the company and try to get along with Mr. Geneen. But I discovered I was supposed to get along with Geneen and try to run the company."

The press release announcing Hamilton's departure attributed it to "policy differences." As often happens in sudden high-level management changes, no one at the company would explain what those differences were, and

Hamilton's leaving was characterized as a resignation rather than a firing. At lower, less visible management levels, allowing an unsatisfactory executive to resign rather than be fired could be viewed as an act of corporate kindness, since it could make it much easier for the executive to find another job. But at the top, firings disguised as resignations save more face for the corporation than for the executives. By publicly firing its CEO, a board of directors would be admitting that it had failed in one of its most crucial responsibilities: choosing a leader.

THE PRESS RELEASE announcing Hamilton's resignation also announced that Rand V. Araskog, forty-seven, senior executive vice president and chief operating officer, would take over as president and chief executive. The Monday morning quarterbacks said Hamilton's greatest error was his inattention to the ego of Harold Geneen, and Araskog lost no time in showing that his sensibilities were more finely tuned. Asserting that he was in charge and Geneen's role would be advisory, Araskog nonetheless volunteered, "We're going to get along. I'm going to make it my business." Saying he planned no major changes, he then proceeded to cancel Hamilton's plans to sell the European consumer-electronics operations.

Only four months after Araskog became CEO, ITT announced that Geneen would relinquish the chairman's job, leaving it to Araskog. But Araskog's political finesse wasn't the only factor in the decision. Geneen's growing outside business affairs had begun to concern several members of the ITT board, who worried about conflicts of interest. According to one source, when Geneen cut a handsome deal for himself, directors wondered why he hadn't brought the deal to ITT. These new pressures from the board forced Geneen to come to grips with what he had not been able to face during Hamilton's tenure: It was time to clear out. To make a clean break, he moved out of

ITT headquarters and into offices maintained by the company in the Waldorf-Astoria. The terms of his departure could not have been sweeter: $450,000 (the salary he would have been paid had he stayed on through 1980, the last year of his contract); $250,000 a year through 1985 for his services as a consultant; and an annual pension of almost $150,000. In 1981, the company added $112,000 a year to his pension. Comfortable as that sounds, it fell short of what Geneen had asked for. Soon after he announced his resignation, he suggested that ITT pay $5 million over a period of five years to buy out his contract.

The ironic postscript to the firing of Lyman Hamilton is that Araskog resumed Hamilton's strategy of selling ITT's subsidiaries to build up the company's financial muscle. Within a year of acceding to the CEO's job, he even sold most of the European consumer-electronics businesses. By the beginning of 1982, he had shed $1 billion worth of ITT assets—more than forty companies in all. Why did Araskog succeed where Hamilton failed? The fact that Geneen found the new CEO's politics more palatable is almost beside the point. The reason Araskog could get away with the transgressions that doomed Hamilton was that this time, after resigning the chairmanship, Geneen was truly out.

THE DISSATISFACTIONS that Geneen had with his first successor have happened often enough in the corporate world for the phenomenon to acquire a name: the second-man syndrome. Simply put, the first heir to a Paley or a Geneen is a marked man because the aging CEO can't resist the urge to eliminate the person now in possession of his prize. Had Charles Revson not died soon after Michel Bergerac took over Revlon, there is a good chance that Bergerac would also be on the list—despite the fact that Revlon would have had to spend $4.5 million to buy out Bergerac's contract.

The second man often succeeds for another reason as

well: In overthrowing his first successor, the old man cashes in all his political chips. Thus ITT directors could be persuaded, on the basis of their great regard for Harold Geneen, to dump one president, but they would not countenance another coup. Aside from whatever moral or professional compunctions individual directors might have felt about getting rid of Hamilton, these sudden, inexplicable management changes are not actions to be taken lightly. They suggest that a company does not know what it is doing, which makes lenders and investors very nervous. Whether Araskog or Hamilton is the better man for ITT is anyone's guess. But because of Hamilton's firing, Araskog is infinitely more secure, and it is conceivable that if Araskog had been the first man, Hamilton would be running ITT today.

Another first man who fell victim to an aging CEO was Robert K. Swanson, who lasted only eight months as president of Greyhound. The older man in the driver's seat, Gerald Trautman, had come to Greyhound in 1963 after representing the company in a number of legal matters. From vice president and legal counsel, Trautman moved up to president and CEO, and in 1969 he added the chairman's title as well. Trautman had not created Greyhound from scratch, as Paley had done with CBS, nor had he presided over spectacular growth in the manner of Armand Hammer and Harold Geneen. But that is not to say he was a man without imperial ambition. "He didn't like being chairman of a bus company, especially one someone else has built," a former executive maintains. So in the early 1970s he acquired Armour & Co., a Chicago meat-packer. Overnight the company known on Wall Street as "The Dog" underwent both major expansion and major diversification.

But meat-packing, except as practiced by a handful of technology-obsessed companies like Occidental Petroleum's Iowa Beef subsidiary, yields more lean than fat. That sad fact left Greyhound to spend the seventies selling a good part of the company Trautman had been so excited to acquire. Trautman defended the sell-offs, arguing that Greyhound got good prices for the operations it didn't want to keep, but others say the proceeds were then plowed back into other low-margin Armour activities.

By 1980, Armour was still a drag on Greyhound earnings, and Trautman was sixty-seven. After considering several of Greyhound's senior executives for the heir apparent's job, he decided to go outside the company. His choice was Robert Swanson, a forty-eight-year-old executive vice-president of General Mills. A hard-charger highly regarded for his marketing and strategic planning expertise, Swanson seemed like just the man to set Greyhound on the right course for the future. But when Swanson showed Trautman just how hard he could charge, Trautman balked. One of the problems, it seems, was that Swanson thought his status as president and chief operating officer meant he could make key decisions without consulting the man who for years had kept Greyhound executives on very short leashes. Not understanding how the game was played, Swanson even recruited a corporate vice president of strategic planning without consulting Trautman or the board of directors. In Trautman's view, the new president was spending too much time on strategy and not enough on running the company. The irony, of course, is that Swanson's planning expertise was one of the things that had made him attractive as a job candidate. Neither Swanson nor Trautman will discuss their short, unhappy relationship, but it is possible that Swanson's emphasis on corporate strategy was a thorn in Trautman's side, reminding him that his efforts to diversify Greyhound had left the company without a sense of direction.

When Swanson was asked to leave after only eight

months, Trautman declined to designate a new heir. Instead he set up an executive office with himself as chairman; a president; and two vice-chairmen. In November 1980, when he announced the plan, Trautman said that all three of the men joining him in the new executive office "have the skills and experience appropriate to, and will be considered for, the role of chief executive officer of Greyhound in the future." Trautman delivered on his promise the following summer, when one of the three, John Teets, was named CEO. A year later, when Trautman retired at the age of seventy, Teets became chairman as well.

With no obligation to submit his plans to Trautman, as Swanson had had to, Teets said he would continue to dispose of Armour operations because they contribute so little to Greyhound's profits—only one-seventh of earnings despite the fact that they accounted for more than half the corporation's revenues. As the second man, Teets may be able to accomplish what the first man could not: improve profitability by dismantling Trautman's empire.

When Trautman decided to create an executive office rather than name a new president to replace Swanson, critics said he was only postponing the inevitable. "It was obviously a decision not to decide," one securities analyst said. But the idea of having two or three heirs apparent instead of only one has an appealing logic. With several executives preparing for the top job, a company reduces its chances of jolting investors' confidence if the first choice doesn't work out. The setup allows a corporation to groom its own chief executives instead of leaving the decision until the eleventh hour and then concluding that the new CEO will have to come from the outside because no one in the organization has the right experience. And from the aging CEO's point of view, the greatest advantage of the arrangement is that it strengthens his influence at a time when people in the organization may be tempted to write him off because he will soon be gone. It is a shrewd power strategy, practiced not only by chief executives but also by elderly baboons. As anthropologists Irven DeVore and Sherwood Washburn found when they studied baboon troops in the African savanna, the dominant male who heads the troop doesn't do it alone; he forms a coalition with two other males. When threats arise, the members of the coalition come to each other's defense, which allows the elderly male to continue his political rule even when he is no longer capable of defeating his aggressors in physical combat.

This method is alive and well at Citicorp, the country's largest bank holding company. Chairman Walter Wriston, due to retire when he turns sixty-five in August 1984, has four potential successors. Each has a major responsibility: institutional banking, consumer banking, legal affairs, and investment banking. The post of president has been vacant since 1982, when its occupant retired, and Wriston sees no need to fill it. Pointing out that General Electric has not had a president for several years, Wriston says, "At Citicorp, the vice-chairmen are really chief executives of their own businesses, so you don't really need a number two to back up the CEO."

Although some critics have suggested that the four-way succession race at Citicorp leads to unnecessary political intrigue, with assorted factions lining up behind the man they think will win, the bank may well benefit if all four turn in the superlative performance necessary to keep them in the running. When the race is over, however, there is the question of what will happen to the losers. Well prepared for the top, they may be tempted to leave if CEO jobs open up elsewhere. That happened at Citicorp in 1967, after Wriston beat out Thomas Wilcox in a competition for the corporate presidency. Wilcox went to Crocker National Bank in San Francisco as chairman, and a number of Citibankers went with him.

Owens-Illinois, a packaging company headquartered in

Toledo, has had a similar contest under way for several years. The competition began in 1976, when one potential successor was named president of Owens-Illinois' domestic business and the other was appointed president of the international operations. A few years later chairman Edwin D. Dodd had the two trade jobs. Now, Dodd feels, both are well prepared to handle the chairman's spot.

Even though a company with a Citicorp-style succession race risks losing the also-rans once the race is over, that risk exists no matter how chief executives choose their successors. After Maurice Valente concluded that he was not a contender for the top job at ITT, he left to accept the presidency of RCA. Robert Frederick, the current president of RCA, left General Electric not long after it named someone else as CEO. Executives burning to run their own companies can hardly be expected to stay in situations where they know they won't have that opportunity.

As easy as it is—especially with hindsight—to fault the succession decisions of William Paley or Harold Geneen (or the adamant nondecisions of Armand Hammer), it is virtually impossible to lay down rules for how the changing of the guard should be accomplished. "There are no formulas," says Edward W. Carter, who has been highly praised for engineering a smooth transition when he stepped aside as CEO of Carter Hawley Hale Stores. Carter, who became CEO at the age of thirty-four, built the company from a three-store operation into one of the country's largest retailers. In addition to its Broadway department stores in Southern California, the Los Angeles-based company owns Neiman-Marcus, Bergdorf Goodman, and Waldenbooks, among others. In Carter's opinion, orchestrating a succession is a complex exercise in judgment, not a matter of following rules. It could hardly be otherwise, for the skills that competent CEOs must have can be acquired only through experience. Not only do they need a comprehensive understanding of their companies and their industries, they also must earn the confidence of the financial community and of political leaders whose decisions affect their corporations.

Carter began thinking about a successor more than twenty years before he expected to retire. "I was extremely anxious that I not be unwilling to relinquish authority when the time came," he says. "I also didn't want to leave a weak successor. Strong builders don't usually leave strong successors because the builders tend to dominate. They squelch creativity, they are often overassured, and they brook no interference." In the late fifties, Carter hired Philip M. Hawley, a young man he hoped would grow into his successor. "He was working somewhere else at the time," Carter says. "I thought he could learn a lot in that job, so I suggested he stay there for a couple of years. I told him that if he would then come to work for me, I'd give him an opportunity to advance if he performed. He did well in every assignment I gave him, so I did everything I knew how to get him to the top. I put him in merchandising, which is the core of retailing. Then I sent him to the Harvard Business School to broaden his perceptions of the world and of business. After that I put him in charge of half of the company's nonmerchandising operations. He eventually became president of Broadway Stores, and then I asked him to come to the corporate office, where I spent several years teaching him what I knew about the company and about the necessity of decentralizing management as far as possible. Gradually I shifted corporate responsibilities to him. I also got him started in community activities to prepare him to be accepted by community, state, and national leaders. He is now one of the leading citizens of Southern California and a leader in retailing. He did it on his own, but I created the atmosphere that made these things possible."

Although Carter was convinced that Hawley was the right man to succeed him, he believes that a CEO's support of a candidate should be only one factor in the ultimate succession decision, which is made by the board of directors. "The important thing is to keep the board informed about your thinking on succession," he says. "That includes being candid when you think there's no one inside the company who can do the job and, if the situation arises, it means telling the board you no longer think a particular candidate is suitable." Even when a CEO believes the right successor has been found and is being well prepared, the succession problem has not been laid to rest, Carter says. "You have to guard against an atmosphere in which subordinates don't know who's boss. If you let people know too early who your successor will be, you can become a lame duck. You have to delegate responsibility to help a potential successor grow, but you have to make sure the successor doesn't have the authority until the board gives it to him."

The board gave Hawley that authority in 1978, when it shifted the title of CEO to him from Carter. Carter stayed on as chairman despite his awareness of the free-for-alls many older entrepreneurs have caused by doing so. "Most times it doesn't work," he acknowledges. "The only way it can work is if you never, ever let anybody know when you and your successor disagree."

That is a tall order, but Hawley claims his former boss has filled it. Long after the changing of the guard, he told *Business Week*, "Carter did a textbook job when he stepped down, because he totally relinquished the reins." As events at CBS, ITT, and elsewhere show, few older entrepreneurs are capable of exercising that kind of restraint. One unusually insightful one who knew he wouldn't be able to stay quietly in the background, as Carter has, was Royal Little, founder of Textron. "I knew I wouldn't be able to sit on the board and shut up," he said. "I'd be a pain in the neck." So at age sixty-six, Little turned in all his epaulets.

Although a handful of corporations have raised succession planning to a high art, their policies are so carefully tailored to the specific needs of their organizations that they could not be successfully transplanted to other organizations. But some of the general types of efforts they are making clearly show how careful attention to succession can minimize the rapid executive turnover that is so disruptive to an organization. At Exxon, where succession is accorded paramount significance, the planning encompasses the advancement potential of every manager and staff professional. Performance is regularly evaluated, and the evaluation is done by several superiors rather than just one, which keeps an insecure boss from hiding a subordinate's talents from executives farther up the ladder. Each operating unit keeps lists of candidates for every existing job, so that when someone leaves or is promoted, the company has possible replacements lined up. Almost every Monday afternoon, Exxon's president, chairman, and several senior vice-presidents meet to go over succession planning and management training efforts. As for choosing the chief executive, the decision lies with Exxon's board of directors, which may agree or disagree with the departing CEO's candidate. But because of the exhaustive attention paid to succession throughout the company, members of the board will already know all the likely possibilities.

At General Electric, human-resources experts outside the personnel department monitor the development of fifty thousand managers, technical people, and staff professionals throughout the company. Performance is appraised annually, and the people followed most closely are those who turn in outstanding performances. Executive vacancies are filled by having two or more star performers compete for the job.

Long past the days when they were run by entrepreneurs, Exxon and General Electric—along with DuPont, Kodak, and a few others—have been able to institutionalize their succession planning rather than leave executive decisions to the caprice of an aging autocrat who cannot bring himself to let go. The managers who survive under a domineering entrepreneur tend to be weak, which leaves a company with shaky leadership once the old man's reign does come to an end. It is too soon to assess how much harm Armand Hammer and William Paley have done by staying on long past their prime, but the jury *is* in on RCA Corporation. There the dictatorship of the company's brilliant founder, General David Sarnoff, set the stage for fifteen years of managerial miscues that eventually toppled a chairman, a president, and two other top executives in the short space of eighteen months.

Chapter 7

His Master's
Voice

RCA and NBC

ON THE NIGHT OF APRIL 14, 1912, a twenty-one-year-old telegraph operator in New York picked up a historic message: "S.S. *Titanic* ran into iceberg. Sinking fast." The young man, David Sarnoff, stayed at his post for the next seventy-two hours, copying the names of the eight hundred survivors so that newspapers could tell their anxious readers the fate of those on board.

This night to remember marked the beginning of one of the most brilliant careers in American technology. A highly imaginative entrepreneur, Sarnoff grasped the commercial possibilities of broadcasting and electronic communication long before his peers. While World War I was still in progress, he deluged his colleagues at American Marconi Corporation with memos on setting up broadcasting networks as a way to get the public to buy wireless contraptions that he described as "radio music boxes." Although Westinghouse beat him to the punch with the first broadcast in 1920, Sarnoff delivered a punch of his own the following year with the first sports broadcast: a boxing match between Dempsey and Carpentier. Sarnoff started building radios shortly after that, and in 1926 he founded the National Broadcasting Company, the network he had been dreaming of. When American Marconi became the Radio Corporation of America, Sarnoff rose quickly to the chairmanship, from which he continued his dazzling series of firsts by building the first televisions and the first color TV sets.

But between these heady beginnings and the late 1970s, so much had gone awry at RCA, and NBC was so firmly in last place among the networks, that the company's link to the *Titanic* had inspired a new genre of mordant humor— the NBC joke. "What's the difference between NBC and the *Titanic*?" one joke began. The answer: "The *Titanic* had an orchestra." Comedian Bob Hope, poking fun at NBC president Fred Silverman's frantic efforts to save the network by jerking dreadful TV shows from one time slot to another, described Silverman as "the only man in America who knows what it's like to rearrange the deck chairs on the *Titanic*."

RCA, the parent of NBC, was in no better shape. By 1982, its management troubles were so well known that they were even the subject of a Charles Addams cartoon in *The New Yorker:* Eight anxious-looking fox terriers (like the Nipper of RCA's famous symbol) sit in a boardroom, their ears cocked toward the Victrola near an empty chair at the head of the table.

Unhappy unless he was pioneering, Sarnoff failed again and again to reap the rewards of his innovations. With radios, TV sets, and color TV's, he was first, betting the company when others said there would be no market for the products of his wild-eyed dreams. The markets always materialized, but by that time Sarnoff was pushing toward some new frontier. The vast opportunities he created were left to be exploited by other companies, like Zenith and Motorola.

By the time David Sarnoff retired in 1966 and left RCA in the hands of his son Robert, the seeds of this weakness had begun to bear disturbing fruit. The solution, as Robert saw it, was to turn RCA into a conglomerate, the quintessential corporate creature of the high-flying sixties. The wisdom of the day held that by owning a variety of businesses, the conglomerate was in a position to shield itself from the ups and downs of a single industry. Robert Sarnoff put together a portfolio of companies that was as diversified as you could get. He acquired a rental car agency (Hertz), the publishing firm of Random House, two food companies, a real-estate operation, a communications satellite business, and a maker of furniture and carpets. He also took RCA into the mainframe computer business, long dominated by IBM.

The computer venture was a disaster. When RCA finally gave up on it, in 1971, computers had saddled the company with a pretax loss of almost $500 million.

The acquisitions didn't pan out, either. After Robert Sarnoff bought companies, he didn't care much about running them, and the conglomerate was never more than a collection of left hands who didn't know what the right hands were doing. With the exception of Hertz, all the companies he bought have been sold. Fed up with Sarnoff's expensive failures, the RCA board of directors in 1975 organized a coup. When Sarnoff came back from accompanying his wife, soprano Anna Moffo, on a concert tour, the board gave him the ax.

RCA is now on its third chairman since Robert Sarnoff. In all likelihood, it will soon have another since the current occupant of the chairman's office, Thornton Bradshaw, is near retirement age. The company also went through a president in short order, hiring and firing Maurice Valente in six months. The cost of this musical chairs at the top? Acute public embarrassment, several million dollars in severance settlements, a severely depressed stock price, and an organization that continued to flounder.

The first man charged with undoing what Robert Sarnoff had wrought was a well-liked, highly regarded RCA veteran named Anthony L. Conrad. But he had barely begun to dismantle the conglomerate, selling the communications satellite company and the maker of furniture and carpets, when a baffling aspect of his life came to light: Anthony Conrad, chairman of one of the world's best-known corporations, had failed to file income-tax returns for the past five years. It wasn't that he was trying to defraud the United States and the state of New York. Through payroll withholding, he'd paid all but about 3 percent of what the tax collectors said he owed. Somehow he just never got around to sending in the proper forms. On the advice of his attorneys, he declined to explain this omission, and to this day there is no solution to the mystery that cost him his $200,000-a-year job and stock options that could have given him a profit of $160,000 for 1976 alone. So in September 1976, only ten and a half months after acceding to the chairmanship, he was reduced to waiting for eight hours in his office while the RCA board decided his fate. There was nothing to do but let him go. Conrad's inexplicable behavior cost RCA more than embarrassment. The board also had to withdraw a planned offering of five million shares of stock for fear that investors would avoid RCA stock because of Conrad's scandal.

Next the board turned to Edgar H. Griffiths, who started his RCA career in 1948 as a $53-a-week bill collector. A gruff, rotund man with an unswerving devotion to the bottom line, Griffiths probably knew RCA better than anyone else at the top. He'd served as president of RCA Service Company, a director of the corporation, a troubleshooter when the conglomerate fell on hard times, and when Hertz faltered, he had engineered a spectacular turnaround. His management style was simple and stern: Monthly targets were set, and every month managers had to report whether the targets had been met. If they hadn't, Griffiths wanted to know why—and when the problem could be corrected. Once when a Hertz manager was having trouble getting his biggest customer to pay a mounting bill, Griffiths ordered him to camp on the customer's doorstep until he got paid. Salvaging RCA, Griffiths believed, was just a matter of looking at the numbers once a month and making whatever managerial adjustments were necessary to maintain a healthy flow of black ink.

For a while it looked as if Griffiths had hit upon the magic formula. By the end of 1978, two years after he became chairman, RCA was in better shape than it had been since the early sixties. Griffiths continued the conglomerate-trimming begun under Conrad, tightened purse strings, and thinned the employee ranks. The proof of his performance was in the bottom line: Revenues had grown by 25 percent since he'd moved into the chairman's office, and net earnings had swelled by more than twice that.

Griffiths was also trying to be an entrepreneur as well as a conservator. RCA engineers had high hopes for their new videodisc player, known as SelectaVision, and Griffiths understood the importance of keeping their efforts well supplied with cash. In addition, he recognized that as RCA unburdened itself of its conglomerate baggage and returned to its roots in electronics and communications, it would need to make some high-stakes bets if it wanted to be a leader in fields where enormous changes can happen overnight. To make sure RCA would have the money it needed for its high-tech gambles, Griffiths hit upon a double-barreled strategy: With RCA's new profits, he would build a nest egg, and he would also buy a cash-rich company that could supply monetary transfusions when necessary.

In 1979 he found his cash cow, a financial services firm

called CIT. With a price tag of $1.4 billion, or $400 million more than its book value, the acquisition didn't seem like such a hot idea to Wall Street analysts. But Griffiths had looked at the numbers and made up his mind. Beyond issuing the obligatory news release to announce the merger, he didn't even want to discuss it. Told of the analysts' doubts, Griffiths said tersely that the acquisition was "a very good deal" and he had no intention of entering into a dialogue with those who disagreed. In acquiring CIT, he had tripled RCA's assets and raised earnings by almost a third. Who could ask for anything more?

There was just one problem: RCA had to take on $700 million of short-term debt to buy CIT, and interest rates were about to take a fast, steep climb. Overnight, CIT was costing RCA almost $80 million a year more in interest charges than RCA had anticipated. This possibility had crossed Griffiths' mind, but he thought he could handle it with the proceeds from selling off more of RCA's subsidiaries and a few of CIT's manufacturing units.

It didn't work out that way. Cash from RCA operations fell, and debt continued to rise. Moody's and Standard & Poor's, the corporate credit rating services, lowered RCA's rating, which meant that RCA had to pay even higher interest on its borrowings. By the end of 1981, CIT bore almost no resemblance to the cash cow Griffiths had tried to buy.

The inevitable belt-tightening shortchanged the very thing that the CIT acquisition was supposed to help—technological pioneering. Short of cash and frustrated in its attempts to find a buyer for Hertz, RCA had to delay capital expenditures that would significantly improve its semiconductors and would make many of its manufacturing operations competitive with the Japanese.

Despite Griffiths' talk about the importance of underwriting new technologies, all-or-nothing gambles of the

David Sarnoff variety were anathema to him. Griffiths was in favor of innovation as long as whatever the gadget was would pay off in three to five years. For a man accustomed to evaluating his managers' performance once a month, five years probably seemed an eternity. But a high-tech company that starves its pure research has almost no chance of being a leader, and a number of electronics-industry observers believe RCA's niggardliness has done irreparable harm.

Griffiths even dragged his feet on the one technology he was willing to bankroll—the videodisc player, which plays prerecorded discs of everything from movies to instructional material on television screens. Unlike videotape recorders, videodisc players cannot record material being shown on the TV screen, but the players cost only half as much as the recorders. After pouring almost $200 million into developing the product, Griffiths held off introducing it because he wanted to make sure the market existed before RCA went all out to capture it. It wasn't until after Griffiths resigned (in January 1981) that RCA began selling its videodisc players. If Griffiths hadn't resigned, his technological tightfistedness might well have done him in. But the RCA empire was full of bêtes noires, and another one caught up with him first.

NBC HAD FALLEN into last place in the network ratings race in 1976 and couldn't seem to get out. Even more nettlesome to Griffiths was the decline in NBC's profitability. In one year, 1978, pretax earnings fell 20 percent, from $153 million to $122 million. Revenues continued to rise, but the net-earnings gap between NBC and CBS had widened to $50 million. Speaking to a group of New York securities analysts in late 1977, Griffiths said he was "determined to overcome the gap." Once Griffiths started streamlining RCA, he was fond of saying that he wanted all the remaining operations to be "preeminent" in their fields. Whatever RCA did, it was going to be a leader, which meant that NBC had a lot of catching up to do.

To cut costs (Griffiths' favorite way of fattening the bottom line), he cleaned house in 1977, moving Herbert Schlosser into the NBC presidency and kicking Julian Goodman upstairs to the chairmanship. Richard Wald, the head of NBC News, was banished (some said for having lost Barbara Walters to ABC). Sports and program chiefs also came and went, along with dozens of key staff people. The broom swept more than three hundred NBC employees out the door.

But the economies failed to improve NBC's picture, and Schlosser's tenure as president of NBC was, in Griffiths' mind, over. At almost the same moment Griffiths was promising securities analysts a rosier future, he was wooing the only man he thought could save the network.

Fred Silverman, the legendary television programmer, had already worked his magic at CBS, increasing its share of the top ten shows from four to nine with series like *All in the Family* and *M*A*S*H*. At ABC, his taste took a nose dive but the results were spectacular. On the strength of inanities like *Three's Company* and *Charlie's Angels,* ABC captured first place for the first time in its history. "He was like the Messiah," said Garry Marshall, the television producer who rode the Silverman wave at ABC with hit series like *Laverne and Shirley* and *Mork and Mindy.* If anyone could save NBC, Griffiths reasoned, it was Fred Silverman, whose ability to spot hits had led *Time* magazine to call him "the man with the golden gut." Griffiths approached him through Jane Cahill Pfeiffer, an RCA consultant who knew Silverman from her days at IBM, when she had worked with him on her company's sponsorship of the ABC miniseries *Eleanor and Franklin*. Since it would never do for the president of ABC Entertainment to be seen in the RCA Building, Griffiths met Silverman in Cherry Hill, New Jersey, on a rainy day late in 1977.

When Silverman's appointment was announced a few weeks later, ABC stock fell $1.75 a share, while RCA's rose $1.25. That made the Silverman deal worth $140 million on Wall Street. ABC hurried to downplay Silverman's value, arguing that he was just one member of a winning team that had been in place before he ever showed up.

Silverman himself was eager to tone down the messiah image. He told *The Wall Street Journal* that he wasn't "going to walk on water," and Griffiths insisted that RCA did not expect him to be a "miracle worker." NBC public-relations people began spreading the word that the network's problems could not be solved overnight, which allowed Silverman to eat his cake and have it too. If he succeeded at NBC, he would be a hero. And if he failed, well, hadn't everybody said he was only human?

But the $1 million a year that Griffiths had agreed to pay him meant that Silverman's neck was on the line from the start. Even though Griffiths was willing to give him time to succeed, Griffiths could not resist saying, less than a month after Silverman started his job, that it was appropriate to have "high expectations" of Silverman. High expectations understood, Silverman had pressed for—and won—a three-year contract. The contract also gave RCA an option to renew for an additional two years if Silverman did improve NBC's fortunes, which, in Ed Griffiths' book, was even better than walking on water.

The redemption of NBC couldn't start right away. Silverman's ABC contract ran until early June 1978, and ABC had no intention of letting its most valuable player leave early. In holding him to his contract, ABC could sabotage NBC's next season because by the time Silverman got to NBC, it would be too late for him to do much about the all-important fall premiere. And once a season is off to a bad start, it is extremely hard to play catch-up because new series that bomb can be replaced only by other new series, which require months to be developed.

So Fred Silverman, in a state of suspended animation, took a long vacation and plotted his strategy for saving NBC. Reasoning that there was probably no way to outschlock the schlock he had brought to ABC—and no doubt sick of being raked over the coals for it by highbrow critics—he opted for the religious experience. Like Saul on the road to Damascus, Fred Silverman became a convert—to quality television. What happened, he explained to the press shortly after he arrived at NBC, was this:

> I would have to admit that a lot of criticism, a lot of the things I read, resulted in quite a bit of soul-searching and a kind of philosophy as to where NBC should go. . . . I can only say that it would be very foolhardy for me to stand here now in front of the world and say that we are moving in a new direction, and then proceed to put shows on the air that are going to be ridiculed. . . . If NBC moves in a direction that is counter to what I've described today, then you have every justification for saying, "He's self-serving, he's a fraud."

One of Silverman's first acts as president of NBC was to hire Jane Pfeiffer as a consultant, and not long afterward he asked her to be chairman—moves that would underscore his commitment to quality. If Fred Silverman, schlockmeister, was going to travel the high road of quality programming, Jane Pfeiffer was the perfect companion for the journey. Her credentials were impeccable: six months in a convent, twenty-one years with IBM (where quality is an obsession), and seats on the boards of the Bache Group, Chesebrough-Ponds, International Paper, J. C. Penney, the Rockefeller Foundation, and the American Red Cross. At first—and even second—glance, Fred and Jane seemed destined to become TV's new odd couple. Fred was a paunchy workaholic who felt uneasy unless he was indoors with one eye on the tube. (Once at a beach in Hawaii, he was seen huddling under a towel and watching a portable TV.) Jane, trim from tennis and golf, looked fresh as all outdoors. Fred was the man who brought "tits and ass" to America's living rooms; Jane didn't like words like that said in her presence. Fred had spent his entire career in an industry reviled for mindlessness; Jane was a product of IBM, where the corporate preoccupation was summed up in one tirelessly repeated imperative: "Think." A child could have seen that this was not a marriage made in heaven.

But the child would have been right for all the wrong reasons. Fred needed Jane. To pry NBC out of third place, he would have to compete against the string of hits that he himself had brought to the airwaves at ABC. Close to fifty million people tuned in every week to watch the likes of *Laverne and Shirley, Three's Company,* and *Charlie's Angels.* Quality was the road not taken in prime-time television, and Silverman thought he was onto something.

The skeptics were quick to call his bluff. After he spoke about his "genuine commitment to quality" in a closed-circuit broadcast to NBC stations around the country, a CBS producer asked, "What else do you expect him to say? He's been accused so long of putting junk on the air." Nevertheless, Silverman stuck to his guns, sounding the theme of quality programming every time he found himself on a podium. The quest for quality suited Jane Pfeiffer down to the ground, and she quickly joined Silverman in spreading the word that NBC's strategy for a comeback revolved around raising television's common denominator. As she told the Academy of Television Arts and Sciences in Hollywood, quality was going to be built right into the system at NBC. She and Fred were "determined to build an operational procedure within the network that is responsible to

NBC corporate management for more and more quality efforts."

Unmistakable class was only one of Pfeiffer's useful characteristics. When Silverman moved from ABC to NBC, he didn't just switch networks, he rose from programming whiz to chief executive. Now, in addition to worrying about prime-time ratings, he had to think about daytime schedules, late-night programs, news, ad sales, the radio and TV stations owned by NBC, a couple hundred NBC affiliates across the country, and a host of financial matters. As a programmer he was battle-tested, but he'd never worn any of the other executive mantles. Pfeiffer had. He understood that she could tend to administration, legal affairs, government affairs, and employee relations, leaving him free to concentrate on programming. In addition, she was expected to bring "a knowledge and judgment of corporate management" and an understanding of "how to run a big company in all of its phases—and a broader view than many [television] executives have."

Just as important, Pfeiffer would help Silverman by serving as NBC's member of the board of directors of RCA, its parent organization. It wasn't so much that Silverman didn't have the time or the desire to serve on the board himself. But if he had become a director, RCA would have been obliged to disclose his $1 million-a-year salary. Worried that fur might fly if it were officially disclosed that hard-pressed NBC was dishing out that kind of money, RCA gave the NBC board seat to Pfeiffer, whose compensation came to less than half that—a salary of $225,000 and a bonus of at least $200,000 (still no niggling sum, and estimated by *The Wall Street Journal* to be more than her husband was earning as senior vice-president of IBM).

Pfeiffer's gender also came in handy for NBC. The year before, the network had had to fork over almost $2 million to settle a class-action suit brought by women employees who felt their opportunities at NBC were less than those of their male counterparts. A woman in the chairman's seat would show that NBC had mended its ways.

All in all, then, even allowing for the odd-couple features, people in the know regarded the Pfeiffer-Silverman alliance as a damn smart move.

Despite the fact that NBC's downhill slide meant that Silverman would have his hands full just keeping bad from going to worse, a couple of rays of hope had recently penetrated the NBC gloom. In an expensive, rough-and-tumble fight, NBC won the right to broadcast the 1980 summer Olympics to be held in Moscow. By shelling out $87 million for the privilege, NBC not only beat CBS, it also delivered a swift uppercut to ABC, which had long dominated TV sports coverage.

Just before Silverman arrived, NBC also scored a ratings coup with its highly acclaimed miniseries *Holocaust*. An audience of 120 million watched *Holocaust*—more than had watched any previous miniseries except *Roots*. Since the subject of the series was genocide, there was monumental insensitivity in NBC's elation over the ratings (and in Madison Avenue's crass view that *Holocaust* was a "great corporate vehicle" for advertising). But NBC could be justifiably proud that it had won the Nielsen race—at least for one week—by offering a moving portrayal of one of history's greatest tragedies.

Holocaust was exactly the sort of high-quality programming Silverman said he wanted to do more of. Since he was the one who had brought *Roots* to the screen, the year before at ABC, he had reason to think he could succeed. (Even though he believed strongly in *Roots*, however, the man with the golden gut lost his nerve when it came time to schedule it. Worried that no one would watch and that the series would drag down ABC's ratings for weeks, he crammed all twelve hours into a single week to get the bad ratings over with.)

NBC's 1978 fall schedule, developed before Silverman arrived, got off to a start every bit as bad as ABC hoped when it held him to the letter of his contract. By the end of November, Silverman had had enough. He canceled nine shows—six hour-long programs and three half-hour ones, which amounted to a third of the twenty-two hours that make up prime time. Less than enthusiastic about most of the midseason replacements, he let it be known that "a fairly decent percentage" of them "were already in development" when he got to NBC.

The one replacement with his unflagging support was *Supertrain,* a series set on a gargantuan nuclear-powered train that traveled a double set of rails between New York and Los Angeles. Working round the clock, carpenters, designers, electricians, and other craftsmen built a $6 million set stretching across three Hollywood sound stages. Tricked out with something for hedonists of every stripe, the train featured a gym, steam room, swimming pool, beauty salon, disco, and boutiques. A medical center on board would allow the producers to toss in a little *Marcus Welby* action from time to time. Nobody knew exactly what *Supertrain* was supposed to be, and the concept that developed was confusing to say the least: a dash of *Love Boat* (an ABC Silverman hit that featured vignettes played out by the crew and big-name guest stars who came aboard as passengers), a bit of *Silver Streak* (a wacky Gene Wilder comedy-mystery set on a train), and a *soupçon* of Agatha Christie's *Murder on the Orient Express.* Television executives said a project the size of *Supertrain* needs at least a year in development, but Silverman insisted the train be ready to roll in six months. The resulting pressures on everyone involved made for wholesale firings and resignations and a show that was roundly denounced by critics. Only a month after its February 1979 debut, *Supertrain* was derailed. The wreck cost NBC $12 million.

*   *   *

THINGS WEREN'T GOING TOO WELL in the chairman's office, either. Almost from the moment Pfeiffer walked in the door, she had to wrestle with something called the unit managers' scandal. It all started when the Marriott World Travel Bureau, which handled trips for NBC's Washington bureau, called to say that NBC employees were returning an unusually high number of airline tickets—either trading them in for cash or exchanging first-class tickets for seats in coach, then asking that the change be given in cash.

Unit managers, in the Washington bureau and elsewhere, oversee the logistics of taking TV crews on location. They rent equipment, buy materials for props, hire local electricians and carpenters, see that crews are fed and lodged, arrange transportation and, on occasion, pay off whoever needs paying off to speed crews through foreign borders, gain access to private locations, and so on. The job requires unit managers to carry large sums of cash, especially in out-of-the-way places where checks and credit cards might be unacceptable. Although unit managers have to keep extensive records, there is often no way to tell whether cash is being spent for the purposes alleged or whether the $100 said to have been slipped to a border guard really ended up in the unit manager's pocket.

Not wanting to be deflected from his programming mission, Silverman entrusted the unit managers' cleanup to Pfeiffer. She went at it with great zeal, determined to do what she no doubt thought was expected of her: find the corruption and yank it out by its roots. First she called in auditors from Price, Waterhouse and attorneys from the New York firm of Cahill, Gordon and Reindel. The airline ticket scam, they discovered, was the tip of a pretty expensive iceberg. Since at least 1972, unit managers had been filing false billings for equipment rentals, using blank receipts from fancy restaurants to turn in expenses for phony meals, buying jewelry and expensive rugs with company funds, and using NBC money to bring home European shoes as presents for other executives. Then there were things like the disappearance of a satchel containing $38,000 in cash—supposedly stolen from a unit manager working with a crew covering a papal conclave in Rome.

By the time all the allegations were out in the open, more than two hundred accountants and lawyers had swooped down on NBC's fifty unit managers to comb their books. According to the auditors' calculations, the skimming had cost the company hundreds of thousands of dollars, perhaps as much as $1 million. In mid-March 1979, six unit managers were dismissed. Some of them later stood trial on charges of fraud and income-tax evasion (for not giving the Internal Revenue Service a share of their ill-gotten gains). In the best tradition of prime-time private eyes, Jane Pfeiffer solved the crime and turned the thugs over to the law.

But life is not television, and that apparently was not the thing to do. RCA chairman Edgar Griffiths had wanted a nice, quiet investigation—the sort of behind-the-scenes wrist-slapping that a family might engage in when an errant member needs to be straightened out. By calling in U.S. attorneys and making the matter public, Pfeiffer had turned an embarrassingly bright spotlight on a whole new facet of NBC ineptitude. It didn't help that the unit managers' dismissals coincided with the resounding flop of *Supertrain*. Or that the tab for Pfeiffer's probe came to more than $4 million—many times the amount that had been siphoned off. To Griffiths, all of this was "like killing a gnat with an elephant gun."

Others objected to the manner in which she had conducted the probe. A unit manager who had been with the company for fifteen years told of being grilled for two hours about three or four thirty-dollar items listed on expense vouchers. After this inquisition, he had to turn in his NBC credit cards, clean out his office in the presence of a guard, and leave. His office door was taped shut behind him.

If the unit managers' scandal had been a project for Business Ethics 101, Jane Pfeiffer would have received an A+. She tackled the problem head-on, brought in outside attorneys and auditors so there could be no accusations of a cover-up, made sure the malefactors faced the music, and saw to it that the company instituted stricter procedures for reporting expenses. But Pfeiffer didn't get an A+. She got a nickname: Attila the Nun.

Asked to comment on the unit managers' scandal, many TV executives could not understand why Jane was making such a fuss. "Everybody does it" was the overriding sentiment. One executive even viewed the skimming as a sort of unit manager perk. The job rarely pays more than $40,000 a year, it's a dead-end position, and it means staying up late to make endless arrangements while everyone else in the crew is out living it up. Letting the poor sods cheat helps keep them happy in what can never be more than a thankless job.

By clamping down, Pfeiffer was being a spoilsport, and just about everyone at NBC resented it. Before long Attila the Nun was not just a nickname, it was a prism for viewing everything she did. If she made a speech about NBC's commitment to quality programming—the song Silverman had been singing since his first day on the job—people said that was Attila the Nun being holier than thou. If she asked that something be done, people said the word had come "down from the Mount." Others insisted that she suffered from a "mother-superior complex: She just always seems to know what's right." Questioning her "was heresy—and heretics get excommunicated."

In a profile of Pfeiffer for *Savvy* magazine, journalist

Michael VerMeulen pointed out that such remarks "smack of a religious bigotry that most people would find revolting if it were directed, say, toward a Jew." But beyond the question of bigotry, any thinking person has to wonder what had happened to the Jane Pfeiffer who was well liked at IBM—the one praised by executive committee chairman Thomas J. Watson, Jr., for her "luster, warmth and charm." Between the time she left IBM, when she married another high-level IBM executive in 1976, and her 1978 accession to the NBC chairmanship, did she somehow change from Dr. Jekyll to Sister Hyde?

Judging by the resolutely venomous terms used to describe her twenty-month tenure at NBC, she did. Except for the puff pastry served to the press by the network public-relations people when Pfeiffer's appointment was announced, it is hard to find a kind word about her in print. If she spoke of NBC's commitment to quality, her critics said she had NBC mixed up with PBS and didn't know anything about commercial broadcasting. When word got around that she was taking scripts home to read (possibly in an attempt to learn more about commercial broadcasting), it was said she was trying to interfere with programming. She was in the classic double bind: damned if she did, damned if she didn't.

But perhaps no offense grated more than her highly public handling of the unit managers' scandal, which dragged on for months. An executive who worked for NBC at the time says morale went from uncertain to dreadful. With programming in such terrible shape, employees didn't need their own chairman beating up on them. Whatever a handful of people had done wrong, hundreds of NBC employees were giving their all to get the network out of last place. Other executives felt that Pfeiffer's actions were designed to let the world know that she was Ms. Clean and that the good ole boys were really pretty bad before she made them straighten up. Like a teetotaler at a drunken brawl, Jane Cahill Pfeiffer was an unpleasant reminder that the group's standards left something to be desired.

Then there was the way she talked. Sure, she could laugh off the Attila the Nun jokes, which she did at a Los Angeles convention of people from NBC-affiliated stations across the country. But her speeches were filled with corporatese, a language not spoken in television. She talked about "operational procedures" and programmers' responsibilities to "corporate management." To people accustomed to seat-of-the-pants decision-making, this kind of talk had no bearing on the task at hand. All it did was show the enormous gulf between an outfit like IBM, where systems are everything, and television, where the one essential ingredient, creativity, defies all systems.

Before long, the word being used by NBC executives to describe Pfeiffer was "intrusive." Perhaps not coincidentally, it was the same word Silverman had used several years before at CBS to describe network president Arthur Taylor, whose straight-arrow personality had much in common with Pfeiffer's. Programmers bent on maintaining high ratings resented his Family Viewing Policy, which complicated their jobs, took away a large measure of their freedom, and implied that they lacked a sense of social responsibility. When Silverman had a chance to leave CBS in 1975 for a bigger job at ABC, he went gladly.

This time around, however, he wasn't about to leave, and whatever his problems with Pfeiffer were, he wasn't ready to ask her to go, either. He had other fires to put out. Many of the new midseason replacement shows had done worse than the ones they'd replaced, and by the end of the season NBC was even farther behind in the ratings than it had been the year before. Its ratings were the worst in ten years.

Since audience size determines what a network can charge advertisers, bad ratings depress revenues. In 1978, first-place ABC could ask $60,000 for a thirty-second commercial in prime time, while NBC could charge only $45,000. For the 1978–79 season, ABC's four-point lead over NBC gave it an extra $200 million in revenues. Poor ratings also hurt the stations affiliated with a network because they too must charge less for local advertising. In the late 1970s, angry NBC affiliates began to defect, either to join another network or to become independent stations.

As bad as things were at the end of his first season, Silverman felt he couldn't be blamed for his predecessors' mistakes, and observers of the television industry tended to agree. In what he referred to as a period of transition, he'd reorganized several departments, including programming, and he felt confident that a new NBC would flow from these new people. Ratings might be down, revenues might be down, but he was heading toward the fall premiere of the 1979–80 season convinced that success lay somewhere in the new shows he had under development. Among the projects: *Crash Island*, starring Harlem Globetrotter Meadowlark Lemon, about a coed swim team stranded on an island after a plane crash; *McGurk*, a situation comedy about four dogs that was set entirely in a doghouse; *Harper and Company*, about four operatives who ski and surf their way through *Mission Impossible*-type exploits; *Sgt. T. K. Yu*, about a Korean detective in Beverly Hills; and *Darn You, Harry Landers*, a sitcom set in the Lost Horizon Retirement Home. If those didn't fly, he had forty-five more shows lined up on the runway.

Silverman also expected that the season would end up on a high note, with the broadcast of the 1980 summer Olympics from Moscow. Even though coverage would be expensive, most of the advertising was already sold, and NBC could use the occasion to plug—over and over, in classic Silverman style—its shows for the upcoming 1980–81 season.

Even the affiliates were willing to give Silverman more time. At their 1979 meeting there was little of the angry criticism that had caught network officials off guard the year before. But their optimism hardly matched Silverman's. The strongest endorsement, made by an affiliate executive from Houston, was at best a left-handed compliment: "There may be confusion [at NBC], but there's action."

According to an old business adage, if you borrow $100 from a banker he becomes your creditor, but if you borrow $1 million he becomes your partner. And so it was with Ed Griffiths, who had invested in Fred Silverman to the tune of $1 million a year. After spending that much, it wouldn't make sense to can Silverman, even though he was more to blame for the $50 million midseason replacement debacle than he was willing to admit. If nothing else, he could be blamed for *Supertrain,* a $12 million mistake. Griffiths had no choice but to give Silverman time to recoup his losses. Still, NBC's wilting profits weighed heavily on the RCA chairman. Revenues for the first quarter of 1979 were up 13 percent, but canceling nine shows and ordering up fifty more had eviscerated net income. Griffiths let Silverman know that he expected an improvement by the end of the year.

Silverman thought he could oblige. In the summer of 1979, when the finishing touches were being put on the fall schedule, he announced that henceforth NBC would build up its success one step at a time. No more wholesale cancellations and replacements. Secure in this new strategy, he could finally fess up to his error: "We tried the shortcut in the midseason and we had disastrous results," he told a group of TV critics in Los Angeles. "You have to learn from your mistakes, and it was just stupid."

What Silverman had learned from his mistakes was unclear when the new season got under way. The critics panned one NBC show after another and took special offense at the tawdry ten-second spots the network was using to promote its shows. T&A, violence, car crashes—the promos were a video version of the lurid headlines in tabloid newspapers. Carrying the titillation into an entirely new realm, Silverman had ordered that the premiere episodes of some supposedly high-quality shows he built around T&A. One featured "The Panhandle Pussycats," a group of jiggly girls from a burlesque house who were called in to cheerlead a football game. The premiere episode of a mystery series was called "Hookers by Day, Housewives by Night." When the critics let Silverman have it for this pandering, he said it was necessary to draw people to the new series. He added that he had no intention of continuing the practice beyond the opening weeks of the season. As soon as the viewers were in place, the titillation would disappear. It is hard to decide whether to fault this ploy for its hypocrisy or its inanity. Viewers drawn to a series because of the sex it offered would hardly stick around if the sex disappeared. The gains—if there were any—would be short-term at best.

Unwilling to predict that he could turn NBC around in the first season for which he was fully responsible, Silverman nevertheless promised that by Christmas 1980 NBC would be Number One. At the end of the 1979–80 season, Griffiths was able to stand in front of RCA shareholders at the annual meeting and report that Fred Silverman had turned the tide. NBC now trailed the leader (CBS this time) by only 2.2 points instead of 4. But a closer look reveals that that improvement was less dramatic than it appeared. NBC's ratings had risen only from 17.0 to 17.4 because CBS had won the 1979–80 ratings race with a 19.6 as opposed to the 21.0 that ABC had chalked up the year before.

From the point of view of ratings, the midseason replacements for the spring of 1980 were a decided improvement over the midseason fiasco of the year before. But two lulus did manage to sneak through. *Pink Lady*, featuring two young Japanese women and an American comedian, made it all the way to prime time before Silverman realized the young ladies could hardly speak English. There was also *The Six O'Clock Follies*, a sitcom set in an armed forces radio station in Saigon during the Vietnam War. Fred Silverman must have been the only man in the country who thought that that war could be made funny.

Despite these boners, even the skeptics were inclined to give Silverman credit for achieving any increase in the face of a devastating blow to his plans. On January 8, 1980, the Soviet Union invaded Afghanistan. An angry President Carter proposed economic sanctions that included a boycott of the summer Olympics in Moscow. There went NBC's dream. Most of the network's investment in the Olympics was covered by insurance, but the millions of viewers—and the expected high ratings—Silverman had counted on had all been snatched away. All the arrangements made with advertisers (who had agreed to pay $165,000 a minute for their Olympics commercials) would have to be renegotiated. Worse, the growing recession was making advertisers think twice about reinvesting their Olympics money in commercials on whatever substitute programs NBC could come up with.

The Olympics weren't the only shake-up that spring. When Silverman and Pfeiffer moved in back in 1978, Silverman had promised there wouldn't be a purge. In the wake of the pruning that Griffiths had ordered the year before, Silverman was expected to build morale and restore confidence. But once the unit managers' scandal started heads rolling, they didn't stop. By May 1980, Silverman had replaced the chiefs of entertainment, news, sports, TV stations, radio, personnel, finance, and operations and engineering. A few weeks later Silverman announced another appointment: Irwin Segelstein would become president of NBC Television and help ease Silverman's administrative burden.

Since administration was supposed to be Pfeiffer's bailiwick, that meant trouble. Perhaps Silverman was trying to corner her into resigning so he wouldn't have to fire her, which Ed Griffiths wanted him to do. The combination of the unit managers' scandal and her outspokenness at RCA board meetings had led Griffiths to conclude that hiring Pfeiffer was a big mistake. He wanted her out, but Silverman couldn't bring himself to lower the guillotine, and Pfeiffer seemed disinclined to take any hints.

Early in July, a month after Segelstein's promotion, the bad blood at the top of NBC found its way into the headlines. *The New York Times* reported that Pfeiffer had been asked to resign. RCA, continuing its tradition of unstraightforward dealings with the press, refused to verify or disavow the rumor. Left holding the bag, Pfeiffer issued her own denial:

No one has asked for my resignation, and I have not offered it. It is apparent that there are some who are trying to use the media to get me to quit. I try to be direct and open and I'll try to be direct and open about this. I won't quit. If anyone wants to terminate my employment contract, I am available to anyone who wants to see me.

Two hours later, unable to take any more heat, Silverman made it official:

During the past two weeks, discussions have been held with Jane Cahill Pfeiffer concerning her status with NBC. I have today relieved her of all responsibilities, and, effective immediately, her organization will report directly to me. We are prepared to continue our discussions regarding her employment contract.

The firing was news to Pfeiffer, who issued another statement:

Yesterday Fred Silverman told me there was no way we could both stay and he wanted his contract renewed now, and for that to happen, I had to make a decision and implement it. He did not ask for my resignation then or ever. He simply stated that the RCA people play hardball, and that he would probably follow me out the door in six months. This afternoon through the media I learned that he had relieved me of my duties as chairman.

Was this true? Had Silverman really fired her without telling her? He wouldn't say. He simply released to the press a two-sentence note to Pfeiffer in which he said he valued the contributions she had made and wished her "all success" in "future endeavors."

As for what went wrong between Pfeiffer and Silverman, they may be the only two who know for sure. Some observers speculate that as NBC's fortunes began to improve, Silverman didn't need her anymore. The animosity between Pfeiffer and Griffiths certainly didn't help, and as Pfeiffer suggested in her statement to the press after she was dismissed, Silverman probably had to let her go to save his own hide.

There was something else, too. By the summer of 1980, Silverman and Pfeiffer were poles apart on the issue of quality programming. Pfeiffer believed in quality for its own sake, while Silverman had seen it as a means to an end: Quality was just a programming gimmick, the strategy he thought could rescue NBC. When the strategy didn't work, he was quick to abandon it, to try to fight schlock with ultraschlock—with shows like *Supertrain*. It is unlikely that Pfeiffer had the stomach for that game. In any event, the accomplishments she cited on leaving office showed that she was still dead set on quality: She had brought live theater back to NBC, instituted management controls (the expense reporting procedures set up after the unit managers' scandal), and persuaded three topflight CBS News people (Richard Salant, William Small, and Roger Mudd) to join NBC News.

However glad Griffiths and Pfeiffer's NBC adversaries were to see her go, the rest of the world couldn't believe what had happened. "It was like what TV shows on the screen," said the dean of the School of Public Communications at Boston University. "If you can't resolve the problem in a half-hour script, you shoot somebody." Even *Broadcasting,* the weekly trade paper that watches the industry with an avuncular eye, reported the event under a headline that summed up the shock: "Rockefeller Center Still Shaking from Pfeiffer Firing." A subhead hinted at coming attractions, saying that Pfeiffer's "acrimonious ouster" raised questions about the "tenure of her boss, Silverman, and his boss at RCA, Griffiths."

For Pfeiffer, there was $705,000 in severance pay—balm for the wounds of being fired—but it wasn't gained without a fight. And to compound the insults, Griffiths had the ill grace to boast about Pfeiffer's settlement at the company's next annual meeting. Contractually speaking, she was entitled to $758,000, he told shareholders. He'd gotten her to settle for $53,000 less.

GRIFFITHS HAD GOOD REASON to stay behind the scenes in the firing of Jane Pfeiffer. He was still smarting from the criticism that followed his blunt dismissal of RCA's new president, Maurice Valente, a scant three weeks before Pfeiffer was axed.

Valente was not Ed Griffiths' first choice for president. But in the fall of 1979, after three fruitless years of trying to speed the growth of presidential timber inside the company and at least four attempts to woo executives from other companies, Griffiths must have been heartened to learn that Valente was interested in the job.

With ITT since 1965, Valente had solid operating experience and a reputation as a good financial man—rather like Ed Griffiths, in fact. As a member of the office of the chief executive at ITT and as executive vice-president in charge of consumer products, Valente said he was happy in his job and not looking for a new one. But when the executive recruiting firm of Heidrick and Struggles came calling at the behest of RCA, Valente was ready to listen. "Being president of RCA with the prospect of becoming the company's chief executive officer seemed like an opportunity to move to the top faster than I could at ITT," he said.

He first learned of RCA's interest in him in mid-October, and he describes the courtship, conducted mainly by Griffiths and RCA vice-president George Fuchs, as "warm and rapid." Less than a month later, the pact was sealed: Valente would become RCA's president and chief operating officer on January 1, 1980. He signed a three-year contract that guaranteed him an annual salary of $400,000 and a yearly bonus of at least $200,000.

By mid-June 1980—only five and a half months after Valente came to work—it was all over. Never one to mince words, Griffiths said Valente's performance "did not meet expectations in terms of the company's long-range needs and objectives." The resounding lack of substance in that statement and in the "explanations" RCA made after the firing suggest that the new president hadn't even had time to make a blunder big enough to be used as a pretext for getting rid of him. How, in such a short time, could Griffiths reach a judgment of such sweep and finality?

Valente's troubles started almost immediately after he arrived. The six operating officers who were supposed to report to him had an average of twenty-five years of RCA service under their belts, and several of them lusted after the prize that had gone to Valente. In addition, without a president, they had been reporting to their friend the chairman, Ed Griffiths, who also had been with the company for many years. When Valente arrived, they were loath to give up their link to Griffiths.

"From the start, I was very aggressive with regard to these reporting relationships," Valente said. "But Griffiths had greater respect for the autonomy of these managers than for me. The way he saw it, I think, was that the new president was attacking the boys, and he had been one of the boys."

What Valente was really attacking was the boys' numbers. At RCA, where each operating unit has a great deal of independence, Valente said, managers are allowed considerable leeway in setting their own procedures for pulling together figures on such matters as cash flow, credit, interest expense, and other items related to financing. Although the figuring is done in accordance with generally accepted accounting principles, the multiplicity of permissible variations on the theme means that it is possible to arrive at a vast assortment of "correct" numbers. The problem, as Valente saw it, was that in letting the operating units determine their own reporting procedures, "managers could come up with any numbers they wanted." It was 180 degrees away from the tightly controlled financial procedures at ITT, where master accountant Harold Geneen had kept close tabs on 280 operating units by requiring each unit's controller to report not only to the head of the subsidiary but also to the corporate controller at company headquarters. "Bringing forth these inappropriate reporting procedures and controls embarrassed the chairman," Valente said.

As well it might. Griffiths had just led RCA to three consecutive record years, and he had done it by paying extraordinarily close attention to the numbers. His entire reputation rested on his skill with numbers. Now some upstart was telling him—and the whole RCA board of directors—that the numbers needed major surgery. It was as if an altar boy had told the College of Cardinals the pope wasn't a good Catholic.

With his immediate subordinates unwilling to report to him and his only superior embarrassed by him, Valente had plenty of cause for reflecting on what his old boss had told him before he came to RCA. "When my appointment as president was announced, Harold Geneen called to congratulate me," Valente said. "He told me it would be a very difficult assignment because of the company's history—especially General Sarnoff's preoccupation with technology, which had not left management in the best shape. But Geneen said that if I worked hard for a couple of years and applied ITT-type financial controls, it was possible that I could help the company realize its potential."

Geneen's vague references to RCA's troubles were the only forewarning Valente had. After RCA expressed interest in him, Valente did surprisingly little to try to get a fix on the company's inner workings. While RCA and Heidrick and Struggles, the search firm, checked Valente's pedigree by contacting at least seventeen and perhaps as many as thirty references on every conceivable aspect of his life, Valente didn't think to give RCA the same sort of scrutiny. Looking back, he saw this omission as a key mistake. "I should have apprised myself of the history of RCA's executive suite, of the situations related to the promotion and dismissal of Robert Sarnoff and Anthony Conrad. And I should have known more about the history of the company generally—about its operations and discipline and controls. If I'd done more checking on the politics and history, I wouldn't have gone to RCA."

In the early weeks of Valente's short presidency, Griffiths told him to take his time, that RCA was a big company and there was much to learn. Despite Valente's discontent with the fact that no one would report to him and his dissatisfaction with financial reporting procedures, he was willing to take his time. It wasn't until four months after he'd started at RCA that he sensed the magnitude of Griffiths' unhappiness. Their first confrontation was about a matter so insignificant that it immediately sets the mind to wondering what the real problem could be: Griffiths chewed out Valente for having used a company car to take a family member to the dentist.

Irrational as it seems, that was the beginning of the end. By mid-June, the RCA board came to the unanimous decision that Valente had to go. "Griffiths called me in one morning and said RCA would like to have my resignation," Valente said. "His explanation was that he didn't feel our future together would be effective. He pointed out that I hadn't had good communication with the operating managers. That was certainly true because he'd let them continue reporting to him. But it was contrary to what he'd told me all along about taking my time, about learning the company first." Valente's impression from Griffiths' earlier advice to take his time was that once he knew the company, he would enjoy the respect of the operating managers, who then would be willing to report to him.

Valente didn't try to defend himself or ask for more time. Griffiths had made up his mind, and he had the whole RCA board behind him. Valente says he and Griffiths talked about the press release that would announce Valente's departure and decided it would say something to the effect that "both sides had agreed to disagree," which would convey mutual consent and an amicable decision. The next thing Valente knew, the media had been given a different—and much blunter—explanation of events: "It was the board's unanimous decision that Mr. Valente's per-

formance over nearly six months did not meet expectations."

The unexpected change of tone in the press release was
the first of several humiliating farewell gifts. For weeks
after Valente left, the business press intimated that the real
reason he was let go was that he'd taken female compan-
ions other than his wife on a company plane. "That story is
ridiculous," Valente insisted, and he said he found these
innuendos "even more debilitating" than the shock of
being fired. He blamed RCA managers, who knew the
rumor to be untrue, for allowing it to spread anyway.

RCA also let it be known that it was dissatisfied with
Valente's "work ethic" but coyly declined to explain what
that meant. Perhaps it was a reference to his indiscretion
in using a company car for a family errand. But since Valente had been coming to the office at seven in the morning
and staying until seven at night in an effort to master the
complexities of RCA, the remark hurt.

Another low blow was the contention by RCA executives that Valente turned out not to be the man they
thought they'd hired. One source claimed that it wasn't
until after Valente came to RCA that the company discovered he was "at least partly responsible" for the decline in
profits of ITT's European, Middle Eastern, and African operations, which he had headed for several years. But with
all the checks RCA ran on Valente before hiring him, it is
hard to believe that an issue as basic as the quality of his
performance would not have surfaced, especially in view
of the *modus operandi* of George Fuchs, the executive vice
president at Griffiths' side during the Valente courtship.
Fuchs reportedly keeps dossiers on RCA managers all over
the world, following their expense accounts and use of per-
quisites. Whatever Valente's warts were, Fuchs and Griffiths undoubtedly knew about them before he was offered
a contract.

Financially, that contract eased the shock of being fired.

Valente was given a severance settlement of $1 million upon leaving RCA and an additional $250,000 on January 1, 1981. Strictly speaking, Valente was entitled to almost twice that much, but he left quietly with his $1.25 million. The following spring, at the same shareholders' meeting when Griffiths bragged about getting Jane Pfeiffer to take $53,000 less than she might have, he was able to point out that RCA had gotten off cheap with Valente, too. And in exchange for the seven-figure understanding that Valente was willing to show, Griffiths praised the ex-president as "an able man" and "a personal friend."

If he had it to do all over again, Valente said, he would ask that his contract also spell out his authority. But, he added, "I don't think there was ever a sincere intent on the part of RCA to honor the contract. The intent and sincerity of both parties are much more important than what's in the contract. The chief executive officer has to give the chief operating officer room to perform to his own and the company's advantage. Pointing out that what happened to him has also happened to others—at ITT, CBS, and Occidental Petroleum—he contended he was another victim of a "chief executive who just wasn't ready to hand over control."

After Valente left, Griffiths had no intention of letting the reins slip from his hands again. Instead of looking for a new president, he announced that RCA's leadership would emanate from an office of the chairman, which included five executive vice-presidents. The search for a successor was put on hold once again.

In firing Valente, Griffiths was removing a stone from his shoe, but the relief would be only temporary. The rapid hiring and firing of a top corporate officer is a mistake that a chief executive can make only once (unless, like Armand Hammer of Occidental Petroleum or William Paley of CBS, he owns more of the company than anyone else). Even though Griffiths got Silverman to do the actual beheading of Jane Pfeiffer, few people were fooled. One RCA executive said he thought Griffiths handled the Pfeiffer situation with "all the finesse of a goat." It wouldn't be long before the tide of the RCA board would begin to move against him.

THANKS TO THE UPROAR caused by the Pfeiffer and Valente firings, Silverman was home free. "Jane Pfeiffer's leaving was Freddie's insurance policy," one broadcasting executive said. "He's all the continuity NBC has. If he leaves, what will it cost them in the stock market? And who will they replace him with?" The Pfeiffer unpleasantness behind him, Silverman could devote himself to what he did best: banking on the future. ("Silverman has an erase button on his memory so he can start each day optimistically," a former NBC executive maintains.) NBC was barreling toward Christmas 1980, the time when Silverman had promised it would be Number One.

The 1980–81 season actually did look like the one that could turn things around. NBC had the World Series, the Super Bowl, a new police series called *Hill Street Blues*, and a miniseries based on James Clavell's best-selling novel *Shōgun*. Ed Griffiths was impressed enough to extend Silverman's contract through 1982.

But the combination of a long television actors' strike and the $33 million in Olympics losses left NBC with 1980 pretax earnings of $70 million—down more than 50 percent from the pre-Silverman high of $152.6 million. And despite the success of *Shōgun*, which pulled in even more viewers than *Holocaust*, there were some big clinkers. The worst was *Number 96*, a steamy series set in an apartment house. Based on a nearly banned Australian show of the same name, *Number 96* featured a transvestite sex expert, a lecherous retired naval commander, and an aspiring actress who thought that all the world was a casting couch. The sex was gratuitous, the dialogue was lame-brained, and the promotions showed torrid embraces shot through keyholes. All in all, it was as far removed as it was possible to get from the high-quality programming Silverman had pledged on his accession to the NBC throne. Three weeks after *Number 96* bowed, it bowed out. When the much-trumpeted Christmas of 1980 finally arrived, NBC's ratings were even lower than before Silverman had come aboard. For the fifth year in a row, NBC finished in the basement.

GRIFFITHS WASN'T HAVING A GOOD TIME, either. In the eyes of the RCA board, he had four strikes against him: his failure to find a successor, his clumsiness in the Pfeiffer and Valente dismissals, the NBC quagmire, and the high cost of carrying CIT Financial's debt. Not even the numbers of which Ed Griffiths was so fiercely proud—four years of record earnings—looked so great anymore. Scrutiny on the bounty revealed that he'd done it all with mirrors. He could declare in the company's 1979 annual report that RCA had achieved its third consecutive record year, but pretax profits had actually fallen $43 million from the year before. Griffiths made up the difference with lower taxes and one-time special items like the $23 million from the sale of a subsidiary. In 1980, another "record" year, extraordinary items came to the rescue once again: an after-tax gain of $11 million from the sale of Random House, a $20 million insurance settlement for an RCA satellite lost in space, and $21 million (after taxes) from the revaluation of CIT assets. Without these extras, RCA's net earnings would have come to less than those for 1978. It was a textbook case of the "paper entrepreneurialism" that Robert B. Reich derided in his provocative book *The Next American Frontier*. Corporate earnings are improved by the clever rearrangement of assets on paper rather than by making productive investments that will pay off in the future.

Early in 1981, the board decided Griffiths had to go. To avoid the appearance of yet another RCA decapitation, the parties concerned worked out a cozy arrangement. Griffiths would stay on until July 1. After that he would serve as a consultant to keep his seat on the board. For five years of consulting he would be paid $1.25 million. Thornton Bradshaw, president of Atlantic Richfield Company and an RCA director for nine years, would succeed Griffiths. At age sixty-three, Bradshaw was not a candidate likely to lead RCA for long, and, in fact, finding a successor was at the top of his list of things to do.

Once Griffiths' exit was arranged, his fair-haired boy, Fred Silverman, was a marked man. Bradshaw, refusing to give Silverman a wholehearted endorsement, would say only that it was too soon to know whether he would go or stay. By June 30, it was all over. Without the expression of unequivocal support Silverman had sought from Bradshaw, Fred Silverman signed off.

IN ONLY EIGHTEEN MONTHS, the RCA empire had unseated four top executives: Valente lasted five and a half months, Pfeiffer twenty months. Whether Silverman's three years on the job gave him enough time to turn NBC around is open to debate. The generous say it would have taken three more years to reverse the NBC slide. But it is fair to ask whether NBC could have afforded three more years of Silverman's desperate experiments: $50 million worth of unwatchable midseason replacement shows, including $12 million for *Supertrain,* plus untold millions on misbegotten projects like *Pink Lady, Number 96,* and *Six O'Clock Follies.* In 1977, the year before Silverman arrived, NBC's revenues had been $152.6 million. In 1980, his last full year on the job, they fell to $70 million, and NBC was still in last place in the ratings.

As an organization, NBC was shaken from top to bottom

during the Silverman reign. More than 80 of its 150 executives at the vice-presidential level and up had been replaced. Scores of staff members came and went with these executives, leaving morale and continuity in tatters. Just as Ed Griffiths attributed magical powers to Fred Silverman, Silverman expected superhuman achievements from the people he hired. When his recruits proved fallible, he felt betrayed and ordered them out.

In severance arrangements alone, the turbulence at the top of NBC and RCA cost $4.7 million. When Griffiths stepped down as chairman in 1981, RCA still hadn't found the president it had been looking for since 1976. The highly public executions at RCA had made the presidential search such a monumentally difficult task that the company had to pay one of its directors, Donald Smiley, $250,000 to devote his attention to the matter.

The price of a new chairman was a classic example of what happens when the revolving door at the top turns at enormous speed: Each replacement costs more than his predecessor. Thornton Bradshaw, who at age sixty-three could never be more than an interregnum chief, nonetheless secured for himself a five-year contract worth at least $4.69 million. At $938,500 a year, Bradshaw would be earning $115,000 more than Griffiths earned in 1980, his last full year as chairman.

By the summer of 1982, after Bradshaw had been in office for a year, RCA was still adrift. The introduction of the long-awaited videodisc players had finally come to pass, but it couldn't be classed as a dazzling triumph. "They waited too long," says one video industry analyst. "While Griffiths was holding back to make sure the customers were there, other companies had the market to themselves for a year. And when RCA finally did get the players into the stores, the demand was so much less than the company had anticipated that they had to cut prices drastically. The profit margins on the players are now so low that when customers come in asking to see RCA's machines, salesmen steer them to products with higher markup."

RCA's greatest flaw, many analysts feel, is at the top, where management has not been able to turn the company's disparate parts—Hertz, NBC, and the electronics divisions—into a unified, well-reasoned whole. The rudder known as strategic planning barely existed at RCA under Griffiths. This failure to give RCA a sense of unity and direction has led one analyst to suggest that everybody would be better off if RCA ran up a white flag and dismantled itself. Sold off one by one, its operations could bring more money than the company as a whole is thought to be worth.

Chapter 8

After the Fall

GETTING FIRED FROM THE TOP is such a touchy subject that it goes entirely undiscussed—even in bland generalities—in the basic texts on executives and management. The silence is equally acute among those who have taken part in such beheadings. Many deny that what took place was a firing, insisting that the executive in question resigned. A man who has served on several corporate boards tells of a drug company chairman who wanted to get rid of his president. The chairman set up a series of dinner parties, inviting the president to all of them. At each party the chairman went out of his way to make remarks he knew the president would find insulting and inflammatory. Unwilling to continue taking this abuse, the president quit his job in the middle of one of the assaults—just as the chairman hoped he would. The chairman called his public-relations man, told him to telephone the news to *The New York Times,* and the next morning's paper announced that the president had resigned. The narrator of this story steadfastly maintains that the president was not fired.

Why the insistence on drawing a distinction between a firing and a resignation that is clearly forced? The question disappears when one considers what went into hiring the fired executive. It is not unheard of for the board of directors of a large corporation to spend a year and hundreds of thousands of dollars—sometimes more than $1 million—to find a new CEO or heir apparent. Executive recruiters scour the countryside for candidates, compensation experts are put to work tying ever-fancier bows on the pay package, and at some companies, a director may be paid a six-figure sum to lead the search. A board of directors would look rather harebrained if it fired an executive chosen so carefully. Having him resign because of "policy differences" or "to pursue other interests" helps the board save face. The memo written by CBS chairman William Paley after he provoked John Backe's resignation is typical of the way a board plays out this charade. Praising Backe's "dedication and hard work" and his "important contribution to the company's progress," Paley added, "We understand his decision to pursue another course in looking toward the future, and we wish him every success and satisfaction." To those who didn't know that Paley had growing doubts about Backe, it sounded as if Backe left because he'd found a better job somewhere else.

An even more fundamental source of the reluctance to call a firing a firing is the highly personal nature of the friction that leads to it. Warren Hirsh grated on the artistic temperament of Calvin Klein. Jane Pfeiffer was the nagging voice of conscience. Lyman Hamilton committed the unpardonable sin of sundering what Harold Geneen had so lovingly joined together. This is not to say that performance is never an issue. Fred Silverman was dismissed after several years of failing to get NBC out of the basement, and the serious decline of AM International's fortunes contributed mightily to the fall of Roy Ash. But when performance is not the issue, CEOs and boards of directors almost never show the candor of Henry Ford II, who admitted he was firing Ford president Lee Iacocca simply because he'd never liked him.

Humiliating as it is to be fired, especially when the event makes headlines for days (and keeps the rumor mills churning for months), it is hard to feel sorry for anyone whose pink slip comes with a check for $1 million or more. The munificence of these severance arrangements is not lost on the executives involved, and Hirsh says his first reaction to being fired from Puritan Fashions was, "Who would have ever thought that Warren Hirsh, a guy from Brooklyn, could make a million dollars for eight weeks' work?" But pointing out how well-off these executives are, and letting it go at that, misses the essence of what it feels like to fall from a peak reached only after a lifetime of climbing. Asked whether it is true, as one management consultant has suggested, that being fired is "a battle star," one deposed chief snapped, "Don't be ridiculous. It's the ass end of the rainbow."

Maurice Valente, who lasted only five and a half months at RCA, agreed. "It was a traumatic experience. I received a lot of phone calls and letters of condolence. Many people were genuinely sympathetic, but many also combined sympathy with curiosity. They were calling more because they wanted to be in the know, to hear from the horse's mouth exactly what happened. And the first shock is the least debilitating. It takes three or four months for it to sink in. Then you begin to seriously question your abilities." In September 1983, Valente was found hanged in an apartment he kept in Rome.

"Initially, I was elated to be out of Puritan," Hirsh says of his firing. "But after two weeks the elation started to turn into depression. I had never been out of work in my life. I hadn't earned under $600,000 a year for three years. There aren't many jobs that pay that well in any industry, especially the garment industry. I felt unsure and indecisive. I would be fine for two hours and then I'd wonder if I ever should have left Murjani to go to Puritan. It was an awful feeling to go from being on top of the world to waiting for the phone to ring." His shock was further complicated by his next business venture, a fiasco with a blouse manufacturer named Zenith-Evans. "Their debts were far greater than the figures shown to me," he says. "In my twenty-five years of working, this was the most unpleasant year I've ever spent. It was even harder than the bad experience at Puritan." After extricating himself from the Zenith-Evans tangle, he made up his mind to leave the apparel business.

As for Puritan Fashions, chairman Carl Rosen died in the summer of 1983 and was succeeded by his twenty-six-year-old son. A few months later, Calvin Klein and his business partner, Barry Schwartz, who were among Puritan's largest shareholders, moved to take over the company.

Although Archie McCardell's departure from International Harvester came about because of the peculiarities of his compensation contract rather than bad chemistry, his experiences after leaving were similar to Hirsh's. "For the first few months, it was great," McCardell says. "I got a lot of sleep and exercise and lost a lot of weight. I ended up in better physical and mental shape. I no longer had to take aspirin to get me going in the morning. But since then it has been an adjustment. I'm on a few boards, but I don't have as many contacts as I used to. I miss the stimulation of that. I consider myself underutilized. If somebody were to come along and ask me if I wanted to take on a troubled company, I'd probably say yes. And I'd be better at it than I was before. I know how to handle a crisis, which is something very few professional business managers know."

Ever the optimist, Roy Ash seems not to have lost any sleep over the coup that removed him from the chairmanship of AM International. "In retrospect, I see how I could have aligned power differently, but events are events.

Madison Fund wanted control of AM, and I stood in the way of that. I became the factor to be eliminated from the equation. All they had to do was figure out how to align their interests with others on the board. It happens all the time. You go on to other things."

In almost all cases, "other things" do not include a perch in the eagle's nest of another large corporation. One rare exception is Robert Swanson's shift from the executive suite at Greyhound to the presidency of Del E. Webb Corporation, a Phoenix-based company that operates hotels and casinos and does construction work. Lee Iacocca's move from Ford to the Chrysler presidency is another of these rarities, as is his long survival in the role of corporate messiah. In most cases, even when it is widely understood that a dismissal came about because of personality clashes rather than performance problems, the fired top executive becomes damaged goods in the eyes of other companies.

Once the shock wears off, most of these fallen chieftains move on to smaller companies or entrepreneurial ventures. Valente started his own telecommunications company. Richard Black, who left AM to sue the company in the hope of recovering the $3.3 million he sank into it when he took over, has turned down job offers to make his own way in high technology, the field Roy Ash said Black didn't understand. In 1983, Black was busy designing a computer for what he sees as an important unfilled niche.

Fred Silverman, thirty pounds lighter and his gray hair blacker than it was in his NBC days, went back to the side of television he knows best: programs. In a joint venture with MGM, he founded a production company to develop new TV shows. High on his list of customers will be all his old employers: NBC, ABC, and CBS. He also started work on a new cable channel.

After overcoming "an incredible sense of injustice and sorrow," former CBS president Arthur Taylor hitched up with RCA and Rockefeller real-estate money in a cable TV partnership to bring high-quality programming to the masses. In 1983, after only ten months on the air, the new channel signed off for good. Just like the cultural cable channel started by Taylor's old boss at CBS, this one failed by aiming too high. As one account put it, Taylor's channel tried "to impose its own lofty programming standards on a marketplace happy with *Dallas* and *Dynasty.*"

Taylor's successor at CBS, John Backe, spent the year after his dismissal considering dozens of proposals before agreeing in 1981 to take the president's job at Tomorrow Entertainment, a television production company. In 1983, still at Tomorrow Entertainment, he and a New York investment firm started their own communications company with the purchase of a TV station in Schenectady.

Lyman Hamilton also found a home in a small company after his ouster from ITT. To the surprise of observers who expected him to go to Wall Street, where his financial skills were much admired, he signed on as chairman of Tamco Enterprises, a private investment company.

Twice burned by the garment industry, Warren Hirsh was in the process of setting up shop as a manager of celebrities when a Hong Kong entrepreneur named Kenneth Fang convinced him to come back to the jeans world. The enticement: Fang promised him a piece of the business. That was the prize Murjani had refused him. Fang also promised the financial and manufacturing support Hirsh had lacked in his last venture. So Warren Hirsh returned to Seventh Avenue as the head of J. Breed Clothing, Inc., makers of Jesse jeans. One wonders what Calvin Klein thought when he saw Jesse's 1982 ad campaign, which was even steamier than the Brooke Shields commercials Hirsh had disliked so. Jesse's posters showed a rugged cowboy and a delicious cowgirl shoulder-deep in a canyon swimming hole. A second handsome cowboy, standing at the edge of the swimming hole, is about to peel off his Jesses and join the fun.

Of all the felled corporados who have managed to rise again, no one has done more spectacularly than Roy Ash, who stumbled onto a gold mine. For once, neither the stumbling nor the gold mine is a figure of speech. In 1961, Ash and his Litton colleague, Tex Thornton, had paid $1.25 million for a ranch in the middle of Nevada. Along with a few thousand head of cattle and a couple of ranch buildings, they made sure they acquired rights to all "hydrocarbon substances and minerals of every kind and nature" under their 223,000 acres. Gold was discovered on the ranch in the mid-1960s by geologists from Newmont Mining, but it wasn't until 1982 that Newmont announced the vastness of the find: over eight million ounces. In the United States, only the famous Homestake Mine in South Dakota is larger than that. The gold on the Nevada ranch is present in microscopic particles rather than in a vein, which means it is quarried rather than mined in the standard underground way. In a procedure that may be as close to alchemy as technology will ever get, the gold-bearing earth is stacked in large mounds and sprinkled with cyanide. The cyanide trickles through the dross, gathering the gold as it goes. Then the cyanide is removed, and *voilà*—pure gold. Although Ash and Thornton's heirs (Thornton died in 1981) are no longer sole owners of the gold rights, royalties could bring them more than $500 million before the mine is played out.

Even without a gold mine or another top corporate job, an executive can survive a fall from the high wire, and that big severance check can go a long way toward making some cherished entrepreneurial dream come true. Watching the dazzling success of entrepreneurs at companies like Apple Computer and Federal Express, many an executive locked into a corporate job would love to test his mettle in a new business. Those who are fired from the top, for all the humiliation and self-doubt they endure, are at least handed a ticket that can take them down the entrepreneurial road, if that is where they want to go. As one of them explained, "It's a big, pleasant change to go from a large corporation to your own small company. You can put your arms around the whole business, you don't have to answer to a superior, and your equity in the business can bring you more financial rewards than you would get from a big company even at the top."

By now, the short-order hiring and firing of top executives brought in from the outside is so well understood that it would be unusual for one of these newcomers not to ask for—and get—a cushy severance clause added to the employment contract. As one management consultant has pointed out, "You never have greater bargaining position than on that day you're negotiating with a company that wants you very badly.... The only barrier when you're negotiating is the limit of your own imagination." The irony is that the big money a corporation spends to hire a savior may well play a large part in his downfall. For those involved in paying stratospheric sums to a new executive, there is a great temptation to slip into circular logic, reasoning that he must be worth it or he wouldn't be getting it. No wonder then that when he makes a mistake, or offends, those who hired him feel they've been had.

But big paychecks and the superhuman expectations they create aren't the only things that make a corporate messiah's life precarious. In a famous experiment with nursery-school children, psychologist F. T. Merei organized relatively passive children into play groups and let them play for several days with the same toys and games. Each group developed its own behavior patterns as well as its own traditions of who played with which toys. Once these patterns were set, Merei added an older child to each group, introducing the newcomer as the leader. (For this role, he chose children who were eighteen months older than the others and who had shown signs of dominance in other situations at the nursery school.) All of these new leaders tried to take charge, but most failed. Merei's explanation: "The group absorbed the leader, forcing its traditions on him." The one leader who succeeded did so only after several group members spent several days smoothing the way.

Corporations are not nursery schools, of course, and a chief executive's position carries considerably more weight than the nominal power Merei conferred simply by announcing to the group that the new member would be its leader. But the enormous pull exerted by a group makes it hard for new leaders to effect any change at all, much less act as quickly as corporate saviors are expected to. Although Roy Ash's attempt to take AM International from low-tech to high-tech did not succeed, he correctly perceived the futility of putting a few electronics engineers into an R&D department filled with electrical and mechanical engineers. Noting that "the big forces for stability would gobble up the little forces for change," Ash decided—not unreasonably—to shut the R&D department and get the electronics he wanted by buying small high-tech firms.

A second problem for the new leader, pointed out by Gil E. Gordon and Ned Rosen of Cornell University in a review of research on leadership succession, is that he cannot "function totally independently of his sponsors and of how those around him expect him to function." Put another way, whatever agenda a new leader may have, the agendas of others must also be attended to. And when these other agendas are unspoken, dimly understood, or denied, the new leader may well fail. The vexations of these hidden expectations can be especially acute if the outgoing leader is an aging entrepreneur. As Lyman Hamilton put it after he was forced to resign from ITT, priority number one wasn't running the company, it was getting along with Harold Geneen.

The combination of unspoken agendas and the aging chief's reluctance to let go mean that the authority of the new leader—despite his lofty title—often is more apparent than real. At RCA, President Maurice Valente found himself bypassed by senior vice-presidents who preferred to continue reporting to the chairman. In not supporting Valente on this issue, the chairman rendered him powerless.

Groups may also be motivated to resist new leaders, Gordon and Rosen suggested. The RCA senior vice presidents resisted Valente because they wanted to preserve their ties to the chairman and because they resented the fact that the presidency had gone to an outsider instead of to one of them. In their view, Valente was not a new leader but a rival to be eliminated. Likewise, Calvin Klein rallied his forces at Puritan Fashions to resist Warren Hirsh as soon as he sensed that Hirsh would interfere with the Calvin Klein way of doing business.

The most telling thing about all these difficulties is that Lee Iacocca of Chrysler and Sanford Sigoloff of the Wickes Companies—two corporate messiahs who succeeded—largely escaped them. Unlike the nursery-school leaders, neither Iacocca nor Sigoloff was absorbed by the group because both came to their jobs with extraordinarily broad powers and moved quickly to replace key members of the group. Neither had to deal with hidden agendas or rival leaders. And at both Wickes and Chrysler, the goal of the leader was survival of the group—something group members had no motivation to resist.

Chapter 9

Raising Lazarus

Sanford Sigoloff and the
Wickes Bankruptcy

IN THE LATE 1970s, the Wickes Companies had a problem. Their main businesses, lumber and building supplies, left them at the mercy of one notoriously cyclical industry: housing. When housing boomed, so did Wickes. But whenever home loan rates went up, potential buyers backed off, housing construction slowed, and Wickes was left in the lurch. To solve the problem, Wickes executives decided to diversify, adding businesses that didn't move in the same cycle. They hoped for a version of the synergy that oil companies achieved when they acquired chemical businesses. Because petroleum is the basic ingredient of hundreds of plastics, fibers, and other chemical products, the same low prices that depress oil company earnings typically lead to lower costs—and higher profits—for the chemical industry. By setting up house together, an oil company and a chemical company can play one set of ups and downs against another.

In 1980, Wickes's quest for that sort of *yin-yang* fit led it from its headquarters in San Diego to the Minneapolis doorstep of Gamble-Skogmo, Inc., a $2 billion-a-year retailer that owned several midwestern chains of supermarkets, drugstores, hardware stores, and clothing stores as well as mail-order and finance companies. On a seesaw of its own, Gamble-Skogmo had managed to double its net income in fiscal 1979 but still was turning in a profit of only about 1 percent. The company's undistinguished performance could be traced partly to a familiar phenomenon: the aging entrepreneur who doesn't want to let go. In this case it was Bertin Gamble, who hung on until age seventy-nine. Finally eased out in 1977, Gamble was succeeded by a president and a chairman both nearing retirement age, which left the company with a leadership vacuum.

Asked why Wickes wanted to marry homely Gamble-Skogmo, E. L. McNeely, the chairman of Wickes, said he felt certain that compatibilities "must exist" between the companies because both operated such extensive small-town chains. Wickes had twelve hundred retail outlets; Gamble, three thousand. McNeely also pointed out that a merger would save both companies millions of dollars on transportation alone. A truck carrying Wickes lumber in one direction might, for example, carry Gamble hardware on the return trip. Since each company spent $100 million a year distributing its goods, the savings from coordinating their efforts could be immense.

As for what Gamble shareholders would gain from the marriage, the answer was money. Gamble stock was selling for $28 a share, and Wickes was offering to buy it for $45.

But by 1982, Wickes's diversification dreams had collided with reality. Unlike RCA, which got into hot water by acquiring CIT Financial with short-term borrowings during a period of soaring interest rates, Wickes had prudently bought Gamble with a $200 million combination of cash and stock. The hitch was that Gamble's dowry included debts of $563 million. Caught in the housing industry's worst downturn in decades, Wickes was falling farther and farther behind in paying off the debt. After the acquisition, Wickes's debt leaped to more than $1 billion from $281 million, and annual interest costs quintupled to $200 million—$50 million more than Wickes earned during the entire year ending January 31, 1981. Now, in the early days of 1982, the company was on the brink, agonizing over how it would make a $70 million loan payment due April 30.

It couldn't be done. The company delayed reporting its earnings for the year ending January 31, 1982, and announced that it expected a loss of $80 million. Creditors were getting nervous. The company's stock wilted to a third of the $17 it had commanded at one point in 1981.

In the face of this precariousness, the compensation committee of Wickes's board of directors saw fit to approve $372,000 in performance bonuses for the company's top managers, including $120,750 for Chairman McNeely. Could it be? Merit bonuses for a management team that couldn't figure out how to keep the company afloat? Perhaps because committee members worried that shareholders would have a hard time grasping a bonus system that rewarded failure, they recommended that the bonuses be postponed until the company turned a profit again. Meanwhile, the bonus money would earn a tidy 15 percent annually for the executives concerned.

The lid blew off during the last week of March. The $70 million for the loan payment was nowhere to be found, and the estimate of an $80 million loss for the year turned out to be grossly short of the mark. Weeks later, when all the numbers were in, the loss totaled a staggering $258 million. McNeely and several top aides were booted out, and five of the company's eleven directors resigned.

For salvation, the remaining directors looked to Sanford C. Sigoloff, fifty-one, a Los Angeles executive who had worked corporate miracles twice before. In the early 1970s he had turned around Republic Corporation of Los Angeles, a discount retailer and maker of health-care products. A few years later he had steered Daylin Corporation, another failing Southern California retailer, through the tricky waters of bankruptcy. The cost of bringing him to Wickes: almost $1 million dollars—a $400,000 sign-on bonus to replace money he would lose by leaving his post as vice-chairman of Kaufman and Broad, a Los Angeles homebuilder; an annual salary of $350,000 (gradually upped to $564,000 over the next several months): and premiums on $2 million worth of life insurance.

Directors also had to grant him powers befitting a czar. "My conditions for taking on a turnaround are always the same," Sigoloff says. "There's only one chief executive officer—me—and he holds all terminal decision-making authority, including authority over the board. You can't succeed in a turnaround if you have to worry about people who have ties and loyalties to the previous management." Within a week of his appointment, five more directors were gone.

Despite the perils of bringing in outsiders to run a large and complex company, a full-scale corporate salvage operation almost demands a new face. As one rescue expert told Donald B. Bibeault, author of *Corporate Turnaround,* "The management reputation of insiders . . . has been tainted. The insider has been a party to those elements that caused the decline and now must draw upon those people involved to act instantly under his direction. The normal reaction is, 'Well, what does he know; he is as much responsible for getting into the hole as we were.' " A second insider problem: the difficulty of breaking commitments made to people hired in better times. "That's impossible for most people to do . . . because it's construed as being deceitful," another turnaround expert told Bibeault. An outsider, with no ties to people in the company, will have an easier time making the unpopular decisions a turnaround requires.

Sigoloff's arrival at Wickes was a textbook example of the chasm between outsiders and former insiders that immediately results from changing the guard for a turnaround. Just before Sigoloff was hired, he met with Wickes chairman McNeely for forty minutes. The two have not spoken since McNeely left.

Trim and intense, Sigoloff thrives on crises. "Being offered the chance to head a company in trouble is like being given a free airline ticket for a Laetrile treatment," he says. "But what makes the challenge exciting is that you're going into a situation where there's an absence of credible intelligence. You have a chance to restore that. It's the challenge of the hundred-piece white puzzle. The form and the substance are there but you have to figure out how the pieces fit."

This time around, the absence of credible intelligence had created a white puzzle with thousands of pieces and debts that ran to $1.6 billion. The white puzzle would have to wait until Sigoloff completed the first task of any turnaround: Stop the bleeding. The technique for doing that is breathtakingly simple—and daring. Cash ebb is transformed into cash flow by putting a hold on payments to creditors as a way of buying time while corporate doctors determine the causes of the hemorrhage. The daring part of the strategy, of course, is that creditors won't tolerate this arrangement for long. For several months before Sigoloff arrived, a number of Wickes suppliers had had it with late payments and excuses, and they were refusing to ship goods to Wickes unless they could collect on delivery. As a result, many of the shelves in Wickes's do-it-yourself retail outlets looked like Old Mother Hubbard's cupboard, which compounded the considerable troubles the company already had in attracting customers.

To make matters worse, mass defections followed the announcement of Sigoloff's appointment. Though he would have assembled his own management team in any case, he says it was "frightening to see how many Wickes people left. They didn't want to make the commitment I knew it would take to turn Wickes around. I needed people who were willing to work six days a week for five days' pay. In three turnarounds, this was the first time I'd ever had to recruit from the outside. The top fifteen executives left."

Why would a turnaround specialist want to keep executives who probably had a hand in making the mess? Eugene E. Jennings, a management professor at Michigan State University, answers the question by telling a story about Ernie Breech, who was hired to turn around Ford in the 1950s. In need of advice on how to begin, Breech went to see Alfred Sloan, retired chairman of General Motors and one of the geniuses of American business. Sloan pointed out that at Ford, Breech would be in the position of an immigrant, and as an immigrant, he would need the natives more than they needed him. To succeed, Breech would need a map, Sloan said, and he counseled him not to fire any natives until he was safely in possession of their maps.

Deserted by the natives, Sigoloff would have to do his own cartography. The problem was compounded by Sigoloff's decision to move corporate headquarters from San Diego one hundred miles north, to the Los Angeles suburb of Santa Monica. Failing companies sometimes relocate in the hope that a large number of employees will choose not to make the move, which eases the dreaded task of handing out pink slips. Sigoloff says that consideration didn't enter into the Wickes move. "I thought I could do a better job in Los Angeles because I would be able to draw from a larger pool of accountants, lawyers, and other support people I would need." On April 24, 1982, less than a month after Sigoloff took the helm, another reason for the move emerged: Wickes took refuge from its creditors by filing a petition under Chapter 11 of the bankruptcy laws. Sigoloff felt more comfortable doing that in the Los Angeles court system, which he knew from the days of Daylin's bankruptcy.

In filing for bankruptcy, Wickes had plenty of company. *The Wall Street Journal* estimated that in the first quarter of 1982, recession-wracked businesses submitted bankruptcy petitions at the rate of thirty-six for every hour of the business day. But with its $4 billion in annual revenues, Wickes was one of the largest U.S. corporations ever to go bankrupt.

Going into Chapter 11 has all the appeal of a trip to Lourdes. It is the course of last resort, the only sanctuary where a company in deep trouble can find the peace it needs to figure out how it will honor its debts. Once a bankruptcy petition has been granted, a corporation is protected from its creditors while it works out a plan of reorganization. Often, but not always, the plan may include selling off all or part of a company's assets in an effort to pay the bills.

When Sigoloff's crisis management team finished adding up the bills, there were fifteen thousand creditors waiting to be paid. In June, five hundred of them came to the Los Angeles Convention Center to hear Wickes explain how it planned to pay back their $1.6 billion. They can be forgiven for their touching hope that Sigoloff really was the messiah. Who else could they believe in? Their great expectations may explain the rumor that circulated in New York after the meeting: Sandy Sigoloff, they said on Wall Street, had appeared before creditors wearing a Superman suit. There was no Superman suit, but Sigoloff did manage to win their confidence with his candor about the magnitude of Wickes's problems. For one thing there was the party favor he gave everyone: a duffel bag containing a fifty-pound computer printout of Wickes's debts—thirty-four hundred pages. The question-and-answer session following a flawlessly prepared slide presentation lasted two hours and was remarkably free of the hostility that claimants typically bring to such gatherings. The meeting ended with applause for Sigoloff—possibly a first in the annals of corporate bankruptcy.

The decline and fall of the Wickes Companies had put creditors over more than one barrel. Not only did they have to worry about collecting back debts, but the suppliers among them had to make a decision that would have confounded King Solomon: whether to continue doing business with Wickes. If they did resume shipping goods to the company's stores, they ran the risk of getting burned again. But if they ended their relationship with the multi-billion-dollar company, they would lose a major customer. Calculators were no help in making the decision. You either believed in Sandy Sigoloff or you didn't.

Getting people to believe is a corporate messiah's most crucial errand. Lee Iacocca did it with his superabundance of confidence. Roy Ash tried to do it with his high-tech dream. Fred Silverman sold NBC on his golden gut. The Wickes suppliers and employees who decided to believe in Sigoloff were inspired not only by his track record at Republic and Daylin but by his frankness. "To get people to follow you, you have to tell them the truth," he says. "At the first creditors' meeting, this was largely a matter of telling them that I didn't know the answer to their most important question—when they would get their money. Inside the company, at group meetings of employees, I told people we were going to go on a diet and that we might conceivably have times that were much harder than a diet."

The diet started with an order from Sigoloff to cut the number of employees by 10 percent. Within two weeks, three thousand people were to be put out on the street in the middle of the nation's worst economic tailspin in fifty years. "When you do that, people look at you as some sort of coldhearted amphibian who comes out of cold, dark recesses and acts without feeling," Sigoloff says. "But unless you do it, you put at risk thousands of other jobs—not just in this company but at suppliers' companies too. Decisions that impact people's lives are not made lightly or just by one person. If unprofitable stores are to be closed, our real-estate people, accountants, and the division president are involved. In closing businesses, we do everything possible to make the process not feel like an invasion. We enlist the help of the people at the store, make them party to decisions, do outplacement for key people, and relocate employees when we can. When you have to let people go, you can do it with dignity and style."

Dignity and style notwithstanding, Sigoloff has had to make many moves that employees have found hard to take. One of the hardest was closing Aldens, Inc., a $300-million-a-year mail-order business in Chicago. Its biggest problems: It had not computerized its record-keeping, which made for great expense and delay while clerks noted orders and kept accounts in a hundred old-fashioned ledgers. Nor had the Aldens catalogue kept pace with the country's demographic changes. Merchandise still was aimed at the tastes of rural residents, many of whom had developed more citified appetites as a result of shopping in the malls that were sprouting everywhere. A costly eleventh-hour turnaround effort failed to convince upscale urban dwellers they needed Aldens. By the fall of 1982, Aldens was losing $1 million a week. In November, Sigoloff flew to Chicago and told Aldens employees he was looking for a buyer for the company. A few weeks later, when no buyer materialized, Aldens closed its doors.

The company's twenty-six hundred employees, who had been there an average of seventeen years, didn't understand what had happened. Even though Wickes felt that Aldens's problems had been long in the making, employees noted that the company had managed to stay in the black throughout the seventies. Since the company didn't begin roaring downhill at full speed until Wickes acquired Aldens in the Gamble-Skogmo merger, there was little Sigoloff could say to convince Aldens employees that Wickes was not the culprit.

Sigoloff has spent uncountable hours visiting Wickes's operations and rebuilding morale, which he views as a top priority. "The average salesperson in any organization doesn't give a damn, but the only way a retailing company can be successful is if it has repeat customers," he says. As obvious as that is, it is terrifically hard to generate enthusiasm in a sales force afraid of being laid off and demoralized by customer complaints about empty shelves and seedy-looking stores. Sigoloff and other top managers have spent much of their time in Wickes's stores, explaining what they are trying to do, and seeking employees' advice on how to do it. Stores also are being spruced up and restocked. Like Lee Iacocca, Sigoloff has taken to the television airwaves to spread the message that his company is on the mend. In rolled-up shirt-sleeves and an open vest (the same thing he wears in the office), Sigoloff pushes a shopping cart through a Builders Emporium store in California. The cart is full, and so are the shelves behind him.

Sigoloff's intense and forthright style also helps to explain why he has been able to pull off the nearly impossible feat of convincing smart, high-octane executives to join a stalled company. Since Wickes was bankrupt, he couldn't entice them with options on stock that might well prove worthless. Nor could he offer spectacular salaries, he says, because "creditors won't cooperate if they think you're getting rich on their sorrows." There could be no promise of job security, either. Still, he says he had no trouble getting the people he wanted. "They're here because they know that in a troubled company they'll grow faster than they would anywhere else."

But the growth has not come without some unexpected pain, which clearly bothers Sigoloff. "This has been my first experience with burned-out executives," he says. "In one week we wiped out three or four executives with the flu, and they just couldn't seem to get well. We're asking people to run night and day, and that has taken its toll. Even though many of us have been through turnarounds before, we've never taken on a project on as large a scale as Wickes." In the fall of 1982, to cope with the burnout, Sigoloff laid down the law about hours. His new rules were astonishing not for their generosity but for what they revealed about the pace at Wickes since the turnaround began: Henceforth almost everyone had to take alternate Saturdays off. A three-day vacation every six or eight weeks became mandatory for top executives, and it was not to be interrupted by phone calls except in emergencies. On Friday evenings, everyone was to be out of the office by six, and no one was allowed in the office after two on Sundays except in emergencies.

It is easy to understand why young executives aching to get ahead would subject themselves to the grueling strains of a turnaround, but Sigoloff's reasons for electing combat duty again and again are different. Beyond the fact that he sees the hundred-piece white puzzle as the ultimate test of his analytical abilities and business experience, he believes that the dictatorial powers granted to a turnaround executive give him "a freedom to do the job that really doesn't exist anywhere else in American industry." Unfettered by board directives, committees, and internecine sniping, the turnaround executive has the luxury of focusing entirely on an agenda he sets.

So far, the burnout at Wickes has left Sigoloff untouched, perhaps because he operates on a clock different from the one that governs other mortals. His days in Los Angeles begin with a run at 5:30 A.M., and his aversion to business travel drives him to put in twenty-two hours a day when he's on the road so he can get home as soon as possible. This hard charging as well as his fearlessness in slashing staff have won him the nickname "Ming the Merciless," but the sobriquet has nothing to do with the tough-guy image the press uses to describe him. Ming, a character in an old science-fiction comic strip, was the leader of a benighted planet named Mongo. "Mongo was a pockmarked, ugly place—like a Chapter 11 company," Sigoloff explains. "It needed a comeback, and Ming had to do all kinds of things to try to make that happen. I adopted the nickname to inject a note of humor. Most of the time, a turnaround is miserable trench warfare. You can't get through it if you don't have the ability to laugh at yourself. There are a lot of nicknames around here—Captain America, Lighter-Than-Wind, Dignity. It's one small way of having fun and making people feel like part of a team."

The news that Ming has mercy may come as a disappointment since it doesn't fit the mystique of the turnaround artist. Unless he inspires fear, the mythology goes, he can't succeed. "Everyone has to be afraid of him," a corporate savior explained in *Corporate Turnaround,* "afraid for his job. . . ." The leader "doesn't even have to use the stick, but he must leave the impression that he's not afraid to use it."

Though Sigoloff has the capacity to be tough, he doesn't see toughness as the key to a successful turnaround. "Succeeding takes two things," he says: "the will to win and even more important, the will to prepare." Central to his idea of preparation is a computerized master calendar listing almost four thousand items in need of attention—everything from executive travel plans and meetings to court testimony and the arrival of visitors. "Every Saturday morning, in what is known as 'the meeting that never ends,' we review the master calendar, look at deadlines for various projects, and sort the critical from the noncritical items on the list," Sigoloff says. "The calendar allows people to focus on short-term and long-term goals. With all the tasks listed on the computer, everyone knows what is to be done by when." Revamped computer systems also have given Wickes weekly cash-flow reports and monthly business reports, which it did not have under the old management.

Not only does Sigoloff contend that turnarounds depend less on toughness than on thorough preparation, he also challenges the belief that only a leader with absolute power can reverse the fortunes of a declining organization. "I do have ultimate control," he concedes. "In the beginning it's important not to relinquish that because you have to act fast to stop the bleeding. But success ultimately depends on how much authority you can give up. To do all the things that need doing you have to delegate authority and responsibility for every task to the lowest possible level. The test of a good executive is not how many decisions he makes but how few. If a CEO attracts the right people, they are the ones making most of the decisions. The only decisions a good CEO makes are the really unpalatable ones, the ones nobody wants to make."

The decisions to be made during the respite provided by Chapter 11 revolve around how the company can shed operations accounting for about $1 billion a year in sales without causing any more damage to its health. Within a week after Sigoloff came to Wickes, the company completed the sale of 75 percent of its MacGregor Golf Company for $17 million. It has closed several furniture stores; sold its agricultural division to Pillsbury; announced plans to sell or close dozens of department stores in Nebraska, Colorado, and Utah; and sold a chain of furniture stores in the South.

The particulars of these transactions would hardly be worth mentioning except for what they reveal about the origins of Wickes's troubles. Like many a red-blooded American corporation, Wickes felt there was greatness in size. The fastest way for a corporation to grow is to buy other companies. The strategy can work if the parent company imposes a high degree of coordination on all operations, but as often as not, conglomerates flounder because the operating units have little or no intrinsic connective tissue. Gathered under one roof with no unifying purpose, disparate businesses tend to drain more energy than they add. As management theorist Peter Drucker has observed, the belief that a diversified business will outperform undiversified companies is mistaken. Complexity, he says, "is a competitive disadvantage. Complex businesses, despite their size and large resources, have again and again shown themselves exceedingly vulnerable to small but highly concentrated single-market or single-technology businesses." Drucker cites the example of Litton Industries, "one of the first conglomerates to preach the gospel of management by 'controls,' that is, by reports, data, and organized information." But because of its complexity, Drucker says, Litton didn't find out about the serious trouble in its office-equipment business until "very late." The unwieldy ITT empire built by Harold Geneen, which circled the globe and came to include everything from Twinkies to satellites, developed similar ailments.

The idea that bigger is better is not peculiar to business executives. Government bureaucrats also dream of presiding over ever-expanding empires, and the association of size with effectiveness even dominates scholarly literature on organization theory. Preoccupied with growth and its consequences, social scientists have paid almost no attention to organizational decline, says David A. Whetten, an organizational theorist at the University of Illinois. That omission is of more than passing interest, since many business leaders—including Sigoloff—believe that a long period of economic retrenchment lies ahead. The traditional American commitment to expansion coupled with a poor understanding of the dynamics of decline will no doubt add to the pain of the coming contractions. Noting that "admitting failure is practically a national taboo," Whetten says that when managers are "forced to admit the existence of decline, they tend to label it as merely a period of temporary consolidation, which is a forerunner of future growth." Shades of Roy Ash, who spent four and a half years characterizing AM International's setbacks as signs of progress.

Sigoloff cherishes no such illusions for Wickes. As he hacks away at the deadwood, he is simultaneously looking for what he calls "the core." The ultimate challenge of the hundred-piece white puzzle, he says, "is to find and burnish the businesses that will allow us to reconstitute a core that will produce the surplus cash flow we need to repay creditors. If we're smart enough and lucky enough, the redefined business will move beyond repaying debt to survive as an employer and a performer of a social good, or at least a service good." Looking at his efforts in a larger context, Sigoloff sees other American businesses taking a leaf from turnaround companies. "From now on businesses will have to be more defensive, more concerned with issues of competitive advantage than with acquisitive crapshooting.

Everybody, not just companies in trouble, has to slim down to fighting weight to survive."

Although Wickes's chances for survival have improved dramatically, the turnaround has a long way to go. On the plus side, after a year in which the company lost $400 million, losses were cut to only $566,000 during the first quarter under Chapter 11. But shareholders' equity has been wiped out by Wickes's indebtedness, and that picture will be long in changing. And without a sustained upturn in the economy, improvements at Wickes will have to come more from streamlining and sharp management than from sales. Wickes has needed two big assists from the economy: interest rates low enough to resurrect the housing industry, and a drop in unemployment strong enough to erase the fears that have made millions of consumers postpone major expenditures such as homebuying and remodeling.

These are major uncertainties, but Wickes has been making progress. Several more subsidiaries have been put on the block, and in February 1983 Wickes presented creditors with the reorganization plan required by the bankruptcy laws. At the time, Sigoloff also predicted that Wickes could emerge from Chapter 11 as early as the middle of 1984. But the success of the plan hinged on just how cooperative creditors were willing to be. If enough of them held out for debt settlements larger than those offered by Wickes in the reorganization plan, Chapter 11 could last somewhat longer.

Sigoloff's survival at Wickes is less of an issue than the survival of Wickes itself. Unlike many corporate messiahs, however, he is not protected by a multiyear employment contract with an expensive severance clause. In April 1982, he and his top managers were given one-year contracts with a guarantee of a year's salary as severance. After that, Sigoloff says, everyone is on his own. And even though Sigoloff handpicked his board of directors, he holds his job totally at their discretion. "When you're the fiduciary of a troubled company, there is no job security," he says. But he will probably stay at Wickes as long as he wants for the simple reason that the company's most critical constituents, its thousands of creditors, desperately want him there.

Chapter 10

Chrysler's Last Stand

Lee Iacocca's Miracle

IN THE SPRING OF 1982, an impeccably tailored businessman settled his six-foot, one-inch frame into a chair in a Washington hearing room to face the formidable Subcommittee on Economic Stabilization of the Committee on Banking, Finance, and Urban Affairs of the U.S. House of Representatives. There was no need for the executive to introduce himself. His rimless eyeglasses, the bulldog set of his jaw, and the bottomless determination he exuded were well known not only to these members of Congress but also to almost everyone in the country because of the television commercials he'd been doing for his company.

On this April day, Lee Iacocca, chairman and chief executive officer of Chrysler Corporation, had come to Washington to tell the subcommittee how his company was faring. Congress had good reason for wanting to know. In 1979, after one of the stormiest debates in history, legislators had lent the full faith and credit of the United States government to Chrysler by agreeing to stand behind $1.5 billion in loans that were supposed to save the failing carmaker. After acknowledging that the thirty-one months since his first congressional appearance had been "thirty-one months of sheer hell" (and after taking time out to excoriate the Federal Reserve Board for the economic havoc created by its high-interest monetary policies), Iacocca began reeling off Chrysler's achievements: an entirely new management team, salary savings of $1.2 billion from white-collar cutbacks, a drop in after-tax losses of $1.2 billion between 1980 and 1981, elimination of $1.3 billion in bank debt, a rise in net worth from $300 million to $800 million, a $900 million cash nest egg, a 60 percent reduction in its debt-equity ratio, the best fuel-economy average of the Detroit carmakers. . . . The list went on and on.

By any standards, it was an impressive list. Iacocca might have gone through hell, but it looked as if he had actually done what he promised Congress he would do: save the company that everyone said couldn't be saved. Only two and a half years earlier, the doomsayers had been everywhere. "Chrysler, like Humpty Dumpty, will fall— with a splat heard round the world," predicted the executive editor of a leading auto industry publication. "All the governments' horses and all Iacocca's men will not be able to put the company together again." In an editorial entitled "They Shoot Horses, Don't They?" *The Wall Street Journal* had argued that federal assistance to Chrysler would only prolong the company's misery. Even the chairman of General Motors, Thomas A. Murphy, went out of his way to kick sand in Iacocca's face, arguing against proposed federal aid on the grounds that if Chrysler were a halfway decent company, it would be able to get help from the banks. "In my judgment," Murphy volunteered, "there's never been a viable business that has lacked for financing." But the obituary writers, obsessed with

Chrysler's rivers of red ink, neglected to take a few things into account. One of them was an intangible asset named Lee Iacocca, whose forceful personality had as much to do with Chrysler's recovery as the $1.5 billion in loan guarantees enacted by Congress.

ON JULY 13, 1978, Lee Iacocca didn't even know exactly where in Detroit Chrysler's headquarters were. He was out in suburban Dearborn in his twelfth-floor office at the world headquarters of Ford Motor Company, waiting to be guillotined in one of the most celebrated firings in American business. The only explanation offered by his boss, Henry Ford II, was this: "Let's just say I don't like you."

So ended a thirty-two-year career studded with marketing triumphs that had brought him all the way to the presidency of Ford.

As a young Ford sales executive in Pennsylvania, Iacocca had dreamed up a sales campaign built around the idea of buying a 1956 Ford with payments of $56 a month. When world headquarters heard about it, "$56 in '56" went national. Brought to headquarters soon afterward, Iacocca quickly worked his way up. His place in the sun was secured in 1964, when he oversaw the development of the Mustang, Ford's most successful product since the Model T. Not only did the sporty styling of the Mustang capture the public's imagination, the car was a magnificent manufacturing achievement as well. Three quarters of its innards were pilfered from a Ford car already in production, the staid little Falcon. The rest was pizzazz pulled from thin air.

For another auto executive, Chrysler chairman John Riccardo, Henry Ford's decision to fire Iacocca couldn't have come at a more propitious moment. During three of the previous six years, Chrysler had run in the red, and

Riccardo knew that more losses lay ahead. Some of the company's problems were those of the entire automobile industry: a dwindling share of the market as ever-larger numbers of car buyers turned to Japanese and European imports, the skimpier profit margins available from making small cars, and the huge cost of complying with federal laws on fuel economy and pollution control.

Other problems were strictly of Chrysler's making. In the sixties, the company had decided to protect itself from the big ups and downs of the American car market by going abroad in search of customers. Acquiring foreign companies right and left, Chrysler came to preside over an international empire as unprofitable as it was vast. The losses from this escapade left the company's Detroit operations short of money for developing new products and modernizing old plants. Desperate for cash by the mid-seventies, Chrysler had to sell most of its foreign subsidiaries for a song. Later, when the recession of 1974–75 put a big dent in auto sales, Chrysler laid off almost a third of its work force and gave most of its engineers a three-month "vacation." Without the engineers, the long-trumpeted debuts of the economical 1976 Dodge Aspen and Plymouth Volare were held up. And when the cars finally did roll off the assembly lines, it was discovered that they stalled during acceleration. The ensuing recalls raised enough doubts about the company's cars to steer significant numbers of potential buyers away from Chrysler showrooms.

Riccardo and his team realized after the Arab oil embargoes of 1973 and 1974 that Chrysler would have to stop making gas guzzlers. But the company was so strapped for cash that it couldn't build the factory it needed to make engines for the new Omni, the fuel-stingy, front-wheel-drive subcompact it wanted to bring out in 1978. Betting that the Omni could start to turn the Japanese tide,

Chrysler hired Volkswagen to build the engines. Unfortunately (as Iacocca would discover in the spring of 1979), 360,000 people wanted Omnis, and Volkswagen could build no more than 300,000 engines. The shortage would send yet another signal that Chrysler couldn't get its act together.

In August 1978, a month after Henry Ford lowered the boom, Riccardo and Iacocca got together at the Waldorf-Astoria in New York. What Riccardo wanted, he said, was a chief operating officer to run the show while he concentrated on getting the banks—and maybe the government—to give Chrysler the legroom it needed to bring its new front-wheel-drive technology to the marketplace. Disenchanted with Gene Cafiero, the company's current president, Riccardo suspected that if Chrysler didn't get a hard-charging new operating man in place, lenders would have little faith in his promise that the new front-wheel-drive cars could start some black ink streaming into Chrysler.

Since Ford had Iacocca on the payroll through the end of October, Iacocca and Riccardo had lots of time to talk. The delay was a blow to Riccardo, who had made up his mind early that he wanted Iacocca. Iacocca wanted the job as much as Riccardo wanted to hire him, but there were a few differences to iron out—like Iacocca's compensation. In joining a Ford competitor, Iacocca would have to give up a severance package worth $1.5 million. The prospect of having to make that up to him didn't thrill Chrysler directors. In addition, the $360,000 a year he had earned as president of Ford, which he wanted as a salary for his new job, was $20,000 more than Riccardo earned. Feeling it would be unseemly for the corporation's chief executive to earn less than its chief operating officer, the directors gave Riccardo a $20,000 raise.

Iacocca wanted something else, too: the chance to be

chief executive officer. Riccardo told him he could have that job in two years. Iacocca held out for one.

When Iacocca's appointment was announced, Gene Cafiero was kicked upstairs to the newly invented post of vice-chairman. Stripped of all meaningful duties, he soon left, but not before telling Iacocca what a mess Riccardo had made of the company. Iacocca wasn't sure who was to blame, but the mess was there, all right—and it was even worse than he'd imagined. Unlike Maurice Valente, who made the mistake of accepting the RCA presidency without knowing much about the company's rough politics, Iacocca had done his homework. As soon as he knew he was leaving Ford, he began thinking about what he would do next. One possibility was some type of international automotive joint venture, and he'd asked the New York investment banking house of Salomon Brothers to research the subject for him. Using the bankers' analysis of Chrysler's prospects, Iacocca came armed with tough questions when he met with Riccardo. Financially, Iacocca knew what he was getting into. But nothing had prepared him for the operating chaos he found when he went to work in November 1978. The organization chart defied all logic. For twenty-five years the company had just growed, like Topsy, and whatever rhyme or reason might once have existed was no longer apparent. With Riccardo's blessing, Iacocca spent his first month drawing up a new organization chart. No longer would a single executive oversee both manufacturing and sales. No longer would purchasing report to engineering. Chrysler Leasing would henceforth report to sales instead of to the chairman's office. And so on.

Iacocca also began bringing in people he knew he could work with, mostly colleagues from Ford. By early 1981, almost every executive above the level of plain vice president would be a new recruit. Aside from wanting to surround himself with people he knew and trusted, Iacocca no doubt enjoyed the thought that what he was adding to Chrysler he was subtracting from Ford. The *Schadenfreude* also included persuading Ford's advertising agency, Kenyon & Eckhardt, to ditch Ford for Chrysler, and writing letters to more than five hundred thousand Ford owners urging them to "put a Ford in your past."

Chrysler's disorganized financial reporting heightened Iacocca's dismay in his first months on the job. At Ford, he'd had access to rigorous and regular financial analysis performed by people who weren't beholden to operating managers. At Chrysler, the numbers people existed largely to tell the operating people what they wanted to hear—when they wanted to hear it. As one of Iacocca's imported executives would later say in complete exasperation, "I have a terrific accountant's report that tells me we lost a billion dollars. What I don't have is an analysis to tell me *how the hell* we lost a billion dollars."

Manufacturing problems were legion, with quality at the top of the list. Buyers of Chrysler products came back to dealers with complaints about their new cars 30 percent more often than Ford and GM customers did. As for the tens of thousands of parts Chrysler used to make its cars and trucks, almost nothing had been done to economize by using the same piece in as many models as possible. Iacocca was appalled to discover that Chrysler vehicles came in no less than thirty-nine hundred colors, including seven shades of white.

The irony was that in spite of all the malfunctions, Chrysler had indeed latched onto something terrific. The company's major investment in front-wheel-drive technology, which gave engineers a way to make cars smaller without reducing passenger space, was exactly what the automotive market needed. The smaller size meant greater fuel economy, which would give Chrysler an edge as gasoline prices moved upward. Like Fred Silverman's "golden gut," Iacocca's automotive feel bordered on the mystical, and he was convinced that Chrysler's new cars were winners. As chief operating officer he was going to leave no stone unturned in his efforts to make these cars as well, as economically, and as successfully as possible.

UNFORTUNATELY, it wasn't going to be that simple. At the end of 1978, when Chrysler toted up its gains and losses for the year, it came out $205 million in the hole. In the next six months it lost even more than it had for all of 1978: $261 million. Riccardo called a press conference at Chrysler headquarters in July and announced he was going to Washington to ask for help. From here on out, Iacocca would have two full-time jobs: finance and operations.

As any American adult without amnesia knows, the Chrysler SOS raised public temperatures like no event since Watergate. Everybody had something to say about it, and in all the talk it was hard to find an encouraging word. "Welfare for corporations," one school maintained. "The antithesis of capitalism," another group said, arguing that if people in a free market chose not to buy Chrysler cars, then Chrysler should be allowed to go down the drain. "The thin end of the wedge," other critics warned: If the government bailed out Chrysler, it would be only a matter of time before somebody else showed up for a handout. Where would it all end? Still others, like GM's Thomas Murphy, asked why the government should take a risk that bankers had shunned. The outrage was palpable.

When Chrysler began telling its side of the story, the critics got even madder. The company said it was asking the federal government for help because the federal government had gotten it into hot water in the first place. Pollution-control and fuel-economy laws passed by Congress had penalized Chrysler more than Ford or GM,

Chrysler said, because Chrysler was so much smaller. With fewer resources, it had to spend a disproportionately large sum to comply with the new rules pouring out of Washington. True, the regulations put a heavier load on Chrysler than on Ford or GM, but beyond that, the reasoning got somewhat specious. As maverick automaker John De-Lorean and others pointed out, if government regulations hadn't forced the American auto industry into manufacturing small cars, Chrysler—and Ford and GM along with it—would have lost an even larger part of the car market to Japan and Europe.

Chrysler also resorted to the red, white, and blue thesis that competition, the soul of free enterprise, would receive a crippling blow if the company went under. Once Ford and GM had the pie all to themselves, Chrysler said, they would start taking it easy and American consumers would have less choice in the marketplace. Chrysler neglected to mention that if GM and Ford didn't take good care of the American consumer, Toyota, Datsun, and a host of other foreign manufacturers would. The same free enterprise that Chrysler said it wanted to protect had seen Japanese imports grow from a mere 2 percent of the market to almost 20 percent in less than a decade.

Infuriated by the critics who said Chrysler should be left to succeed or fail on its own, Iacocca insisted that "the free-enterprise system has gone to hell. Other companies have gotten federal aid, but it was 'different.' The Federal Housing Administration loan guarantees are 'different.' The agricultural subsidies on tobacco are 'different.' Everything is 'different.' "

He had a point. Even Senator William Proxmire, one of the most vituperative opponents of Chrysler aid, had bent his rules to vote in favor of a $19 million tax break for American Motors, which happened to be based in his home state of Wisconsin. And in 1971 the government had stepped in with loan guarantees worth $250 million to snatch the Lockheed Aircraft Corporation, a major defense contractor, from the jaws of bankruptcy. As the largest producer of tanks in the non-Communist world, Chrysler could say it was as worthy of rescue as Lockheed. Equally important to the analogy was the fact that the Lockheed bailout had succeeded.

But the most compelling arguments in the automaker's brief posited a Chrysler-less world so grim that Congress had to sit up and take note. According to a widely accepted estimate, one out of seven jobs in the U.S. economy depends on the auto industry. In addition to the assembly-line workers and staff employees of the auto companies themselves, millions of Americans in steel mills, rubber factories, tool-and-die shops, car dealerships, and hundreds of small-parts manufacturers owe their livelihood to Detroit. Chrysler calculated that if it went out of business, six hundred thousand jobs would be lost, raising the national unemployment level six-tenths of one percentage point. Michigan's unemployment rate would jump by four percentage points, Detroit's by ten. A Congressional Budget Office study estimated that the absence of Chrysler would reduce federal tax revenues by $11 billion and require an expenditure of $2 billion in unemployment benefits.

Chrysler lobbyists armed with computer printouts visited congressmen one by one and showed them how many jobs would disappear from their districts if Chrysler didn't get help. Alarmed by the impact such massive unemployment could have on their 1980 reelection prospects, Congress finally began to take Chrysler seriously. The debate shifted from whether the government should help Chrysler to whether the assistance would enable the company to survive.

THE ANSWER to that question would have to come from Chrysler's new chairman and chief executive officer, Lee

Iacocca, who took over in mid-September of 1979—six weeks earlier than Riccardo had promised. Riccardo's doctors, worried about his heart, had told him he had to retire or risk losing his life. There were those who thought Iacocca's combativeness wouldn't work in Washington and that his impatience would lose more votes than it would win. Having looked at Chrysler's new technology and having made a good start on overhauling the company, Iacocca was convinced his cause was just. With anyone who didn't see it his way—which included President Carter, most of Congress, and virtually all of the media—he was operating on a shorter and shorter fuse. He'd explained his position until he was blue in the face. Yes, Chrysler had made every mistake in the book, but all it was asking for was time to clean up the mess. Despite what the newspapers and television commentators had been telling people, it wasn't going to cost taxpayers a cent. Chrysler simply wanted the government to guarantee the bank loans the company would get from commercial lenders. Was that too much to ask to save six hundred thousand jobs?

There was nothing humble about the way Iacocca presented his case to Congress. He thrusted, jabbed, parried, brandished, swaggered, bellowed, snapped, paced, punched, wheeled, and pounded. The skeptics took to calling him "the Iacocca," as in "the Ayatollah." Looking through his testimony, speeches, and the interviews he gave to anyone who would listen, one is impressed by how rarely he expresses himself in conditional terms. Instead of "We think we can," it is, "We can" or "We will." He was confidence incarnate. Although he was breaking all the rules by refusing to tread softly in the corridors of power, his pugnacity did not have the untoward effects that old Washington hands predicted. The man was a walking conviction, six feet of pure passion, and that was hard to resist.

Outside Washington and outside the headlines, the public at large got its first taste of Lee Iacocca at about the time he became chairman. With public opinion dead set against aid to Chrysler and with the continuing misimpression in the media that the government would lend Chrysler the money rather than just guarantee the loans, Iacocca fought back with one of the most powerful weapons money can buy: advertising.

In a series of newspaper and magazine ads that carried his signature, Iacocca addressed all the points Chrysler's critics raised, but the ads raised these points as questions rather than conclusions: Is Chrysler building gas guzzlers? Has Chrysler done everything it can to help itself? Would a loan guarantee for Chrysler set a dangerous precedent? Does Chrysler have a future? Iacocca's case, of course, was even more fiercely partisan than the arguments advanced by his opponents. But for once he was allowed to peel away the confusion and get down to what he saw as the bare bones. No, Chrysler wasn't building gas guzzlers; it had the best average gas mileage of the Big Three. Yes, Chrysler was doing everything it could to cut costs, improve manufacturing, and tighten financial controls. No, the loan guarantees would not set a precedent, dangerous or otherwise; federal loans and guarantees worth more than $400 billion already were on the books. Yes, Chrysler had a future; the company had been in business for fifty-four years, almost all of them profitable.

There is nothing new about corporations buying advertising to tell their side of a story. Mobil has done it regularly for years, and other companies do it on occasion to counter bad publicity, as Union Carbide did in 1982 after critical media coverage of one of its pesticides, or to correct what they regard as inaccurate reporting, as Eastern Air Lines did after a front-page story in *The Wall Street Journal* suggested that the company had a fistful of serious problems. But the typical reaction—fairly or unfairly—is that such ads are self-serving and dyspeptic. Although the Chrysler ads were as self-serving as anything in the genre, what came through even more strongly was Iacocca's confidence that if Congress passed the loan guarantees, he could put Chrysler back on its feet. "The loans will be repaid," he promised. "With interest. The loan guarantee will cost the taxpayer nothing. You can count on it." We plan to be around for at least another fifty-four [years]. You can count on it."

By December 1979, Iacocca, the salesman's salesman, the man who had cooked up "$56 in '56" and the Mustang, had sold Washington on the wisdom of saving Chrysler. Like all good car salesmen, he was selling dreams, and like old men who buy sports cars, congressmen bought because they believed he would make them come true. They were counting on it.

How HE WOULD DO IT was another matter. Iacocca had made quite a splash in August 1979 when he announced he was cutting his salary from $360,000 to $1 a year. With that single stroke he convinced the country he was giving heart and soul to his rescue operation. But it was going to take millions to keep Chrysler afloat. In early 1980, a few weeks after Congress approved the loan guarantees, Chrysler reported its 1979 financial results. The bottom line: a $1 billion loss. Even the $1.5 billion tourniquet supplied by Washington couldn't stop that kind of bleeding.

Iacocca knew that.

So did the Treasury Department, which would oversee the implementation of the loan guarantees. Congress had bought the idea that Iacocca could save Chrysler, but before any money was handed out, Treasury wanted to make sure that the messiah had plenty of cooperative apostles. Sacrifices had to be made, and everybody had to kick in:

Chrysler employees, the company's banks, and its suppliers. United Auto Workers members who worked for Chrysler had to agree to a two-year wage freeze, bankers had to buy the forthcoming Chrysler notes, and suppliers were going to have to wait for their money.

It wasn't until the summer of 1980 that Chrysler got the first of the guaranteed loans—$800 million worth. That was enough to tide the company over for the rest of the year, but when the accountants closed their books on 1980, the company was even deeper in the hole. Damages for the year came to a staggering $1.7 billion. The critics were more convinced than ever that Iacocca had sold Congress a bill of goods.

A GRIM IACOCCA flew to Washington in January 1981 to convince the loan board to put up another $400 million, which would bring the company's federally guaranteed borrowings to $1.2 billion—within $300 million of the $1.5 billion agreed to by Congress. With his indefatigable optimism, Iacocca explained that 1980 had gone fine until November. The company had chopped $1 billion from its annual fixed costs, closed eight plants, and turned several others into the most modern front-wheel-drive manufacturing facilities in the world. In addition, independent surveys had ranked the quality of Chrysler's new cars ahead of Ford's and GM's. But between October and November, Iacocca reported, American car sales took a nose dive, and in December, when the prime rate hit 21.5 percent, sales dried up altogether.

Iacocca didn't like asking for the $400 million any more than the Loan Guarantee Board liked listening to him ask. The publicity brought the doomsayers out of the woodwork and drove customers away from Chrysler dealers. "People won't buy a car if they don't have faith that the company will be around to make good on its warranty and provide service," explained Maryann Keller, an auto industry securities analyst in New York. "It's not like buying a sweater or a pair of shoes, where the financial health of the company doesn't make any difference to the consumer." Iacocca himself estimated that the public jitters caused by Chrysler's loan requests probably cost the company fifty cents in sales for every dollar it secured in loans.

But time was running out. Without the $400 million, Iacocca told the loan board, Chrysler would be bankrupt by February. To convince the loan board it could operate on an even thinner shoestring, Chrysler had to exact another round of concessions from workers, bankers, and suppliers. So the United Auto Workers gave up $622 million in wage and cost-of-living increases in addition to the $462.5 million they had given up the previous summer. White-collar workers added wage and benefit concessions of $161 million to the $137.9 million they'd made earlier. Suppliers had to agree to price freezes and price cuts worth $72 million in 1981 on top of the $63 million they'd given up when the first guaranteed loans were made. Cities, states, and foreign countries where Chrysler had operations pitched in with $357 million in loans and grants. Chrysler's banks had to agree to the conversion of $568 million in loans and deferred interest to preferred stock, and they had to accept 30 cents on the dollar for another $500 million of Chrysler debt.

This was it. Chrysler had cashed in all its chips. Iacocca vowed he would sell his children before he went back to Washington to ask for the last $300 million. Months earlier, Douglas Fraser, the president of the United Auto Workers and a Chrysler director, had said he didn't see "any light at the end of the tunnel—unless it's an oncoming locomotive." The situation was even more desperate now.

*　*　*

DESPITE THE BLACK OUTLOOK, morale had never been higher at Chrysler than it was in the winter of 1981. One reason was that going to work was the only way Chrysler employees could get away from the vultures who circled the company waiting for their dire prophecies to be fulfilled. "You couldn't pick up a newspaper or turn on the television without hearing that the company was going under," says the manager of a Chrysler design and development unit. "Nobody in the media ever just said 'Chrysler Corporation' anymore. It was always 'Financially Troubled Chrysler Corporation.' You began thinking that's how you should answer the phone at work."

Working in this pressure cooker took its toll, but it was so much better than *not* working that Chrysler employees were disinclined to complain. Those who survived the massive layoffs, which saw the number of Chrysler employees drop from 131,700 in 1978 to 68,700 by the summer of 1982, seemed determined to do everything conceivable to keep Chrysler going. Some of the survivors were old-timers, hoping to ward off early retirement as long as possible. But many, only eight or ten years along in their careers, had turned down opportunities to go elsewhere. "I've had job offers," said a personnel director at one of the company's operating units. "A lot of managers and engineers here have. Aerospace manufacturers and electronics companies have come to town and run big newspaper ads to lure people away. Ford even held a dinner for Chrysler engineers at a hotel in Dearborn. But I'm staying where I am because I think Chrysler's going to make it."

Besides, moving away wasn't as simple as it sounded. By the winter of 1981, unemployment in Detroit had hit 20 percent, and mortgages costing 15 or 16 percent had turned the housing market to sludge. Selling a house took four months—if you were lucky. Backs to the wall,

Chrysler's surviving employees welcomed the chance to throw themselves into their work. "Going to the office didn't make the problems go away, but you could feel as though you were making progress," one computer analyst recalls.

The problems certainly weren't going away, despite the fact that the auto magazines were heaping praise upon Chrysler's new front-wheel-drive K-Cars and saying the company's products were the best they'd ever seen. Industry analysts contended that Chrysler's front-wheel-drive strategy was well conceived and well executed and that Chrysler offered more for the money than either Ford or GM. But the combined effects of high interest rates and consumer uncertainty caused by the spreading recession were keeping people from buying new cars. The low sales confounded auto executives who kept predicting that the "pent-up demand" for automobiles would break loose at any minute and that sales would take off. It didn't happen. Customers who were lured into the showrooms by promises of rebates took one look at the prices, developed the ailment known as sticker shock, and fled. With the average new car selling for $9,370 by the summer of 1982—twice what a new car cost in 1975—many people decided to spend a few hundred dollars patching up their old clunkers.

Potential customers were also puzzled by the unfriendliness of car dealers. Instead of bending over backward to make sales, they were surly and short-tempered. Why? Little by little, to save money, Detroit had narrowed the gap between the dealer's cost and the sticker price. The dealer who used to get a car for 25 percent less than the amount on the sticker now got a discount of only 9 or 10 percent on some models. Bowled over by the high prices, most prospective customers had a hard time believing that dealers had very little room to bargain.

In addition, the same high interest rates that made consumers reluctant to take on car loans were affecting dealers, who had to finance their inventories with borrowed money. Between 1980 and the summer of 1982, twenty-seven hundred car dealerships went out of business. Defying all theories of pent-up demand, car sales continued to fall. Between 1979 and mid-1982, Detroit watched 40 percent of its market dry up as sales of American-made cars dropped from 8.3 million to 5.2 million a year. Foreign carmakers were also hurt by the four-year slump, but as the pie got smaller, their piece got larger. By 1983 three of every ten new cars sold in the United States were built in Japan or Europe.

STILL, THE WORSE THINGS GOT, the more heroic Iacocca seemed to become. Surveys taken for Chrysler's ad agency, Kenyon & Eckhardt, revealed that by mid-1982, eight out of ten Americans knew who Lee Iacocca was. All those people who used to complain about crybaby Chrysler and deride Iacocca as an arrogant huckster either disappeared or changed their minds. Back in the fall of 1978, when John Riccardo announced that Iacocca was coming to Chrysler, the smart money said he was the wrong man for the job. Chrysler needed a turnaround artist, they said, someone who knew finance backward and forward. Iacocca was a marketing man, a tire kicker.

No one fully appreciated that properly handled, his marketing tinsel could be turned to pure gold. With the same prestidigitation that had transformed the dowdy Falcon into the racy Mustang, Iacocca would create a new Chrysler. And, in fact, one of his first acts on becoming chairman was to give the company a personality transplant. By dubbing it "The New Chrysler Corporation," a phrase that appeared in all the company's sales literature, Iacocca began the necessary process of separating the company from its past mistakes. In late 1979 he also began appearing in the company's television commercials, coming on for a few seconds at the end to challenge car buyers to test-drive his new products. When "The New Chrysler Corporation" was unveiled, he appeared again to deliver his personal pledge that the company would survive. In 1980, when the long-awaited K-cars were almost ready, Iacocca made another series of commercials to explain what the new front-wheel-drive cars were all about. By the time they came to market, two of every five Americans—an extraordinarily high proportion for a new product—were aware of them. When Iacocca talked, people listened.

Mystique, by definition, defies rational explanation, and even Chrysler's advertising executives can only dance around the edges when they talk about the Iacocca mystique they helped to create. "TV tends to diminish people," says Ron DeLuca, vice-chairman of Kenyon & Eckhardt. "Iacocca's personality is big enough so that it's not diminished. He's intense, he's intelligent, he has tremendous natural poise and bearing. When he walks, which is difficult to do well on film, he looks like General MacArthur—you can almost see the swagger stick. None of this is taught. The way Iacocca comes across on TV is pretty much the way he is. As for why all this works, what's star quality? Nobody really knows. But whatever it is, he's got it."

Building on this star quality (an off-balance-sheet asset that probably no other *Fortune* 500 company can claim), Kenyon & Eckhardt has carefully crafted the larger-than-life Iacocca who now appears on television. In the course of three years, he grew from a seller of cars to chief executive of The New Chrysler Corporation to industrial statesman, praising the high quality of American technology as emphatically as he praised the cars made by his own company. "The time has come," he said in one commercial as he strode purposefully through a futuristic-looking factory, "to restore the confidence of the American carbuyer in American technology, American workers, and American cars. It's time we in the auto industry convince you that you can make a long-term investment in the quality of a new car and not have to worry about it." After a brief pitch for Chrysler's five-year, fifty-thousand-mile warranty, he returned to statesmanship: "We in the car industry must make 'Made in America' mean something again. We owe it to you." From there he moved directly into one of Madison Avenue's best fillips: "So we invite GM and Ford to follow Chrysler." In that single sentence, Iacocca put Chrysler at the head of the Big Three and, by omitting foreign carmakers, implied that they aren't in the same league with the Americans. His parting shot was pure confidence: "If you find better protection, take it. If you can find a better car, buy it."

But star quality doesn't necessarily sell products, and it looks as if the commercials have sold Iacocca more successfully than they've sold automobiles. At the company's 1982 annual meeting, one person after another rose to compliment the chairman on the ads. With no trace of humor, he told those admirers what to do: "If you like them so much, go out and buy a car."

Iacocca isn't the only one concerned about the fact that his image overshadows the company's. In the summer of 1982, Marc Stepp, the UAW vice president who oversees the union's relations with Chrysler, was approached by a stranger who had just seen him on television discussing the union's upcoming contract negotiations with Chrysler. "You guys aren't going to hurt Iacocca and Chrysler, are you?" the stranger wanted to know. The stranger was more than a little out of order. To keep Chrysler going, UAW members gave up more than $1 billion of wages and benefits, and more than forty-thousand blue-collar jobs disappeared. Stepp's encounter shows the power of television, which has made millions of people think that Iacocca saved Chrysler all by himself.

Wrongheaded as that is, the myth probably will persist. As business after business came unglued in the long recession, Iacocca symbolized the possibility of a comeback. Alone among public figures, he offered the confidence and the hope that a disillusioned country genuinely needed. "He's the classic underdog," says Ron DeLuca of Kenyon & Eckhardt. "Like Rocky, he picked himself up off the canvas and kept on fighting. People love that."

A December 1982 poll by the Gallup Organization for *The Wall Street Journal* bears out DeLuca's observation. Asked which business leaders they admired most, a majority of executives in small businesses said "Nobody." But more than a quarter chose Iacocca. Theorizing about the results of the poll, Iacocca said, "Misery loves company." If the poll had been taken while he was making $1.5 billion a year for Ford, he added, he wouldn't have fared nearly as well. "Admiration goes up directly proportional to the adversity and the ability to deal with it."

In keeping with Hegel's observation that no man is a hero to his valet, it might be expected that the Iacocca mystique would wear thin among the people who see him every day. Although Chrysler employees do not attribute to him the superhuman powers his television fans do, they are extravagant in their praise. "He's the greatest single corporate treasure we have," says one design manager. Variations of that remark emanate from every quarter of Chrysler. Iacocca even has legions of admirers among the sixty-three thousand Chrysler employees who have lost their jobs since 1978, says Arvid Jouppi, a Detroit securities analyst who specializes in the auto industry. "Chrysler's greatest strengths aren't on the balance sheet," Jouppi says. "Lee Iacocca has generated tremendous loyalty." Although Iacocca hasn't worked the miracle by himself, Jouppi adds, "he has been the catalyst for it."

BUT THE ISSUE of who saved Chrysler deflects attention from an even more basic question about the company: Has it in fact been saved? On the spring day in 1982 when Iacocca went to Washington to tell Congress what Chrysler had achieved since the black days of 1979, it was clear that something close to a miracle had taken place. The fact that it had happened in the middle of the country's most acute economic distress in fifty years added to the impressiveness. Iacocca—with a tremendous assist from employees, dealers, banks, and suppliers—had done everything he said he would. And he'd done it against odds that lengthened considerably after he'd made his audacious promises.

In July 1981, Chrysler announced its first profitable quarter in more than two years: only $12 million, but it was black ink. For the year Chrysler still would register a loss ($475 million), but in 1982 the company turned a profit despite the fact that sales continued to slide.

There were many secrets to this success. One was the sale of a subsidiary (Chrysler Defense, the tank manufacturer the company had earlier told Congress was a critical reason for endorsing the loan guarantees). Without the $348.5 million gain from that sale, the company would have had a first-quarter loss of $200 million. In the second quarter, however, the profit—all $106.9 million of it—was almost entirely from operations. The New Chrysler Corporation was no longer just a Madison Avenue slogan, it was a reality.

But the Chrysler of 1982 bore almost no resemblance to the Chrysler of 1978. More than sixty thousand workers were gone, the vast majority for good. Twenty factories had closed their doors. Robots that didn't demand cost-of-living raises had come to build cars, and computers allowed engineers to design parts in hours instead of weeks. Most important, these changes meant that by 1983 The New Chrysler Corporation needed to sell only 1.1 million cars to break even. The old Chrysler had had a break-even point more than twice that size.

And the old tire kicker wasn't through yet. In the dreary spring of 1982, with more than ten million Americans out of work and the recession's end nowhere in sight, Iacocca unveiled a Dodge and a Chrysler that made people feel good all over: the first convertibles built in this country since 1976. The cars were important not only because they would bring the company an extra $100 million profit in 1982, but also because of what they revealed about The New Chrysler Corporation. With every ounce of flab gone, the company now had enough flexibility to respond quickly when it spotted an opportunity. Bob Marx, the product planning project manager who mid-wifed the convertibles, says the company will introduce minivans and front-wheel-drive limousines in other efforts to fill empty niches in the car market. Like the Mustang, all of these products are spin-offs of cars already in production.

The convertibles also show manufacturing changes that foreshadow other changes in the company's structure. The 1982 Dodge 400s and Chrysler LeBarons earmarked for convertible use came off the assembly lines as hardtops, then were taken to a small specialty-car firm, Cars and Concepts of Brighton, Michigan, for transformation into convertibles. "In the old days, before robots, assembly-line workers could do the special fitting and hand-finishing needed to build a convertible," Marx explains. "The robots don't have that capability." In addition, safety modifications have led to changes in the way cars are engineered, making the roof into a more important part of the frame than it used to be. So when the top is sawed off to make a convertible, the car has to be reinforced with a beam running from one end to the other.

Although the new assembly lines cannot perform these out-of-the-ordinary tasks, the fact that Chrysler can subcontract such chores gives the company a financial flexibility that far outweighs the robots' rigidity. In the future, says auto analyst Arvid Jouppi, "Chrysler will probably build less and buy more" of the special services and supplies it needs. It can save enormous amounts of overhead, especially when hard times leave a plant with inventories for which there is no market and workers for whom there is no work. The old Chrysler, Jouppi says, "had been moving toward the 44 percent level of manufacturing integration that GM has. Now Chrysler is making only 25 percent of the parts it puts in its automobiles. They might be able to reduce this even further. As long as they hold onto design, engineering, and marketing, they'll have an automobile company. Who makes all the parts isn't important."

The problem of high parts inventories is also being tackled at American car companies with a "just-in-time" system known in Japan as *kanban*. Instead of keeping factories humming at peak efficiency, cranking out parts whether they are needed or not, the *kanban* system orders up only those parts actually needed for current production levels. But even with *kanban* and the other improvements Chrysler has made in every aspect of its operations, it is unlikely that the company will regain the robust health it once enjoyed. Probably no U.S. auto manufacturer will. In the best years, Jouppi says, "Chrysler enjoyed a net profit of 5 percent, Ford 7 percent, and GM 9 percent. Now we're looking at a world in which GM will probably average 5 percent, Ford 3 percent, and Chrysler 1 percent."

One percent is thin ice. Jouppi praises Chrysler's ability "to get well in a recession," but, he adds, "even though the company is out of intensive care, it is still in the hospital." So far, the born-again Chrysler is holding its own among American car manufacturers, but neither it nor the other U.S. carmakers have managed to stop the Japanese. The 9.3 million vehicles built by U.S. automakers in 1981 amounted to only four-fifths the number of cars and trucks built by the Japanese that year. Only a few years earlier, American auto companies turned out 10 million vehicles a year—half again as many as the Japanese. Although U.S. auto executives expect their production to improve, not even the most optimistic see a day when they will again lead the Japanese by such a wide margin. And despite all Detroit has done to trim manufacturing costs, it is losing $1,000 or more on every subcompact it sells. Unable to beat the Japanese at the small-car game, U.S. automakers are swallowing their pride and hiring the Japanese to build subcompacts for them. Chrysler has done it in partnership with Mitsubishi, and General Motors hopes to join Toyota in manufacturing a Toyota-designed car in California. Ford has considered similar possibilities.

To hear the American consumer tell it, the appeal of Japanese cars is simply that they offer more for the money. But Lee Iacocca's version is that the Japanese are being allowed to steal America blind. When he made his spring 1982 report to Congress, he argued that "the Japanese automakers have an unfair tax and trade advantage which is denying hundreds of thousands of Americans a fair shot at the job. The United States of America loses $1,750 of taxes on every Japanese car sold in this country, a portion of it the result of a Japanese tax policy which allows a Toyota to be sold for less in Washington, D.C., than it sells for in Tokyo."

Orthodox capitalists argue that if Americans want Japanese cars, they should be allowed to have them, with as little government interference as possible. But Iacocca and other American auto executives are quick to point out that the Japanese aren't willing to play by these same free-trade rules. Foreign cars coming into this country are subject to charges of about 25 percent, while fees on American cars entering Japan run 100 percent or more.

Whatever happens between the United States and Japan, the American auto industry barely resembles what it was in 1979, when Chrysler sent its distress signal to Washington. With half as many workers, it still can produce the same number of cars. And now that a new car costs more than $9,000—52 percent of what the average U.S. worker earns in a year—few people will be able to indulge in the old all-American pleasure of trading in their cars for new models every two or three years. Car sales in this country are expected to grow by only 1.5 percent a year for the rest of the decade. In 1980, car sales hit a sixteen-year low, 1981 was even worse, and 1982 ended with another drop. To exacerbate matters, the average cost of driving rose by a third between 1979 and 1982. Thanks to higher fuel prices, rising car prices, and high interest rates on auto loans, it now costs $2,790 a year to drive a car. Faced with that expense, many families have decided to make do with one car instead of two, further reducing the demand for automobiles. A further complication: Americans are driving less. Since 1978, the average number of miles driven each year has been falling. The combination of higher driving costs, a willingness to keep cars longer, and less driving could permanently shrink the new-car market by more than 20 percent.

No one has a greater stake in this new scaled-down game than Chrysler. In a world of narrowed profits, Chrysler's are the narrowest. With no fat left to trim, it cannot afford a major blunder. Iacocca, true to form, insists that big mistakes are a thing of the past. His optimism is no longer the simple faith of the salesman who has no choice but to believe in tomorrow; it is grounded in dollars and cents; Chrysler managed to hang on through the auto industry's worst slump in decades, the company has tucked away more than $1 billion in cash, and the tax credits it gets as a result of its losses will sweeten the bottom line for the rest of the decade. In 1983's first quarter, for example, Chrysler's net income came to $172 million, almost half of that courtesy of tax-loss carry-forwards. The good news sent Chrysler's stock soaring in the bull market that began in the summer of 1982, enabling Iacocca to exercise options that added $1.2 million to his salary and bonus of $366,000. In December 1983, Chrysler promised Iacocca 150,000 shares of stock plus options on 300,000 more—a package worth $12 million at the time it was offered. To collect, Iaccoa has to stay on as chairman for three years. If he stays for four, he'll get 50,000 extra shares and options to buy another 100,000.

By the spring of 1983, Chrysler was feeling confident enough about the future to make two sizable financial moves. It offered to make an early repayment of its federally guaranteed loans. And it announced plans to buy a factory from Volkswagen of America, which had made the mistake of expanding its manufacturing capacity in 1980, just as the recession was taking hold. Chrysler needed the extra space to alleviate the crowding that resulted from closing so many plants.

But to focus on financial transactions is to miss the point about Chrysler and about Iacocca. The numbers are the effect, not the cause of the company's spectacular recovery. Iacocca's success is not so much a lesson in leadership as a case study in the totally neglected subject of followership. His leadership is so interwoven with his individuality and his personal style that it would be pointless for budding executives or business school students to try to copy it. There is only one Iacocca, as there was only one F.D.R.

Beyond his marketing genius, his thirty-five years of auto industry experience, and the first-rate financial expertise he has acquired in rebuilding Chrysler, Iacocca has, in superabundance, a quality that cannot be taught: confidence. More important, he possesses the ability to communicate his confidence, to make people believe he can lead them to the Promised Land—if they will just follow him.

They not only have followed, they look upon the company's hard times as the greatest adventure of their lives. Marc Stepp, the United Auto Workers vice-president in charge of relations with Chrysler, describes himself "as the most fortunate man in all of the UAW for having the opportunity to mobilize the union for saving Chrysler. I feel as good about being a union leader in this situation as I'm sure Iacocca feels about leading Chrysler." Considering the long-standing animosity between unions and auto companies, Stepp's words are nothing short of amazing.

In the fall of 1982, however, the UAW's enthusiasm for Iacocca dimmed a little. After months of hearing the Chrysler chairman crow about the company's new financial strength, the union decided it was time for Chrysler to start returning part of the $1 billion UAW members had given up to help Chrysler through its darkest hours. Chrysler's labor negotiators were left in the uncomfortable position of explaining that although the company's finances had improved, they were not all that robust. The UAW thought Chrysler was bluffing. When UAW president Douglas Fraser, a Chrysler director, ventured his opinion that a big wage increase would do serious damage to the company, the rank and file accused him of selling out. UAW members at Chrysler's Canadian plants decided to strike, and after a five-week walkout, they won a 10 percent raise in wages and benefits. If Iacocca had exercised more restraint in proclaiming Chrysler's triumphs, the strike—which cost the company $100 million in lost sales—might never have happened, and Chrysler might have convinced the union to settle for a smaller raise.

Despite that setback with blue-collar workers, Iacocca still enjoys immense popularity among Chrysler's white-collar work force. One after another claims to be exhilarated by the company's struggles to survive. "The challenge is irresistible," says the manager of a design unit. "In the old days we might have come up with three or four design possibilities for some minor components. Now we can afford only one. You have to get it right the first time. Naturally, there are frustrations, but when you do pull something off, everyone feels elated." Adds another manager: "At Chrysler, where there is so little staff and so little money, you're not just a cog in the wheel. You're the whole wheel."

Eugene E. Jennings, a professor of management at Michigan State University, says that the esprit de corps at Chrysler is "a combat mentality." "Morale is highest when an organization has to fight for its existence," he explains. "That's as true of families as it is of corporations. The Chrysler experience brings out an important managerial principle we often lose sight of: People work hardest when they understand a goal and believe in it."

The achievement of Lee Iacocca is not that he saved Chrysler, for it is still too early to tell whether survival is a certainty. For the short term, the company looks secure, but it still has unfunded pension liabilities of $1.5 billion, and $125 million more a year in labor costs because of its 1982 agreement with the UAW. Iacocca's biggest achievement may be that he convinced more people to follow him than any business leader has ever done before. Like Moses, he understood that he had to hold out the hope of a Promised Land before he could get dozens of competing factions to put aside their differences and unite. The importance of hope in such a situation cannot be overestimated. As Eric Hoffer noted in *The True Believer,* those "without hope are divided and driven to desperate self-seeking." Hoffer cited the experience of the Donner party, trapped in a mountain snowstorm. Members of the party cooperated as long as they believed they would be rescued but turned against each other when they lost hope.

Iacocca was also able to capitalize on what Hoffer calls "the will to follow." Churchill, Hoffer points out, was a well-known but largely unheeded figure in Britain during the 1930s "until disaster shook the country to its foundation and made autonomous individual lives untenable." Churchill the great leader could not exist until the British developed the will to follow him. Iacocca arrived at a similar point in Chrysler's history. The threat of extinction not only created the need for a strong leader, it created the will to follow. By offering hope and a way out of the wilderness, Iacocca convinced Chrysler's employees, lenders, and suppliers to make the sacrifices necessary for Chrysler's survival. But unlike Moses, Churchill, or any other leader of the mass movements analyzed in *The True Believer*, Iacocca did not ask for selfless sacrifice. He told his constituencies that the sacrifices were worth making because they would ultimately benefit their own interests. Workers would keep their jobs, suppliers would not go out of business, bankers would see their loans repaid. If the psychological and sociological literature on leadership is any guide, this was not just brilliant strategy, it was probably the only strategy that could have worked. Academic studies of the leadership succession lay out countless theories to explain what works and what doesn't, but there is one point on which all the theorists agree: A leader will not be followed unless the followers believe he will produce results that benefit the group. Iacocca made his followers believe, and he has sustained their belief by delivering on his promises.

Chapter 11

Unholy Grails

Number Worship, the
Japanese Shrine, and
Technorapture

THE COMING OF the corporate messiah during the troubled years of the late 1970s and early 1980s was just one of several signs that business was ready to place new faith in the power of individual leaders. Writing in the *Harvard Business Review* in 1977, social psychologist Abraham Zaleznik spelled out the differences between managers (a pragmatic breed) and leaders (visionaries who can inspire others to join them in realizing the vision). Business needed both, Zaleznik said, but he wondered whether business schools were turning out too many managers and too few leaders.

In a 1981 book called *The Leader,* another social psychologist, Michael Maccoby, listed the traits he thought contemporary leaders should have: They should be willing to share power, should stress cooperation over competition, and should show more flexibility and tolerance. More intriguing than Maccoby's ideas was the fact that only five years before he had posited quite a different ideal leader. In a book on management styles, Maccoby delineated four types of executives and argued that one of them, the gamesman, was best suited to the corporate world as it was. The gamesman (after whom the book was named) viewed his career as a game—to be won, of course. The gamesman loves taking calculated risks "and is fascinated by techniques and new methods. He thrives on competition . . . he communicates his enthusiasm, energizing his peers and subordinates. . . . [He] competes not to build an empire or pile up riches, but to gain fame, glory, the exhilaration of victory." In the 1980s, however, the gamesman's strengths have become weaknesses, Maccoby has concluded. Because the material resources at the gamesman's disposal are limited and competition is fierce, the gamesman can't spur on subordinates with promises of ever-larger rewards. And the competition he inspires can be at loggerheads with the cooperation needed for survival in hard times.

Implicit in the new meditations on leadership, as well as in the search for corporate messiahs, was the idea that there were flocks waiting to be led. Despite the restraint and seriousness of the new scholarly studies of leadership, it was irresistibly tempting to leap to the conclusion that problems would disappear if only the leader could galvanize his followers, as Lee Iacocca had done. Search firms began hearing from clients that they were looking for managers with "charisma" and "vision." It was the desire for the quick fix all over again.

Oversimplified versions of other ideas also became holy writ with amazing speed as businesses searched for a way out of the deepening abyss of the recession. Quantitative analysis, long considered a useful tool, assumed all the trappings of a religion: Thick computer printouts became as revered as Bibles, the anointed spoke in a language only they could understand, priests were summoned to interpret the signs, and there was little or no tolerance for information at variance with the creed. Thousands also came to worship at the shrine of Japanese management in the hope that their willingness to practice the faith would lead them to the light. And the pews were packed at the church of high technology, where the believers waited for microchips and robots to deliver them to the Promised Land. As with individual leadership, the dangers in these new religions lay not in the creeds themselves but in the fervor of the faithful.

NUMBER WORSHIP

Sifting through the economic wreckage of the long recession of the early eighties, trying to figure out what went wrong, many critics fastened a large share of the blame on American business schools. A business professor at the University of California at Berkeley asked why the United States and Great Britain, "the nations with the most developed systems of professional management education," were doing so poorly when Germany and Japan, which "provide almost no professional management training . . . have been the outstanding successes" in the years since World War II.

Because the B-schools emphasize quantitative analysis, they are accused of turning out human calculators who function superbly in the tidy world of numbers but can't manage anything as messy as the average human being, much less a full-blown crisis calling for highly subjective judgments. In 1982, a midwestern business professor unhappy with the standard M.B.A. curriculum stepped behind a pseudonym and spoke his mind in *The New York Times:* "In the last 10 years, the annual output of master's degrees in business administration has doubled. During that decade, America has tumbled into the worst recession in 40 years. Is there a cause-and-effect relationship between M.B.A. inflation and economic recession?" The main problem, he said, was that business students spend their time "in concentrated study of subjects such as management information systems, operations research, forecasting and quantitative management. All these are actually forms of accounting and math." Although he acknowledged that managers "need to know accounting" and "should understand the mathematics of finance and business forecasting," he concluded that the focus on numbers has led to an obsession with good-looking bottom lines, which "often are illusions based on short-term manipulations and temporary tax advantages."

The early eighties were vintage years for lambasting M.B.A.s, but the critics almost always failed to mention a key point: The quantitative analysis taught in B-schools is taught largely because that is what corporations say they want M.B.A.s to know. M.B.A.s are the victims, not the cause, of the business world's fatal fascination with numbers.

The thought of running even a small business without numbers is patently absurd, and in large organizations, much of what goes on can be measured, expressed, and understood only in numerical terms: Sales were down compared to last year, inventories were up, average salaries rose, the cost of borrowing fell. All too often, however, the focus is placed on the numbers themselves instead of the issues they represent. As Archie McCardell discovered in his first weeks at International Harvester, once the company's group presidents calculated that the upcoming year would not be as profitable as the current one, they were content to sit back and let it happen. And one of Lee Iacocca's lieutenants at Chrysler complained about being presented with an accountant's report that told him the company had lost $1 billion but didn't say a word about why.

Another problem with numbers is the ease with which they can be massaged—especially by someone who has mastered the fine points of quantitative analysis. "Send a financial man out to manage a division," says a veteran management consultant, "and in two years he can really milk it. He can cut costs by lowering quality and letting a plant go to hell. His bottom line looks spectacular on paper, which helps him land a great job for more money somewhere else. By the time the damage starts to show, he's long gone."

In *The Next American Frontier*, Robert Reich criticized this "paper entrepreneurialism" because it gives the impression that a corporation has increased its wealth when in fact it has not. But sometimes the results are even more serious than that. The most pernicious of these entrepreneurs resort to accounting fictions, making their profits out of whole cloth instead of paper. That appears to be what happened at AM International, where sales were overstated and inventories were said to be worth more than they actually were. Although cooking the books is emphatically not business as usual, the Securities and Exchange Commission decided in 1983 that the practice was sufficiently widespread to merit special investigative attention. Ironically, it is the numbers themselves—particularly the pressure they exert—that drive executives to commit the frauds that concern the SEC. In addition to the intense focus on each quarter's bottom line, managers face a proliferation of highly specific sales and production goals now that computers are so widely used in corporate planning. And executive compensation plays a pivotal role, since more and more managers find their pay tied to delivery of the right numbers. When auditors confront a manager with evidence of financial wrongdoing, the tale they hear is almost always the same: He (or she) didn't mean to commit a crime. The phony numbers were a desperation move to get through lean times, and the intent was to set things right as soon as business picked up again. The ultimate victims of these accounting misrepresentations are not the corporations involved but unwitting investors, which is why the SEC has given the matter a high priority.

Thomas J. Peters and Robert H. Waterman, Jr., in the book *In Search of Excellence,* raised further objections to the preoccupation with numbers. As they saw it, "the numerative analytical component has an in-built conservative bias. Cost reduction becomes priority number one," and not enough attention is paid to quality, value, or new product development. "A buried weakness in the analytic approach ... is that people analyze what can be most readily analyzed, spend more time on it, and more or less ignore the rest." Too often, Peters and Waterman said, "the rest" includes the most crucial aspects of a situation. The conservatism that comes from leaning too heavily on numbers also sets off a destructive chain reaction: an overeagerness to veto new ideas simply because the uncertainties involved cannot be quantified, which causes a reluctance to experiment, which in turn leads "inevitably to overcomplexity and inflexibility." In the end, the highly analytical organization becomes so rigid it cannot respond quickly enough when change is called for.

Robert Reich looked at number worship from a different perspective but reached a similar conclusion:

As the bureaucratic gap between executives and production workers continues to widen, the enterprise becomes more dependent on "hard," quantifiable data. . . . "Softer," less quantifiable information—about product quality, worker morale, and customer satisfaction—may be at least as important to the firm's long-term success. But such information cannot be conveyed efficiently upward through layers of staff.

Even if soft information occasionally does find its way to the top, Reich said, it is often ignored because it does not lend itself to "quick decisions and crisp directives."

Although the perils of number worship are clearer now than they have ever been, little has happened to reduce the primacy of quantitative analysis. If anything, numbers are assuming even more importance, largely because computers do such a dazzling job of generating them. (As psychologist Abraham Maslow has said of this trend, "When the only tool you have is a hammer, everything begins to look like a nail.") Decision-making, an arena where intuition and experience should play leading roles, has become a highly mathematical affair complete with computer models designed to reduce subjectivity and translate the qualitative into the quantitative. Although such models may be useful in forcing executives to clarify the issues they are trying to resolve, the real appeal of mathematical decision-making may lie in the fact that it shifts responsibilities for decisions away from managers. By basing their decisions on numbers, corporate managements can absolve themselves of much of the blame for plant closings, layoffs, and other unpalatable moves. And if a decision leads to disaster, managers can defend themselves by saying the decision was made with the best numbers (that is, the most "rational" information) available.

There is no question that qualitative information—anecdotes, feelings, values, hunches, opinions, and the like—complicates decision-making. It does not yield easily to rational analysis, and its usefulness is not always immediately apparent. But even when this kind of information cannot be precisely understood, it can be absorbed. It can be especially valuable in spotting problems before they get bad enough to show up in the numbers (in coping with workers' discontent before it escalates into a costly strike, for example). Qualitative information is equally critical to innovation, since the dearth of numbers on any radically new development tends to "prove" that it will not work. The point is not that business would be better off without so many numbers but that in devoutly practicing the religion of quantitative analysis, the number worshipers are gathering only half the intelligence they need.

THE JAPANESE SHRINE

American business can learn much from Japan's astonishing successes of the past twenty-five years, but the bloom of economic good health will not be restored by following the Japanese prescription. In their eagerness to copy the Japanese, Westerners seem to have paid attention to the wrong things—and even these have been grossly misunderstood.

As the story is usually told in the United States, one of the main reasons Japanese laborers are loyal and hardworking is that their companies offer them lifetime employment. Some companies even have their own cemeteries, providing what is known as "eternal employment." Those who want to transplant lifetime employment to American soil argue that it would boost productivity, enhance job satisfaction, and reduce friction between unions and management.

But the issue is considerably more complicated than that. For one thing, lifetime employment in Japan is not nearly as widespread as most Americans believe. At most, only a third of Japan's workers fall into the category of permanent employee. And what lifetime employment does exist may spring as much from the traditional Japanese system of corporate finance as from idealistic notions of how employers should treat employees. With most financing needs handled through bank loans rather than the sale of stocks and bonds, the big businesses of Japan have escaped the investor pressures that lead American corporations to push for quarter after quarter of increased earnings. Without this pressure, the Japanese have been free in hard times to cut stockholder dividends instead of employee payrolls. But now that they have begun selling more securities abroad (to beat high interest rates at home), they will find themselves facing investors who demand short-term performance rather than long-term promises.

Fully two-thirds of Japan's labor force is considered temporary. It is not unheard of for workers to stay at "temporary" jobs for ten years without getting the fringe benefits and higher pay that go to permanent employees. Layoffs are not an everyday occurrence among temporary workers, but if production slows enough, these workers are considered expendable. Women are the most expendable of all. When business slacks off, they are often urged to take "voluntary" leaves, and even though they make up half the labor force, they rarely gain permanent status.

The split between permanent and temporary workers also dictates the work each class does. At one steel mill, temporary workers not only work longer hours for less pay, they are also expected to do the worst jobs: "climb under hot oxygen furnaces to clean them, bend over short shovels to recondition the tracks where hot metal will flow and work close to earsplitting noise."

In most companies, "lifetime" employment ends at age fifty-five (although this is slowly changing). This retirement age was set after World War II, when life expectancy in Japan was fifty, but by the 1980s, life expectancy had risen to seventy-four. Since the Japanese government provides little in retirement benefits and since company pensions rarely cover the cost of living, many Japanese need to work long after the official retirement age. Often they stay on with the same company—at lower pay. (Americans, who save only 4 percent of what they earn, frequently are urged to follow the example of the Japanese, who save 20 percent. Although the U.S. personal savings rate is deplorable, the model behavior of the Japanese may owe more to the stark realities of old age in Japan than to abstract ideals of discipline and thrift.)

American blue-collar workers who saw their jobs disappear forever in the long recession of the early eighties must look with envy upon the promise of lifetime employment. But even the minority of Japanese workers lucky enough to land these permanent jobs forfeit something most Americans would find hard to give up: the opportunity to change employers. It is not illegal to move from one company to another in Japan, but it is seldom done. Not only does leaving run counter to the Japanese ideal of group loyalty, but the job training received at one company is so specific it would be difficult to use in another organization. As Japan expert B. Bruce-Briggs has noted, "Japanese corporations . . . are rather like Fraternity Row on an American campus—once pledging the Betas, you cannot switch to the Deltas. . . . As in a small American town, where you work in the mill or not at all, lifetime employment reflects a lack of choice." That is no minor consideration, he points out, since most Americans do not leave their companies because of layoffs or firings but because they have found better jobs elsewhere.

If there is any lesson to be learned from Japan's lifetime employment, it concerns the commitment that management makes to permanent employees. As manufacturing authority Robert Hayes of Harvard has pointed out, by constantly upgrading the skills of these workers through training programs and changing work assignments, management turns workers into experts who can keep factories running smoothly.

The nature of Japan's famous Ministry of International Trade and Industry (MITI) has also been lost in translation. In the fifties and sixties, MITI had the power to grant (or not to grant) foreign-trade licenses. A company without a MITI license could not import natural resources or export its products, and in a country with as few natural resources as Japan, a MITI refusal amounted to a death warrant. The cumulative effect of MITI's decisions was to give Japan a cohesive national industrial policy, with banks, businesses, and government all rowing in the same direction.

MITI's decisions are no longer legally binding, but even when its word *was* law, it was not the flawless planning machine so lovingly described by many of those who think the United States needs a strong industrial policy. Despite frequent American claims to the contrary, the industries MITI chose to support were not always the ones with the brightest futures. Agriculture and shipbuilding have been heavily subsidized because of political pressures, and billions have been poured into the inefficient government-owned Japanese National Railroad. Even Japan's most spectacularly successful business, the auto industry, prospered in spite of MITI rather than because of it. As Peter Drucker explains, MITI "views the private automobile as a self-indulgence and as the opening wedge of a consumer society, which it finds abhorrent. . . . It has also been quite fearful that a large automobile market would provoke irresistible demands to open Japan to foreign imports, the one thing it has been determined to prevent." Furthermore, Drucker says, MITI has argued that the greater the success of the auto industry, the worse for Japan's balance of trade because car manufacturing "requires the two raw materials that are in shortest supply in Japan: petroleum and iron ore. It also requires the diversion of scarce resources—both food-growing land and capital—to highways and highway construction."

Given the magnificence of Japan's achievements, it would be petulant to dwell on MITI's shortcomings just to point out that the Japanese aren't perfect. But with a "Should we or shouldn't we?" industrial policy debate taking shape in the United States, it is vital to understand what MITI has—and has not—accomplished.

The legendary productivity of Japanese workers is as misunderstood as MITI and the concept of lifetime employment. True, the Japanese can make in thirteen man-hours the same car it takes General Motors more than twice as long to build. And there is no dismissing the fact that postwar Japan's improvements in productivity have been four times greater than American gains. But increases in Japanese productivity have slowed dramatically in the past few years, and per capita output of U.S. workers still outstrips that of their Japanese counterparts.

Even the Japanese willingness to work long hours is not quite what it seems. To demonstrate their loyalty, workers in many offices must stay until their bosses leave. "Their superiors stay late for the same reason," writes an American editor who worked in Japan for several years, "so by about 7:30 P.M. most of the people still in the offices are sitting at their desks for appearance's sake, more likely to be writing letters or reading novels than working." Other visitors to Japan have remarked on the same phenomenon.

Not that the Japanese don't work hard. Workaholism is chic, especially among executives, and the standard workweek runs five and a half days in some companies, six in others. But this too is changing. Workers no longer pass up vacation time, as they once did, and the average workweek is getting shorter.

And however productive Japanese workers are, more companies are finding they are no match for robots. So far, the world's appetite for Japanese goods has enabled the economy to grow fast enough to keep the unemployment rate well below 3 percent, but the spread of robots is causing Japanese labor officials to express some of the same concerns felt by their American counterparts. Unions are to be consulted before robots are installed, and at least one big manufacturer, Toyo Kogyo, maker of the Mazda, has promised that robots will not lead to layoffs. At Fanuc, which manufactures robots, the issue was not layoffs but shrinking union dues as a result of making robots by robots instead of by humans. Management sympathetically responded to the problems by offering to pay union dues for the robots, but the Labor Ministry vetoed the idea. In Japan as in the United States, it seems, no one has yet come to terms with the brave new world that has such creatures in it.

As for the quality circles often said to be the secret of Japan's manufacturing excellence, Robert Hayes of Harvard discovered in his tour of Japanese businesses that they played a smaller role than he had expected. The purpose of quality circles, which provide a formal means for workers to discuss production problems and product defects, is to improve the quality of manufacturing. But at most of the plants Hayes visited, he found that companies had had problems with quality circles for several years after they were introduced. "Moreover," he writes, "most of the companies I talked to already had enviable reputations for high-quality products by the time they adopted QCs." At one company on his itinerary, quality circles were "secondary, peripheral activities," and another said it had discontinued them—"temporarily." Hayes also found that the absence of quality circles did not reduce quality. One more sign of the minor importance the Japanese attach to quality circles: Few of the Japanese companies that have built plants in the United States have bothered with them.

When the Japanese management fad first hit American business, quality circles were seized upon as the quickest way to involve workers in raising the quality of the goods produced. But American workers did not exactly leap at this new opportunity. Since many of the first U.S. quality circles were imposed by management fiat rather than started as joint ventures with unions, workers viewed them as yet another management attempt to get something for nothing. After a while, even management turned against quality circles. As Japan expert Robert E. Cole of the University of Michigan put it, managers and workers grew tired "of being told how the Japanese do everything better." The Japanese mystique had become so powerful that when research psychologist Srully Blotnick put a Sanyo label on an RCA electronic device and asked nine hundred people to compare it to an identical device with the RCA label, 76 percent said the Sanyo was better.

Almost every American executive who visits Japan comes home filled with admiration for the harmony between management and labor in Japanese factories. Cooperation, not confrontation, is the order of the day, workers take pride in keeping their work stations clean, and when union members have demands, they paint them on posters or wear them on armbands instead of going on strike. But U.S. managers who think they will make their workers happy by bringing Japanese-style human relations to American factories would do well to ask workers whether they want that. One of the most unflattering appraisals of the Japanese way appeared not in a staid American business journal with an interest in defending the status quo but in a labor union magazine, the AFL-CIO *American Federationist,* which criticized everything from Japan's employment practices to the difficulties of individual expression in a society where hierarchy and harmony are so highly valued.

Even more surprising was a major Indiana University study that concluded that U.S. workers are more satisfied with their jobs than their Japanese colleagues are. The study paired more than thirty-five hundred Americans with Japanese workers in similar jobs and similar industries. Nearly 90 percent of the Americans claimed to have a family feeling about their employers compared to only a third of the Japanese. Although 68 percent of the Americans said they would be willing to work harder, only 44 percent of the Japanese would. The Japanese also were less satisfied with the tasks performed in their jobs, their supervisors, and how they spent their lives. The Japanese did prove more loyal to their companies, however, with 43 percent saying they would turn down better-paying jobs elsewhere; only 24 percent of the Americans were willing to go that far. But since the idea of changing employers is much less acceptable in Japan than in the United States, this finding may reveal less than it seems to.

The most valuable lessons to be learned from the Japanese are not about management but about manufacturing. Building on the ideas of W. Edwards Deming, an American statistician who was an adviser to Japan's postwar occupation government, the Japanese have applied statistical quality control to every step of manufacturing—from participating in the design of their factory equipment to continuous polling of customers to make sure that products measure up. In an eternal quest for "zero defect" production, the Japanese collect data on each manufacturing stage—charting, analyzing, and correcting all deviations from desired patterns. As the Japanese wave crested in the United States, it was fashionable to point out that much of the marvel could be traced to an American, but to put the focus on Deming's techniques is to miss the most important part of the story. The Japanese started with Deming, but they succeeded because of their own extraordinary diligence in applying his ideas.

To the surprise of many Americans, Hayes found that Japanese manufacturing facilities are neither more technologically sophisticated than American ones, nor are they the factories of the future. What they are, in the words of the *Harvard Business Review*, "is the factory of the present, operating as it should." Assembly lines run more slowly, which prevents breakdowns and lengthens the life of factory equipment. Workers are taught how to do routine maintenance of their equipment, and unlike their American counterparts, they have the right to stop the line when they spot a problem. The slower pace of the line and the freedom to shut it down give the Japanese an opportunity for quality-consciousness that is denied the typical American factory worker. And rather than settling for off-the-shelf machinery, Japanese manufacturers actively participate in the design and construction of their factory equipment. That way they get equipment tailored precisely to their needs, which means they don't have to adapt their manufacturing processes to fit standard machines.

In addition, Japanese manufacturers work closely with suppliers to eliminate defects in the parts that will be used on assembly lines. In an interview with *The Wall Street Journal,* an American supplier of plastic parts to a Japanese plant in Tennessee compares his experience with American and Japanese manufacturers:

There is not any comparison between the quality [Japan's Sharp Corporation] demands and that demanded by RCA and Zenith. . . . [Sharp] helped us with our quality-control layout and training. They developed hourly audits of our assembly line to isolate problems sooner. . . . They are providing us with the expertise of their top management. At American companies, if they find a problem in your product, it's your problem. At Sharp, we work it out together.

Equally important, the Japanese accord manufacturing a place of honor in their organizational hierarchies. In the

United States, fast-track young managers typically are steered away from manufacturing, and the top ranks of the biggest industrial corporations are much more likely to be filled with accountants and lawyers than with former plant managers. Operations management is one of the least popular areas of study in M.B.A. programs, partly because it does not pay as well as management consulting or investment banking and partly because it is seldom the road to the top. As a result, most of what happens on American factory floors is overseen by foremen with little training in engineering or management.

It wasn't always that way. Speaking to *Business Week*, Hisashi Shinto, president of Nippon Telegraph and Telephone Public Corporation, recalled an era when American manufacturing was the envy of Japan—and the rest of the world:

In 1955, when I visited factories in the U.S. I remember many young capable engineers working to improve manufacturing technology.... And they trained the workers so they would perform better....

But today I cannot find such qualified people ... working on the shop floor.... Most production managers I have seen have come up through the foreman route and are not college educated. They do not have the intellectual capability to devise improvements in manufacturing to make the product better. This is the key reason why the productivity gap is growing between our two countries.

One school of Japan-watchers argues that the United States will never be able to duplicate the Japanese success because so much of it flows from Japan's unique culture and history. That is an attractive thesis; if the Japanese have triumphed because of their Japanese-ness, there is no point in going to the bother of trying to copy them. Typically the argument rests on three points: the shared experience of defeat in World War II; high esteem for group harmony, which in business manifests itself as teamwork, intense company loyalty, and acceptance of one's place in the hierarchy; and Confucian and Shinto values, which stress loyalty and hard work.

But however strong the sweep of these currents, they may reveal less about the Japanese success than does a factor that is too often downplayed: From all over the world, the Japanese have borrowed the best of what industrial countries had to offer—the best product ideas, the best management ideas, the best technology. And they have been indefatigable in making the best better. The intriguing question is not how the Japanese managed to learn so fast but how their older cousins in Europe and the United States managed to forget the lessons they once knew so well.

TECHNORAPTURE

As a cure for the economic malaise of the past several years, high technology—the shimmering worlds of microchips, robots, and genetic engineering—is bound to disappoint. For one thing, the millions of blue-collar workers who lost their jobs in the recession of the early eighties cannot be moved en masse, or even in significant numbers, from the world of the smokestack to the wonderland of electronics. Although some of these workers can and will be retrained for high-tech work, that is only a small part of a large and complex picture. Many jobs being created by the new technologies are not high-tech at all, and two Stanford University researchers, Henry M. Levin and Russell W. Rumberger, say that high technology probably will lower the skills required for most U.S. workers. Citing occupational forecasts by the U.S. Bureau of Labor Statistics, they point out that between 1978 and 1990, the country will need 150,000 new computer programmers but 800,000 more fast-food workers and kitchen helpers. The need for custodians and janitors will outstrip the need for computer systems analysts by three to one—600,000 to 200,000. More than twenty years ago, a Harvard Business School study of automation's impact on job skills required in U.S. industry found that they rose at first but fell sharply as mechanization increased. Levin and Rumberger believe high technology could do the same, making work tasks simpler and more routine and "reducing opportunities for worker individuality and judgment."

In addition, many of the jobs in high-tech factories pay only half as much as workers earn on the assembly lines of Detroit or in the steel mills of Pittsburgh. And even though the new technologies will create hundreds of thousands of new jobs between now and the end of the century, there is no guarantee these jobs will stay in the United States. On Washington's birthday in 1983, Atari—an all-American high-tech success story if ever there was one—made headlines by announcing that to cut costs it was closing its California manufacturing operations. The work would be done at Atari's plants in Hong Kong and Taiwan. There went 1,700 American high-tech jobs. It was a stunning decision, and no group was more taken aback than the so-called Atari Democrats, the informal congressional coalition that favors an industrial policy to encourage "sunrise" industries like high-tech. "Sunset" industries, like steel and rubber, would be left to die quietly in the night.

In *The Next American Frontier,* industrial policy theorist Robert Reich argued that the sunset industries have too much political clout in Washington, and the sunrise industries, because they are new and small, don't have enough. As a result, Reich said, U.S. policies such as tariffs and price supports and loan guarantees encourage investment capital to flow to older, declining businesses rather than to emerging industries. Reich's point is well taken, but as the Atari incident demonstrates, capital can be made to flow not only to the most promising industries but also to the most inexpensive sources of labor. That augurs well for the world's consumers, who will benefit from low prices, but it raises at least two unnerving questions: Where will Americans work? And with less and less to export, how can they afford to import more and more?

The question of where Americans will work is most often answered by pointing out that most of them aren't employed in manufacturing as it is. They work in services, doing everything from checking groceries and setting broken bones to programming computers and writing airline tickets. But many services may prove to be no more immune to exportation than manufacturing is. Thanks to the links provided by communications satellites, much of the data processing needed by U.S. companies could now be done anywhere in the world. It is not inconceivable that a nation like India, with its vast pool of cheap labor, could become a major supplier of data processing services for corporations in other countries.

With their spacious lawns and sleek, low-slung buildings, the high-tech industrial parks that have sprung up in American suburbs during the past two decades are a decided improvement over the sprawling, belching factories that have marred the landscape for most of the century. Inside the modern parks, work life is a good deal less hazardous and more pleasant than in most industrial factories. The noise, the heat, the noxious smells—all these intrusions on body and spirit are blessedly absent. But much of the clerical work spawned by computer technology has an assembly-line quality that threatens, in the view of one critic, to make work in the vaunted office of the future as grueling as in the factory of the past. The villain: computerized monitoring of office workers' productivity. The same video display terminals (VDTs) that enable clerical workers to be more efficient also have, in many cases, built-in monitors that track output and error rates. Karen Nussbaum, executive director of 9 to 5, the National Association of Working Women, says that at one large insurance company, the productivity of workers at VDTs is measured in units of six and a half minutes, which subjects workers to horrendous stress. Nussbaum says that one major American study showed that "people who work at VDTs suffer even more stress than air controllers do." Another study, by the National Institute of Occupational Safety and Health at Blue Shield in San Francisco, found a higher incidence of anxiety, depression, fatigue, and related symptoms among 250 workers monitored by computer than among 150 workers in a control group that did not work under the electronic whip.

Nussbaum also blasts the organization of work in highly automated offices, where many jobs involve repetition of a single task all day long—typing names and insurance policy numbers, for example. "You don't need a college education to hate that kind of work," she says. Arguing that "nothing inherent in the work demands that kind of specialization," she urges that jobs be structured to include several tasks. Without the variety, Nussbaum says, "the potential for alienation is enormous."

Workers aren't the only ones dismayed by the size of the canyon between high-tech dreams and low-tech realities. Despite the impressive achievements of genetic engineers, who have figured out how to make synthetic versions of natural substances ranging from insulin to bull semen, much of the biotechnology industry seems to be in a limbo between the lab and the marketplace. Since many of the new "designer genes" cost a fortune to produce and many more have yet to be refined beyond experimental stages, it could be years before the promises of genetic engineering reach even modest fulfillment.

The robotics industry has also been long on fanfare and short on delivery. Part of that owes to the length and breadth of the recession, which left many manufacturers unable to acquire the marvelously productive "steel-collar workers." As one steel executive put it, "We know what we need [in terms of automation]. We just don't have the money to buy it." Other manufacturers, also operating at a fraction of their peak capacity because of dried-up markets for their products, won't even consider installing robots until demand perks up again. One notable exception is Deere & Company, a farm-equipment maker, which saw robots as an investment in the future and began putting them in even when it was still feeling the effects of the troubles in the farm economy.

The robotmakers have scared away more than a few manufacturers by building equipment that cannot communicate with gear made by other robot companies. The strategy forces customers to buy all their robotic equipment from one source or design elaborate computer systems to topple this high-tech Tower of Babel. When Westinghouse Electric wanted to put state-of-the-art manufacturing equipment in a North Carolina plant that forges turbine blades, it had to spend almost two years developing a computer setup that lets nine different machines talk to each other.

As for how many American factory workers will lose their jobs to robots, no one knows. But it would be naïve to hope that the robotics industry will create enough jobs to offset the number that will be lost. In a study for the state of Michigan, economist Tim Hunt of the W. E. Upjohn Institute for Employment Research pointed out that only seven thousand robots were on the job in the United States in 1982. Hunt doubts that there will be a mechanical population explosion in the eighties, which means, he says, that "it just won't take that many people to build and maintain the robot ranks."

Cities and states competing for a slice of the high-tech pie are also discovering that the dream may not be all that it's cracked up to be. Across the country, countless chambers of commerce and economic development commissions are trying to grow their own versions of California's fabled Silicon Valley and Boston's Route 128. Akron, the tire city, has billed itself as "Polymer Valley." Chicago's high-tech hustle includes proposals to underwrite scientific research and provide seed money for promising new ventures that agree to locate there. At least a dozen states regularly buy ads in business magazines to persuade executives to move their companies. By one 1983 estimate, thirty-three states have either spent or plan to spend a total of $250 million to woo high-tech. Although these efforts have been a boon to high-tech businesses, showering them with all manner of tax breaks and other incentives to relocate, there just isn't enough high technology for everybody who wants it. Interested companies can play cities against each other to get the best deal for themselves, but inevitably there will be a few winners and a crowd of losers.

In his 1970 book *Future Shock*, Alvin Toffler pinpointed the problems created by accelerating change and what he described as "the premature arrival of the future." Today's problem, at least in the world of high-tech, is that the future is not arriving fast enough.

Chapter 12

The Next Messiahs

IF TECHNOLOGY, Japanese management, and sophisticated quantitative analysis can't save American business, and if the experience of most corporate messiahs shows that salvation cannot be bought, is there *anything* to believe in?

Perhaps. The economic upheavals of the late seventies and early eighties did bring promises of repentance and reform from almost every industrial quarter. Managers said that they had learned their lessons, that they would run leaner and meaner, that they would look to the long term.

If the economy continues to improve and corporations shift their energies from survival to growth, the new messiahs probably will come from marketing rather than finance. Unlike the business expansion of the sixties and seventies, which came about largely through diversification and acquisition, the item to be expanded in the eighties is market share. One of the first messiahs for this new era is John Sculley, named CEO of Apple Computer in 1983. IBM and other competitors have taken a large bite out of the personal computer market, which was created by Apple, and it will be Sculley's task to set that right. Sculley went to Apple from PepsiCo, a company renowned for its aggressive and successful marketing. He was promised a salary and bonus of $2 million for his first year, $1 million in severance pay if things didn't work out, and options on 350,000 shares of Apple stock.

Atari took a similar tack, hiring James J. Morgan of Philip Morris, another organization well known for its marketing. Warner Communications, Atari's parent, offered Morgan the job just two days after he met Warner chairman Steven Ross at lunch. Morgan's seven-year contract was conservatively estimated to be worth $10 million. His job, like Sculley's, will be to increase his company's share of the personal computer market.

The human calculators will not disappear, but when desperate corporations need financial expertise, it probably will come from committees of bankers, not individual messiahs. In cases where the stakes are as large as they were at International Harvester, bankers will be apprehensive about putting the job in the hands of one person. The one-person approach may disappear even from corporations that aren't in trouble. More and more multibillion-dollar organizations are being run from an office of the chairman, which divides the CEO's responsibilities among several executives.

Although stockholders' complaints about overly generous executive compensation have been duly recorded in the minutes of annual meetings and the excesses of "golden parachutes" have drawn clucks of disapproval from the SEC, the seven-figure paycheck will never be an endangered species. As economist Thorstein Veblen noted long ago in *The Theory of the Leisure Class*, the average American worker doesn't dream of overthrowing the rich but of becoming one of them.

As for the next management religions, they seem to revolve around ideas of creative destruction: a breaking up of existing structures with the idea of reassembling the pieces in new ways. Between 1980 and 1982, corporate divestitures rose 31 percent—a strong signal that the credo of "bigger is better" is on the way out. Sociologist Max Weber observed that as organizations grow, entrepreneurs are replaced by bureaucrats, and one of the lessons of the past several years may well be that the bureaucratic style has reached its limits. The authors of *Industrial Renaissance: Producing a Competitive Future for America* have argued that America's industrial dinosaurs can survive only if they move beyond bureaucracy to "de-maturity"— by changing the focus of their innovation "from the refinement of existing concepts toward disruptive change in the concepts themselves." The courage to make these disruptive changes—to bring about creative destruction, in other words—will be vital to the success of anyone who hopes to save industries such as steel, textiles, and rubber.

Just how far can this creative destruction go? If the thriving economy of the Italian textile city of Prato is any model, chaos may be the most elegant of all organizational arrangements. The town's fifteen thousand businesses have an average of five employees each. One firm may design fabrics and take orders for them, but then it farms out weaving, dyeing, and spinning to many other small companies. Inefficient as it sounds to do a bit of business here and a bit there, with none of the economies of large-scale production, the system keeps the capital-equipment costs of each manufacturer extremely low. That in turn permits remarkable flexibility. As a Prato-born student at the London School of Economics explained to *Forbes*, "You can change your product almost overnight." And Prato, let it be noted, has almost no unemployment—perhaps because its manufacturers can make the goods customers want rather than cajoling customers into wanting the goods it makes, as U.S. auto companies have so often tried to do.

No one knows what will emerge from this creative destruction, but whatever happens, the next corporate messiahs, like the last ones, are sure to live in interesting times.

Notes

Abbreviations used in this section:

BW = *Business Week*
NYT = *New York Times*
WSJ = *Wall Street Journal*

CHAPTER 1

CORPORATE MESSIAH

Page

11 "... he will succeed me." Susan Alai, "Rosen: Hirsh Is Eventual Puritan Chief," *Women's Wear Daily* (July 22, 1980), p. 1.

12 a "one-man show," Susan Alai, "Murjani: The Show Goes on amid Hunt for New U.S. Exec," *Women's Wear Daily* (Aug. 12, 1980).

12 Profits were down. "Puritan's Profits Decline 93.7% in Second Quarter," *Women's Wear Daily* (Aug. 1, 1980).

14 about 4 percent. Daniel F. Cuff, "End of the Line for a Family Business," *NYT* (Dec. 4, 1983), p. F6.

14 "The Feminist." "Sultry Jeans Ad Banned by WABC, WCBS-TV," *NYT* (Nov. 20, 1980), p. D1.

14 about the switch. *Women's Wear Daily* (Sept. 20, 1980).

16 more than doubled. Douglas Bauer, "Why Big Business Is Firing the Boss," *NYT Magazine* (Mar. 8, 1981), p. 24.

17 "... for the next 20 years." John Rutledge, "Decision-Makers Now Confront Disinflation," *WSJ* (May 24, 1982).

21 "... sour very quickly." Bauer, op. cit., p. 25.

CHAPTER 2

MAD MONEY: Executive Compensation

Page

23 Smith of Federal Express. "The $50 Million Man," *Forbes* (June 6, 1983), pp. 126–54.

23 $1.6 million for a year's work. Mark Green, "Richer Than All Their Tribe," *New Republic* (Jan. 6 and 13, 1982), p. 21.

23 ". . . the way some people chew vitamins." Milton Moskowitz et al., *Everybody's Business: An Almanac* (New York: Harper & Row, 1980), pp. 207–9.

24 price tag came to $4.5 million. "Michel C. Bergerac," *Financial World* (Mar. 15, 1977), p. 34.

24 swelled to $1,125,000. "Executive Compensation: Looking to the Long Term Again," *BW* (May 9, 1983), p. 102.

24 personal financial planning. "Executive Pay Raises Likely to be Less in 1981; Bonuses and Perks Keyed to Job Performance," Jill Bettner, *WSJ* (Nov. 17, 1980), p. 50.

24 $1 million bonus for coming aboard. "A Good Seven Months for Thomas Wyman," *Broadcasting* (Mar. 23, 1981), p. 87.

25 pay back a dime. Carol J. Loomis, "Archie McCardell's Absolution," *Fortune* (Dec. 15, 1980), pp. 89–90.

25 ". . . substantial incremental profits." Robert B. Scott, Jr., "A Look at Management Incentive Plans," *Journal of Accountancy* (June 1981), p. 76.

25 ". . . less than they're worth." Robert M. Bleiberg, "Good for General Motors?" *Barron's* (May 29, 1978), p. 7.

26 ($2,996,036 in 1982). "The $50 Million Man," p. 127.

26 a few years before. Arthur M. Louis, "The Crucible: Out of the Great Depression, Tycoons," *Across the Board* (June 1981), pp. 37–40.

26 tripled between 1975 and 1980. Lynda Schuster, "As Bosses Go, Mesa Pete's T. Boone Pickens Is Doing Very Well— Too Well, Some Say," *WSJ* (Apr. 14, 1981).

27 down considerably. G. Christian Hill, "T. Boone Pickens' Mesa Option Yields Slimmer Pickin's," *WSJ* (Oct. 15, 1982).

27 "... a garbage collector." Donald B. Thompson, "Are CEOs Worth What They're Paid?" *Industry Week* (May 4, 1981), p. 73.

28 for playing baseball. Glen Waggoner, "Money Games," *Esquire* (June 1982), pp. 49–60.

28 $69,630 in 1981. "Haig, as Secretary of State, Is Making 10% of Salary Level at United Technologies," *WSJ* (Apr. 15, 1981).

28 "... on the shop floor." Bleiberg, op. cit.

30 "... the wrong man." George Bull, "Worthy of Their Hire," *Director* (June 1980), p. 3.

30 if he meets certain goals. R. Lubar, "American Leads British Steel back from the Brink," *Fortune* (Sept. 21, 1981), p. 88.

30 basic soldier's pay. John C. Baker, "Are Corporate Executives Overpaid?" *Harvard Business Review* (July–Aug. 1977), pp. 51–56.

30 $902,176 for the year. Green, op. cit., p. 26.

31 for half that amount. Green, op cit., p. 25.

31 rose 6.5 percent. "Pay at the Top Mirrors Inflation," *BW* (May 11, 1981), p. 58.

31 about the same amount. "How America's Top Moneymakers Fared in the Recession," *BW* (May 9, 1983), p. 84.

31 would not bring many big salary increases. "Hard Times Hit the Executive Suite," *WSJ* (Jan. 18, 1983), p. 1.

31 higher retirement benefits. "Top Officers' Pay Raises Slowed," *WSJ* (Apr. 26, 1983), p. 1.

32 UAW president Douglas Fraser. "GM Chairman Sets Pace: Cuts Pay by $135 a Month," *WSJ* (Feb. 1, 1982).

32 forced GM to back off. "GM Stubs Its Toe, Again," *BW* (May 10, 1982), p. 176.

32 earnings dropped 43 percent. "How America's Top Moneymakers Fared in the Recession," op. cit., p. 84.

32 the biggest paycheck. Carol J. Loomis, "Incredible Shrinking Norton Simon," *Fortune* (Mar. 7, 1983), p. 90.

32 $13,222 a month. "Playboy's Execs Know a Rabbit's Foot When They See One," *Magazine Industry Newsletter* (Nov. 17, 1982), p. 2.

33 "... justify their huge salaries." William Steve Albrecht and Philip Jihn, "The Million Dollar Men," *Business Horizons* (Aug. 1978), pp. 9–14.

34 bonus climbed 67.1 percent. Alfred Rappaport, "Executive Incentives vs. Corporate Growth," *Harvard Business Review* (July–Aug. 1978), pp. 81–88.

34 "... on incentive pay." Jude T. Rich and Ennius E. Bergsma, "Pay Executives to Create Wealth," *The McKinsey Quarterly* (Winter 1983), pp. 25–26.

35 frequently corporate officers themselves. Baker, op. cit.

35 bigger the bonuses. Edward Meadows, "New Targeting for Executive Pay," *Fortune* (May 4, 1981), pp. 176–84.

36 the executive's performance. Rappaport, op. cit., p. 85.

37 "... essential to the growth and earnings," Exxon, *Notice of Annual Meeting May 14, 1982 and Proxy Statement*, pp. 52–55.

37 his employment contract. Paul A. Gigot, "First Chicago Says Earnings Rose 19% for First Quarter," *WSJ* (Apr. 13, 1981), p. 1.

38 at least $938,500 a year. "RCA Paying Dismissed Executives," *NYT* (Mar. 11, 1981).

38 severance provisions in their contracts. Roger Ricklefs, "Top Bosses More Likely to Get Axed, and Big Settlements When They Do," *WSJ* (July 14, 1980), p. 17.

38 complexities of compensation plans. Baker, op. cit., p. 53.

38 "... straightforward salary." Meadows, op. cit., p. 177.

38 bonus of at least $200,000. Jeffrey A. Tannenbaum, "RCA Forces President of Six Months to Quit," *WSJ* (June 19, 1980), p. 2.

39 Araskog's New York apartment. Carol J. Loomis, "The Madness of Executive Compensation," *Fortune* (July 12, 1982), pp. 42–43.

40 "golden parachutes." Kenneth B. Noble, "S.E.C. Panel Asks Curb on Golden Parachutes," *NYT* (May 14, 1983), p. 33.

40 up to $2.2 million. Robert J. Cole, "Agee Quits Allied and Bendix Jobs," *NYT* (Feb. 9, 1983), p. D1.

41 after the acquisition. "Why There's Room at the Top," *Forbes* (Apr. 25, 1983), p. 10.

41 five highest-paid officers. "A Clearer Look at Top Executive Pay," *BW* (Sept. 15, 1980), pp. 43, 46.

42 ". . . a target already." Aljean Harmetz, "For Film Moguls, Salaries in Megabucks," *NYT* (Dec. 14, 1981).

42 burdensome and confusing. "Concealing the Boss's Pay," *NYT* (Feb. 14, 1983), editorial.

CHAPTER 3

SOWING AND REAPING: Archie McCardell and
International Harvester

Page

43 salary of $460,000. "McCardell Starts Things Moving at International Harvester," *Dun's Review* (Apr. 1978), p. 28.

45 eight thousand employees . . . in a single year. "International Harvester: Axing the Fat off a Company Gone Flabby," *BW* (June 26, 1978), p. 66.

46 lowest in the industry. Jill Bettner with Lisa Gross, "Planting Deep and Wide at John Deere," *Forbes* (Mar. 14, 1983), p. 120.

46 twice as much per employee. Hal Lancaster and Sue Shellenbarger, "Chrysler and Harvester Typify the Hard Times of the Industrial Giants," *WSJ* (Jan. 28, 1983), pp. 1ff.

46 to boost earnings in the short run. Carol J. Loomis, "Archie McCardell's Absolution," *Fortune* (Dec. 15, 1980), p. 90.

47 rejecting their budget proposals. "Axing the Fat off a Company Gone Flabby," p. 66.

47 ". . . 180 degrees." R. Hamermesh and E. T. Christansen, Harvard Business School Case 9-381-053 (rev. June 1981), p. 9.

48 should have hit $800 million. Ibid., p. 3.

48 from 93,000 to 90,000. "Axing the Fat off a Company Gone Flabby," p. 66.

48 beaten his $100 million goal by $40 million. "International Harvester's Crash Diet," *Financial World* (Sept. 15, 1979), p. 27.

48 Harvester's profitability fell. Loomis, op cit., p. 90.

48 make the plants more efficient. Carol J. Loomis, "The

Strike That Rained on Archie McCardell's Parade," *Fortune* (May 19, 1980), p. 93.

49 high price of UAW labor. Richard Hamermesh, Harvard Business School Case Number 4-381-054 (B2), p. 3.

49 a dozen or so showed up. Ibid., p. 2.

50 didn't have them. Ibid., p. 1.

51 Round One went to the UAW. "International Harvester: Axing the Fat off a Company Gone Flabby," p. 71.

51 goal of $240 million. "International Harvester's Crash Diet," p. 27.

51 until he had wrung out $500 million. "Axing the Fat off a Company Gone Flabby," p. 71.

51 Inventory systems. Ibid.

51 rivals listed in McCardell's contract. Loomis, "The Strike That Rained on Archie McCardell's Parade," op cit., p. 94.

52 "distinguished performance." Loomis, ibid., p. 90.

53 loss of $479 million. Loomis, ibid., p. 94.

53 from $45 a share to $27. "Harvester Falls Flat on Its Bargaining Goals," *BW* (Apr. 7, 1980), p. 34.

54 ". . . pulled down the average to 9.15%." Loomis, "Archie McCardell's Absolution," pp. 90, 94.

55 "food weapon" against OPEC's "oil weapon." Stephen Kindel and Laura Sanders, "Please Come Back, W. J. Bryan," *Forbes* (Aug. 30, 1982), p. 110.

55 one farmer could feed seventy-eight people. Ibid., p. 109.

55 sold for $3.41. Ibid., p. 109.

56 soybean business up and running. Ibid., pp. 110–11.

56 $50,000—up almost fourteen times. Norman Peagam and Hal Lancaster, "Farm-Machine Slump Strikes Far Beyond Ills at Harvester, Massey," *WSJ* (June 3, 1982), p. 1.

56 33 percent less than in the late seventies. Steven Leuthold, "Grim Reapers: The Great Bull Market in Farmland Is Ending," *Barron's* (Aug. 9, 1982), pp. 6–7ff.

56 ". . . like a rope supports a hanged man." Ibid., p. 16.

57 almost no profit. Claudia Waterloo, "Harvester Dealer Struggles to Overcome His Suppliers and the Recession," *WSJ* (Nov. 30, 1982), p. 56.

57 operating loss of $375 million. Phillip H. Wiggins, "Inter-

national Harvester Says Its Loss Rose by 70% in 1981," *NYT* (Nov. 28, 1981), pp. 1ff.

57 dividends would be eliminated. Ibid., pp. 1ff.

58 $650 million less than in fiscal 1981. "Harvester to Reduce Costs by $650 Million for Its Oct. 31 Year," *WSJ* (Apr. 15, 1982), p. 56.

58 loss came to $635.7 million. Heywood Klein and Meg Cox, "Harvester's Team Gains Trust, But Doubts about Long Run Persist," *WSJ* (Nov. 14, 1982), p. 33.

59 should have concentrated on strategy. "International Harvester: Can It Survive When the Banks Move In?" *BW* (June 22, 1981), p. 69.

59 ill equipped to handle the UAW. Maurice Barnfather and Lisa Gross, "The Bankers' Partner," *Forbes* (Nov. 23, 1981), p. 43.

59 even more money. "How International Harvester Hopes to Return to the Black," *Fortune* (Jan. 25, 1982), p. 8.

60 to restructure $4.9 billion of Harvester's finances. "The Growing Obstacles to a Harvester Bailout," *BW* (Sept. 28, 1981), p. 33.

60 an emaciated $350 million. Ibid., p. 34.

60 development work for the vehicles. Norman Peagam and Paul Ingrassia, "Harvester's Finances Deteriorate, Leaving Its Future in Doubt," *WSJ* (Sept. 21, 1981), pp. 1ff.

61 some $300 million less than book value. "Harvester Sees Bigger Charge in Sale to Dresser," *WSJ* (Sept. 7, 1982), p. 12.

61 take its business to suppliers who would. "Harvester Studies Plan to Close Several Plants," *NYT* (Nov. 11, 1982), p. D4.

61 trim waste in management. Norman Peagam, "Harvester Faces Dec. 23 Deadline to Push to Complete Refinancing of $4.15 Billion," *WSJ* (Dec. 11, 1981).

61 management pay cuts. "How International Harvester Hopes to Return to the Black," p. 7.

62 "... looking out for yourselves." Winston Williams, "Harvester Declares $299.4 Million Loss," *NYT* (Feb. 19, 1982), p. D3.

62 "... equality of sacrifice." "Harvester Gives Managers Bonuses Totaling $6 Million," *WSJ* (Jan. 18, 1982).

63 instead of making them in-house. "Why Harvester Talks Are Reaping Anger," *BW* (Feb. 1, 1982), pp. 18–19.

63 notice of plant closings. "New Harvester Pact Approved by UAW, Early Returns Indicate," *WSJ* (May 3, 1982), and Winston Williams, "Harvester and UAW in Pact on Concessions," *NYT* (Apr. 30, 1982), p. D1.

63 wanted to sell in Canada. Laurel Sorenson, "Two Towns Fight to Keep Harvester Plants, Knowing that Only One Will Remain Open," *WSJ* (Sept. 8, 1982), p. 35.

65 Fort Wayne matched that. "Fort Wayne Offers Plan to Harvester," *NYT* (May 12, 1982).

65 another $11 million. Sorenson, op. cit.

65 a blow to Fort Wayne. "Harvester to Switch Indiana Truck Unit to Plant in Ohio," *WSJ* (Sept. 28, 1982).

66 below the level specified in the debt agreement. "Harvester May Need a New Debt Deal," *BW* (Mar. 8, 1982), pp. 29–30.

66 repayment of a $3.5 million loan. Winston Williams, "Harvester Bank Loan Repaid," *NYT* (Apr. 6, 1982).

66 bigger ratio of debt to net worth. Norman Peagam, "Harvester Asks Lenders to Reduce Required Net Worth," *WSJ* (Apr. 23, 1982), p. 23.

68 tightening their grip. Hal Lancaster and Norman Peagam, "Harvester's Ex-Chief Probably Refused to Accept Diminished Role, Bankers Say," *WSJ* (May 5, 1982), p. 4.

68 a change of leadership to restore confidence. Hal Lancaster and Norman Peagam, "Harvester Chief McCardell Ousted; Outside Director Menk Is Successor," *WSJ* (May 4, 1982), p. 3.

CHAPTER 4

HIGH-TECH DREAMS: Roy Ash and AM International

Page

70 underdeveloped countries. Milton Moskowitz et al., *Everybody's Business: An Almanac* (New York: Harper & Row, 1981), pp. 829–32.

70 council on executive organization. "If at First You Don't Succeed," *New Republic* (Dec. 23, 1972), pp. 11–12.

70 extensive federal contracts. Ibid.

71 from its all-time high of $120 to $12. Ibid.

71 Proxmire of Wisconsin. Don Irwin, "Nixon Shuffles Cabinet Posts," *Los Angeles Times* (Nov. 29, 1972), pp. 1ff.

71 "... 'everything's coming up roses' public attitude." Les Aspin, "The Case Against Roy Ash," *Nation* (Feb. 26, 1973), pp. 264–68.

72 of duplicating equipment. N. R. Kleinfield, "AM's Brightest Years Now Dim Memories," *NYT* (Apr. 15, 1982), p. D1.

72 dominated the market for forty years. *AM International* (Norwalk, Conn.: International Resource Development, 1981), p. 16.

72 change in leadership. Louis Kraar, "Roy Ash Is Having Fun at Addressogrief-Multigrief," *Fortune* (Feb. 27, 1978), p. 47.

73 double his money. Ibid., p. 48.

74 Ash's $2.7 million was now worth $4.2 million. Ibid., p. 52.

74 three hundred thousand shares, just like Ash. Ibid., p. 48.

74 "... seen to be intelligent and effective," quoted in Donald B. Bibeault, *Corporate Turnaround* (New York: McGraw-Hill, 1982), p. 163.

75 "... learn how to chew it." "Conversation with Roy Ash," *Organizational Dynamics* (Autumn 1979), p. 50.

75 "... all businesses are the same." Kraar, op. cit., p. 50.

75 cash on hand of $42 million. Susie Gharib Nazem, "How Roy Ash Got Burned," *Fortune* (Apr. 6, 1981), p. 72.

75 he would catch up with them. Kraar, op. cit., p. 48.

77 "... resignation of people we really didn't want anyway." Stephen J. Sansweet, "Chairman Trautman Finds Greyhound Post Remains a Hot Seat," *WSJ* (Nov. 20, 1980), pp. 1ff.

78 not nearly as threatened ... as the company had feared. Kraar, op. cit., p. 50.

78 "... turned in another direction." Terrence E. Deal and Allan A. Kennedy, *Corporate Cultures* (Reading, Mass.: Addison-Wesley, 1982), p. 175.

79 slicing headquarters staff in half. Kraar, op cit., p. 50.

79 80 percent of the company's management. "AM International: When Technology Was Not Enough," *BW* (Jan. 25, 1982), p. 62.

79 four presidents in two years. "The Unflappable Roy Ash," *Forbes* (Dec. 18, 1980), p. 39.

80 more than thirty executives. "AM International: When Technology Was Not Enough," p. 68.

80 mechanical duplicators priced between $10,000 and $20,000. "AM International: When Technology Was Not Enough," p. 68.

81 sales of $667 million. "Up from the Ashes," *Forbes* (Apr. 16, 1979), p. 104.

82 losing $20 million a year. "AM International: When Technology Was Not Enough," pp. 65, 68.

82 before reaching this conclusion. Ibid., p. 65.

82 "going over the peak right now." Kathryn Harris, "AM International Predicts Loss for the Quarter," *Los Angeles Times* (Oct. 10, 1979), Section 3, p. 17.

82 troubles were now safely consigned to the past. "AM International: The Cash Bind That Threatens a Turnaround," *BW* (Aug. 18, 1980), p. 121.

83 earnings came from AM's old businesses. "Up from the Ashes," p. 108.

83 rental contracts on some of AM's equipment. "AM International: The Cash Bind That Threatens a Turnaround," p. 121.

83 three years earlier. Ibid.

83 ". . . by greater accomplishments." Nick Galluccio, "The Unflappable Roy Ash," *Forbes* (Dec. 8, 1980), pp. 38–39.

84 firing his chief financial officer. Ibid., p. 38.

84 Interest expense outstripped operating income. Ibid.

84 debt had actually begun to exceed shareholders' equity. Thomas C. Hayes, "Ash Forced Out of Two AM Posts," *NYT* (Feb. 21, 1981), pp. D1ff.

84 buy AM a little staying power. Galluccio, op. cit., p. 39.

85 a 14 percent stake. Hayes, op. cit.

85 he resigned and left the meeting. "Why Ash Was Ousted at AM International," *BW* (Mar. 9, 1981), p. 34.

86 Richard B. Black of Maremont Corporation. Hayes, op. cit.

86 AM shares jumped $2.875 in one day. Hayes, op. cit.

CHAPTER 5

LOW-TECH REALITIES: Richard Black and AM
International (Again)

Page

88 earnings per share. AM International, Inc., 10-K (year
ended July 31, 1981), p. 27.

88 recorded the transaction as a sale. Richard L. Hudson,
"AM International Inc. Inflated Results before Chapter 11 Filing, SEC Charges," *WSJ* (May 3, 1983), p. 2.

89 between 1979 and 1981. AM 10-K (1981), p. 18.

90 severance bonuses . . . and relocation bonuses. AM 10-K
(1981), pp. 24–26.

90 made on the basis of misleading information. Meg Cox,
"New Chairman Trying Another Strategy to Save AM International, Deep in Debt," *WSJ* (Oct. 12, 1981), p. 29.

90 would lose $175 million for the year. Ibid.

90 even gloomier $250 million. "AM International Is To Re-
port Unaudited $250 Million Deficit," *NYT* (Dec. 3, 1981),
p. D3.

90 defaulted on more than $100 million. "AM International Is
Back in Default Status as Waiver on $106 Million of Debt Ex-
pires," *WSJ* (Oct. 27, 1981).

90 United States, Canada, and Great Britain. "AM International Enters $109 Million Amended Loan Pact," *WSJ* (Dec. 16,
1981).

90 final figure was $245 million. Heywood Klein, "AM Inter-
national Has $245 Million Fiscal 1981 Loss," *WSJ* (Dec. 17,
1981), p. 52.

90 a loss of $19 million for the first quarter. "AM International
Posts Deficit of $19.3 Million," *WSJ* (Jan. 13, 1982), p. 6.

90 laid off 850 employees. Thomas Petzinger, Jr., "AM International Cuts Wages 8%, Trims Jobs 5%," *WSJ* (Jan. 7, 1982).

91 another accounting firm. "AM International: When Technology Was Not Enough," p. 65.

92 new debt default. Heywood Klein, "AM International Reports Net Loss for Jan. 30 Period," *WSJ* (Mar. 25, 1982).

92 forced to declare bankruptcy. "AM Files Chapter 11 Petition," *NYT* (Apr. 15, 1982), p. D1.

92 liabilities ran to more than $500 million. Ibid.

92 a misbegotten strategy. "An Aftershock Stuns AM International," *BW* (Mar. 22, 1982), p. 31.

92 more black ink than red. "AM International: When Technology Was Not Enough," p. 64.

CHAPTER 6

THE LONG GOOD-BYE: Aging Entrepreneurs and the Quest for the Chosen Son

Page

95 "That is not spoken of at Polaroid." Paul W. Sturm, "Choosing the Next Boss: Why So Many Bosses Do It Badly," *Forbes* (Oct. 2, 1978), p. 44.

95 had sunk to $20. "Polaroid Profit Drops; Founder Quits Last Post," *WSJ* (July 27, 1982), p. 2.

95 off limits when Land ran the company. Louis A. Fanelli, "Polaroid Needs Brighter Image," *Advertising Age* (May 4, 1981), p. 4.

96 of the country's major airlines. "Delta: The World's Most Profitable Airline," *BW* (Aug. 31, 1981), p. 70.

96 to the tribe. Sir James George Frazer, *The New Golden Bough* (ed. Theodor H. Gaster) (New York: S. G. Phillips, 1972), pp. 224–25.

96 ". . . as long as God will permit me." Peter W. Bernstein, "Armand Hammer's Other Collection," *Fortune* (Sept. 8, 1980), p. 48.

97 Hammer's condition. Linda Grant, "At 82, Hammer Continues to Set a Defiant Pace," *Los Angeles Times* (May 21, 1980), p. 1.

98 were selling for six. Linda Grant, "Abboud Replaces Merszei as President of Occidental," *Los Angeles Times* (Aug. 5, 1980), Section 4, p. 1.

98 "Go back to Buffalo." Stephen J. Sansweet, "Meeting Is Mirthful as Hammer Marks His 82nd Year," *WSJ* (May 22, 1980), p. 26.

99 assortment of cabinet ministers. Edward Jay Epstein, "The Riddle of Armand Hammer," *NYT Magazine* (Nov. 29, 1981), p. 72.

99 Britain's Queen Mother. Bernstein, op. cit., p. 48.

100 salable in the United States. Armand Hammer, letter to the editor, *NYT Magazine* (n.d.), p. 110.

100 dealings with the Soviets. Epstein, op. cit., pp. 72–73.

100 were a bit cross. "U.S. Hopes to Bar Occidental's Hammer from Building Siberia-Moscow Pipeline," *WSJ* (Oct. 8, 1982), p. 5.

100 contributions to cancer research. John Noble Wilford, "Hammer Offers $1 Million Prize for Cancer Cure," *NYT* (Dec. 4, 1981), p. A32.

101 for their beef. Epstein, op. cit., pp. 71–72.

101 international oil market. Epstein, op. cit., p. 73.

101 deals for Occidental. Grant, "At 82, Hammer Continues to Set a Defiant Pace," loc. cit.

101 "the best acquisition I ever made." Susie Gharib Nazem, "Occidental Petroleum's Odd Couple," *Fortune* (Nov. 19, 1979), pp. 70–72.

102 modernize Hooker plants. "A Swashbuckler Tries His Talents at Oxy," *BW* (Oct. 22, 1979), pp. 176ff.

102 where zoning laws forbade expansion. Ibid.

102 $122 million write-off. Tom Redburn, "Occidental President Out, Ex-Dow Chemical Chief In," *Los Angeles Times* (July 25, 1979), Section 3, p. 16.

102 controls and reporting systems. Nazem, op. cit.

103 $8 million fight. "Occidental Taps Zoltan Merszei as President; Baird Quits Post Held Since '73 after Rumored Rift with Chairman Hammer," *WSJ* (July 25, 1979), p. 5.

103 $300,000-a-year paycheck. Grant, op. cit.

103 ". . . learn a tremendous amount from him." "A Swashbuckler Tries His Talent at Oxy."

103 limelight fall on Hammer. "Role of Occidental Petroleum President Stressed to Analysts, Merszei Discusses Operations of Company but Doesn't Steal Show from Hammer," *WSJ* (Nov. 7, 1979), p. 15.

103 twice as large as equity. "A Swashbuckler Tries His Talent at Oxy."

103 chlorine and caustic soda. Ibid.

103 twenty-year pact. Milton Moskowitz et al., *Everybody's Business* (New York: Harper & Row, 1980), p. 518.

104 driving the price down. "A Swashbuckler Tries His Talent at Oxy."

104 supplies of superphosphoric acid. "Oxy's Swap with Russia Seems Back on Track," *BW* (May 11, 1981), p. 35.

105 "... just running Hooker." Bernstein, op. cit., p. 47.

105 eight-year reign at First Chicago. Grant, "Abboud Replaces Merszei as President of Occidental."

105 heard in the hallways. From *Fortune* (Apr. 21, 1980), quoted in Moskowitz, op. cit., p. 524.

105 stocks to buy. Grant, "Abboud Replaces Merszei as President of Occidental."

105 "... do whatever the doctor wants done." Bernstein, op. cit., p. 48.

105 "... discarded immediately." Stephen J. Sansweet, "Hammer Names Abboud President in Occidental Management Shuffle," *WSJ* (Aug. 5, 1980), p. 29.

105 being sold off. "Oxy's Bold Bid to Ease Its Need for Foreign Oil," *BW* (Aug. 30, 1982), p. 23.

106 management of Iowa Beef. Alexander Stuart, "Meatpackers in Stampede," *Fortune* (June 29, 1981), p. 68.

106 largest individual shareholder. "Oxy's Bold Bid to Ease Its Need for Foreign Oil."

107 an office building. Leslie Wayne, "A Costly Merger for Occidental," *NYT* (Jan. 23, 1983), Section 3, pp. 1ff.

107 too good to pass up. "The Big Winner if Oxy Gets Zapata," *BW* (Sept. 21, 1981), p. 32.

108 honor the trust. "CBS: When Being No. 1 Isn't Enough," *BW* (May 26, 1980), p. 129.

108 ad sales to corporate finance. William Paley, *As It Happened* (Garden City, N.Y.: Doubleday, 1979), p. 345.

108 bought in 1928. "Mr. CBS Is Stepping Down," *Broadcasting* (Sept. 13, 1982), p. 31.

108 broadcasting and nonbroadcasting. Paley, op. cit., p. 346.

109 "... further apart." Paley, op. cit., p. 347.

110 which was fatal. Paley, op. cit., pp. 349–50.

110 Renaissance history. "Paley Springs Trap under Arthur Taylor," *Broadcasting* (Oct. 18, 1976), p. 23.

110 New Jersey Symphony. Sally Bedell, *Up the Tube* (New York: Viking, 1981), p. 97.

111 five pennants in a row. Stratford P. Sherman, "CBS Places Its Bets on the Future," *Fortune* (Aug. 9, 1982), p. 71.

111 justifying their expenses. Bedell, op. cit., p. 97.

111 before nine at night. Bedell, op. cit., pp. 100–1.

112 followed him out the door. "CBS Prospers, but Paley Wields the Ax." *BW* (Oct. 25, 1976), p. 41.

112 $400 million in cash. Bedell, op. cit., p. 190.

112 the next two days. "Paley Springs Trap under Arthur Taylor," p. 21.

112 $250,000 in 1977 and 1978. "Settlement Helps to Put Taylor Second on CBS's '76 Salary Scale," *Broadcasting* (Mar. 28, 1977), p. 98.

112 ". . . bad chemistry." "Paley Springs Trap under Arthur Taylor," p. 21.

113 ". . . my successor is in place." Paley, op. cit., pp. 352–53.

113 ". . . be the savior." Bedell, op. cit., p. 190.

113 almost $500,000 each. Ibid., p. 189.

113 *Charlie's Angels.* Ibid., pp. 213–14.

113 ratings down even farther. Ibid., p. 191.

114 out of a job. "Behind the Executive Shake-up at CBS," *BW* (Oct. 31, 1977), pp. 57ff.

114 make them better. "CBS: When Being No. 1 Isn't Enough," p. 130.

114 promoting from within. "A Conversation with CBS's John Backe," *Advertising Age* (Mar. 28, 1977), pp. 53ff.

114 rather than looking for scapegoats. "Backe: Taking a Humanistic Approach to Make Things Run," *Broadcasting* (Jan. 3, 1977), p. 97.

115 toy manufacturer. "CBS: When Being No. 1 Isn't Enough," p. 129.

115 *Dallas.* Bedell, op. cit., p. 284.

115 "video abundance." "More Bearishness Toward Cable," *Broadcasting* (May 31, 1982), p. 25.

115 70 percent by 1990. Sally Bedell, "What's Gone Wrong at Black Rock," *NYT* (Oct. 31, 1982), business section, p. 8.

116 "... social set talk about." Bedell, *Up the Tube,* p. 304.

116 in the annual report. Maurine Christopher, "Backe Ouster Hints of Upcoming Clashes," *Advertising Age* (May 19, 1980).

116 right man for the future. "The Backe-Paley Disconnection," *Broadcasting* (May 19, 1980).

116 "... think of what might happen." Ibid.

116 he resigned. "History Repeats at CBS; Backe Out as President," *Broadcasting* (May 12, 1980), p. 25.

117 "on the track." "The Backe-Paley Disconnection."

117 "... pursue another course." "History Repeats at CBS; Backe Out as President," p. 26.

117 "... at General Electric than at CBS." "CBS: When Being No. 1 Isn't Enough," p. 129.

117 "I think he changed." Ibid.

117 "Frank was terrific." "The Backe-Paley Disconnection."

117 "... one of the best opportunities." "The Backe-Paley Disconnection."

118 two years' pay. John E. Cooney, "From Food to Media: CBS Chooses Wyman of Pillsbury to Succeed Backe as Its President," *WSJ* (May 23, 1980), p. 2.

118 "... a master's degree in it." Ibid.

118 "... it's for real." Sherman, op. cit., p. 70.

118 and a consultant. Sally Bedell, "54 Years after Founding CBS, Paley Is Resigning," *NYT* (Sept. 9, 1982), p. 1.

118 his elegant suite. "Paley: This Is My Company," *Broadcasting* (Oct. 18, 1976).

119 "... 200 channels to watch." "Wyman's Case for Big Investments in Lean Times," *Broadcasting* (Mar. 8, 1982), p. 58.

119 the bottom line. Sherman, op. cit., p. 71.

120 "... adjusted for inflation." Jean A. Briggs, "I Like It Here," *Forbes* (Mar. 15, 1982), p. 35.

120 several senior vice-presidents. "GAF Creates Office of Chairman, Won't Name New President," *WSJ* (Nov. 24, 1981), p. 42.

120 more than $400,000 a year. Briggs, op. cit., p. 35.

120 runs until 1986. Pamela G. Hollie, "Dissidents Elected in GAF Fight," *NYT* (Dec. 14, 1983), p. D1.

121 $766 million. Robert J. Flaherty, "Harold Geneen Rests His Case," *Forbes* (June 15, 1977), p. 42.

121 $16.7 billion. "Tinkering with Geneen's Growth Machine at ITT," *BW* (May 15, 1978), p. 58.

121 Twinkies and Wonder Bread. Milton Moskowitz et al., op. cit., p. 825.

121 decidedly parsimonious. Jean A. Briggs, "What Might Have Been," *Forbes* (Aug. 30, 1982), p. 46.

122 devote himself to accounting. Moskowitz et al., op. cit., p. 827.

122 better than they are. Geoffrey Colvin, "The De-Geneening of ITT," *Fortune* (Jan. 11, 1982), p. 39.

122 ". . . exaggerating their importance." Ibid., p. 36.

122 office of the president. "ITT's New Chief Executive Gets Down to Work," *International Management* (Jan. 1978), pp. 19–20.

123 seventeen briefcases. Julie Connelly, "Lyman Hamilton: ITT's Mr. Outside," *Institutional Investor* (Nov. 1976), p. 43.

123 the withering question. "Tinkering with Geneen's Growth Machine at ITT," p. 64.

123 as in "Jesus." "Why America's Big Brothers Are in Trouble," *The Economist* (July 21, 1979), p. 77.

123 it solved them. Jeffrey A. Tannenbaum, "ITT's Araskog Reverses Geneen Formula, Sheds Units to Improve Company Fortunes," *WSJ* (Apr. 1, 1981), p. 34.

123 ". . . you'll make your year." Colvin, op. cit., p. 36.

124 election in a foreign country. Michael H. Crosby, "ITT's Chile Confession: A Definite 'Maybe,'" *Business and Society Review* (Summer 1976), p. 67.

124 Keep The Hartford Insurance Group. "Tinkering with Geneen's Growth Machine at ITT," p. 60.

125 ". . . testimony about the case.)" Moskowitz et al., op. cit., pp. 827–28.

125 made since then. Jeff Gerth, "Report Lists More ITT Payments," *NYT* (May 14, 1982), p. D1.

126 "International This & That." Bill Abrams, "How ITT Shells Out $10 Million or So a Year to Polish Reputation," *WSJ* (Apr. 2, 1982), pp. 1ff.

126 the company's performance. "Is It Time to Dump ITT?," *Financial World* (Sept. 1, 1979), p. 26.

126 Supreme Court justices. "Tinkering with Geneen's Growth Machine at ITT," p. 64.

126 joined ITT in 1962. "The Fastest Antelope of Them All," *Fortune* (Mar. 1977), p. 17.

127 wasn't going to increase its borrowings. Connelly, op. cit., p. 44.

127 12 percent in 1975. Ibid.

127 consumer products and services. Ibid.

127 ". . . a blaze of glory." "Geneen's Heir Is Still Not Apparent," *BW* (Dec. 20, 1976), p. 22.

127 Rand V. Araskog. Ibid.

128 Nixon's reelection campaign. "The Fastest Antelope of Them All."

128 stay on as chairman. Ibid.

128 did a good job. Flaherty, op. cit., p. 47.

128 rather than acting alone. "Why America's Big Brothers Are in Trouble," p. 77.

128 daily operations of the company. "High Politics at ITT," *Fortune* (Aug. 13, 1979), p. 31.

128 times had changed. Terrence E. Deal and Allan A. Kennedy, *Corporate Cultures: The Rites and Rituals of Corporate Life* (Reading, Mass.: Addison-Wesley, 1982), p. 42.

129 support Hamilton, not oppose him. "Tinkering with Geneen's Growth Machine at ITT," p. 64.

129 selling six companies. "High Politics at ITT," p. 32.

129 was asked to resign. Colvin, op. cit., p. 37.

129 control of the board. Tim Metz and Priscilla S. Meyer, "Harold Geneen Is Seen as Driving Force behind ITT Switch in Top Management," *WSJ* (July 13, 1979).

129 ". . . try to run the company." Priscilla S. Meyer, "Araskog Emphasizes He Is ITT's Chief," *WSJ* (Aug. 10, 1979), p. 3.

129 ". . . policy differences." "High Politics at ITT," op. cit., p. 32.

130 president and chief executive. Priscilla S. Meyer, "Lyman Hamilton Resigns as ITT President, Chief," *WSJ* (July 12, 1979), p. 2.

130 "... make it my business." "Araskog Emphasizes He Is ITT's Chief," p. 3.

130 consumer-electronics operations. Colvin, op. cit., p. 37.

130 leaving it to Araskog. "ITT Chairman Geneen Intends to Resign January 1," *WSJ* (Nov. 15, 1979), p. 4.

130 deal to ITT. Colvin, op. cit., p. 39.

131 in the Waldorf-Astoria. Ibid.

131 $112,000 a year to his pension. "ITT's Chief Araskog, after Adding a Title, Is Being Paid 47% More," *WSJ* (Mar. 31, 1981).

131 buy out his contract. Priscilla S. Meyer, "Geneen Is Expected to Ask ITT's Board to Buy Out His Contract for $5 Million," *WSJ* (Dec. 12, 1979), p. 12.

131 consumer-electronics businesses. Colvin, op. cit., p. 37.

131 more than forty companies in all. Ibid.

132 "... someone else has built." Stephen J. Sansweet, "Chairman Trautman Finds Greyhound Post a Hot Seat," *WSJ* (Nov. 20, 1980), p. 1.

133 low-margin Armour activities. Ibid.

133 running the company. Alexander Stuart, "Greyhound Gets Ready for a New Driver," *Fortune* (Dec. 15, 1980), p. 59.

134 "... in the future." Barnaby J. Feder, "New Chief Named by Greyhound," *NYT* (Aug. 21, 1981), p. D1.

134 one-seventh of earnings. Paul B. Brown, "Gentlemen, This Is a Bus," *Forbes* (Sept. 27, 1982), p. 70.

134 "... decision not to decide." Stephen J. Sansweet, "Greyhound Taps Batastini as President, Revives Executive Office after 5½ Years," *WSJ* (Nov. 21, 1980), p. 8.

135 in physical combat. Described in Melvin Konner, *The Tangled Wing: Biological Constraints on the Human Spirit* (New York: Holt, Rinehart and Winston, 1982), pp. 39–40.

135 "... to back up the CEO." "After Wriston," *Forbes* (Jan. 3, 1983), p. 262.

135 in San Francisco as chairman. Julie Salamon, "Citicorp Names Three as Vice Chairmen, Extending Their Race to Succeed Wriston," *WSJ* (June 16, 1982), p. 7.

136 the chairman's spot. John Koten, "At Owens-Illinois,

Chairman Has Created Unusually Public Competition for Top Job," *WSJ* (May 25, 1982), p. 33.

136 named someone else as CEO. Andrew Pollack, "RCA Names a President and Likely Heir to Chief," *NYT* (Sept. 8, 1982), pp. D1ff.

138 "... relinquished the reins." "Following the Corporate Legend," *BW* (Feb. 11, 1980), p. 66.

139 all his epaulets. Ibid., p. 65.

139 know all the likely possibilities. John Perham, "Management Succession: A Hard Game to Play," *Dun's Review* (Apr. 1981), p. 54.

139 compete for the job. Ibid., p. 58.

CHAPTER 7

HIS MASTER'S VOICE: RCA and NBC

Page

141 those on board. Milton Moskowitz et al., *Everybody's Business: An Almanac* (New York: Harper & Row, 1980), p. 843.

142 first color-TV sets. Jefferson Grigsby, "RCA: Off the Roller Coaster, onto the Escalator?," *Forbes* (Feb. 15, 1977), p. 26.

142 "... on the *Titanic.*" Sally Bedell, *Up the Tube* (New York: Viking Press, 1981), p. 255.

142 head of the table. *The New Yorker* (Apr. 19, 1982), p. 49.

143 dominated by IBM. "RCA: Still Another Master," *BW* (Aug. 17, 1981), p. 80.

143 almost $500 million. Grigsby, op. cit., p. 26.

143 gave him the ax. Moskowitz et al., op. cit., p. 844.

144 furniture and carpets. "RCA: Still Another Master," p. 80.

144 said he owed. "Conrad Out at RCA; Griffiths New President," *Broadcasting* (Sept. 20, 1976), p. 25.

144 for 1976 alone. "Griffiths, Conrad and Goodman Top RCA Salary Scale," *Broadcasting* (Mar. 14, 1977), p. 62.

144 withdraw a planned offering. "Conrad Out at RCA: Griffiths New President," p. 25.

144 a spectacular turnaround. "The Managers Were Already in Place," *Electronic News* (Nov. 1, 1976), p. 6.

145 until he got paid. Robert J. Flaherty with Anne Bagamery, "Upturn at RCA: It's for Real," *Forbes* (Oct. 27, 1980), p. 138.

145 thinned the employee ranks. "How Ed Griffiths Brought RCA into Focus," Bro Uttal, *Fortune* (Dec. 31, 1978), p. 49.

145 more than twice that. Ibid., p. 48.

146 more than its book value. Laura Landro, "RCA Considered, Then Rejected, Selling CIT Financial as Part of Divestiture Plan," *WSJ* (Jan. 29, 1982).

146 lowered RCA's rating. A. F. Ehrbar, "Splitting Up RCA," *Fortune* (Mar. 22, 1982), p. 66.

146 those who disagreed. "RCA Merger with a 'Sleepy' CIT Produces Yawns on Wall Street," *Broadcasting* (Aug. 27, 1979), p. 29.

146 almost a third. Alice L. Priest, "RCA Chooses Financing over Technology," *BW* (Sept. 3, 1979), p. 88.

146 competitive with the Japanese. Ehrbar, op. cit., p. 62.

147 to $122 million. N. R. Kleinfield, "Fred Silverman's NBC: Still Out of Focus," *NYT* (July 13, 1980), Section 3, p. 1.

147 ". . . overcome the gap." "RCA's Griffiths Gives NBC Goal of Profit Parity with CBS," *Broadcasting* (Nov. 14, 1977), p. 63.

148 out the door. "The Turmoil Awaiting NBC's New President," *BW* (Feb. 6, 1978), pp. 42–43.

148 ". . . like the Messiah." Bedell, op. cit., p. 182.

148 *Eleanor and Franklin.* Bedell, op. cit., p. 221.

149 rose $1.25. "Networks Go Back to Work as Silverman Surprise Begins Wearing Off," *Broadcasting* (Jan. 30, 1978), p. 36.

149 ". . . walk on water." Ellen Graham, "TV Taskmaster: Fred Silverman Wages Uphill Fight as He Bids to Lift NBC Ratings," *WSJ* (Jan. 18, 1979), p. 1.

149 "high expectations." "Griffiths Tells NBC Affiliates Silverman Has Carte Blanche," *Broadcasting* (June 26, 1978), p. 23.

149 "a miracle worker." "NBC Plans Its Climb out of TV's Last Place," *BW* (July 3, 1978), p. 28.

150 "... 'he's a fraud.'" "Silverman Says It Once More: He's Out for Program Quality," *Broadcasting* (July 3, 1978), p. 61.

150 "genuine commitment to quality." "Checking in with the Affiliates," *Broadcasting* (June 19, 1978), p. 44.

151 "... junk on the air." "Taking a Fix on Freddie," *Broadcasting* (June 26, 1978), pp. 69–70.

152 "... more quality efforts." "Pfeiffer Seconds the Motion," *Broadcasting* (Sept. 24, 1979), p. 30.

152 and employee relations. "Jane Pfeiffer Named NBC Chairman," *Broadcasting* (Sept. 18, 1978), p. 28.

152 "... broader view." "NBC's Jane Pfeiffer: Making Overachieving Seem Ever So Easy," *Broadcasting* (Oct. 23, 1978), p. 89.

152 senior vice-president of IBM. "Pfeiffer Seems to Be Highest Paid Female after Move to NBC," *WSJ* (Mar. 7, 1979), p. 29.

153 their male counterparts. "The High Price of NBC's Deal with Its Women," *Broadcasting* (Feb. 21, 1977), pp. 63–64.

153 TV sports coverage. "Schlosser Eschews NBC's Past Glory in Hard Look at Today's Challenges," *Broadcasting* (May 23, 1977), p. 46.

153 except *Roots.* James P. Forkan, "NBC Execs Assuaged by 'Holocaust' Ratings," *Advertising Age* (Apr. 24, 1978), p. 3.

153 "great corporate vehicle." Ibid.

153 get the bad ratings over with. Bedell, op. cit., p. 169.

154 when he got to NBC. "Silverman Putting Distance between Himself and NBC's Second Season," *Broadcasting* (Jan. 29, 1979), p. 51.

154 *Murder on the Orient Express.* Tom Buckley, "TV: 'Supertrain' Chugs," *NYT* (Feb. 8, 1979), p. C18.

154 wholesale firings and resignations. "An Executive Exodus at Hard-Pressed NBC," *BW* (Mar. 26, 1979), p. 28.

155 given in cash. Ralph Blumenthal, "U.S. Is Investigating Alleged Embezzlement at NBC," *NYT* (Mar. 15, 1979), p. C23.

156 conclave in Rome. Ibid.

156 came to more than $4 million. Michael Ver Meulen, "The Corporate Face of Jane Cahill Pfeiffer," *Savvy* (May 1980), p. 30.

156 ". . . with an elephant gun." John E. Cooney, "NBC's Silverman Fires Ex-Ally Pfeiffer as Chairman," *WSJ* (July 9, 1980), p. 2.

157 taped shut behind him. Blumenthal, op. cit.

157 living it up. Les Brown, "Inquiry Focuses on Role of Unit Managers," *NYT* (Mar. 17, 1979), p. 43.

157 "down from the Mount." Ver Meulen, op. cit., p. 27.

157 ". . . heretics get excommunicated." "Rockefeller Center Still Shaking from Pfeiffer Firing," *Broadcasting* (July 14, 1980), p. 23.

158 ". . . toward a Jew." Ver Meulen, op. cit., p. 27.

158 "luster, warmth and charm." "Jane Pfeiffer Named NBC Chairman."

158 about commercial broadcasting. Cooney, op. cit.

158 interfere with programming. Colby Coates, "Silverman's Renewal Seen as Pfeiffer Axed," *Advertising Age* (July 14, 1980), p. 81.

159 stations across the country. Ver Meulen, op. cit., p. 24.

159 "corporate management." "Pfeiffer Seconds the Motion."

159 the year before. "An Executive Exodus at Hard-Pressed NBC," op. cit., pp. 28–29.

160 could charge only $45,000. Bedell, op. cit., p. 254.

160 Lost Horizon Retirement Home. "Program Development Multitude at NBC," *Broadcasting* (Mar. 26, 1979), pp. 118–19.

161 ". . . but there's action." "NBC-TV Emerges Mostly Unscathed after Meeting with Its Stations," *Broadcasting* (Mar. 19, 1979), p. 78.

161 by the end of the year. "Nielsen Numbers Haunt NBC," *Advertising Age* (Apr. 30, 1979), p. 94.

161 ". . . it was just stupid." Bob Marich, "Silverman Hinting at New NBC Look," *Advertising Age* (July 2, 1979), p. 10.

162 NBC would be Number One. "Silverman: Troops Home by Christmas '80," *Broadcasting* (Oct. 29, 1979), p. 31.

163 during the Vietnam War. Bedell, op. cit., pp. 288–89.

163 programs NBC could come up with. James P. Forkan, "NBC Mulls Olympic Fill-In," *Advertising Age* (Apr. 21, 1980), pp. 2ff.

164 operations and engineering. "On the Upside with Fred Silverman," *Broadcasting* (May 19, 1980), p. 33.

164 administrative burden. "Segelstein Adds Stripes," *Broadcasting* (June 9, 1980), p. 24.

164 "... anyone who wants to see me." Tony Schwartz, "NBC Chairman Relieved of Duties Following Refusal to Quit," *NYT* (July 9, 1980), p. 1.

164 "... her employment contract." Ibid.

165 "... duties as chairman." Ibid.

165 "future endeavors." Tony Schwartz, "Mrs. Pfeiffer Officially Quits NBC Position," *NYT* (July 11, 1980), p. D1.

166 to join NBC News. Ibid.

166 "... you shoot somebody." "Messy Firing of Mrs. Pfeiffer Astonishes, Offends—and Entertains," *WSJ* (July 10, 1980), p. 21.

166 "... boss at RCA, Griffiths." "Rockefeller Center Still Shaking from Pfeiffer Firing," p. 22.

166 for $53,000 less. "Griffiths's Last Bow," *Broadcasting* (May 11, 1981), p. 48.

167 yearly bonus of at least $200,000. "RCA Gives Up on Valente as President," *Broadcasting* (June 23, 1980), p. 28.

167 "... needs and objectives." Jeffrey A. Tannenbaum, "RCA Forces President of 6 Months to Quit," *WSJ* (June 19, 1980), p. 2.

168 three consecutive record years. "RCA Gives Up on Valente as President."

171 "... did not meet expectations." "Why Valente Is Out at RCA," *BW* (June 30, 1980), p. 38.

171 "work ethic." "RCA Forces President of 6 Months to Quit."

171 master the complexities of RCA. Jeffrey A. Tannenbaum, "RCA's Valente Tells His Side of Firing," *WSJ* (July 17, 1980), p. 23.

171 "at least partly responsible." "Why Valente Is Out at RCA."

171 offered a contract. "RCA: Still Another Master," p. 86.

172 an additional $250,000. "RCA Paying Dismissed Executives," *NYT* (Mar. 11, 1981).

172 "a personal friend." "RCA Gives Up on Valente as President."

172 five executive vice-presidents. "Griffiths's Last Bow."

173 "... replace him with?" Tony Schwartz, "NBC Extends Silverman's Pact," *NYT* (Sept. 4, 1980), p. C17.

173 "... start each day optimistically." John E. Cooney, "Judgment and Style of NBC's Silverman Near Final Test as Fall Season Approaches," *WSJ* (Aug. 27, 1980), p. 27.

173 pre-Silverman high of $152.6 million. "NBC Reaffirms Faith in Silverman; New TV Entries," *Broadcasting* (Jan. 19, 1981), p. 90.

173 more viewers than *Holocaust.* "Week for 'Shogun' Is Week for NBC," *Broadcasting* (Sept. 29, 1980), p. 60.

173 it bowed out. "NBC Hopes Viewers Visit 'Number 96,'" *Broadcasting* (Dec. 22, 1980), p. 91.

174 less than those for 1978. Ehrbar, op. cit., p. 65.

175 be paid $1.25 million. "RCA Paying Dismissed Executives."

175 would succeed Griffiths. John E. Cooney, "Griffiths's Resignation at RCA Follows Year of Turmoil, Criticism," *WSJ* (Jan. 26, 1981), p. 1.

176 ordered them out. "The Decline and Fall of Fred Silverman," *Broadcasting* (July 6, 1981), pp. 24–25.

176 attention to the matter. Ehrbar, op. cit., p. 76.

176 last full year as chairman. "RCA's Annual Report Shows 28% Profit Drop," *Broadcasting* (Mar. 16, 1981).

CHAPTER 8

AFTER THE FALL

Page

179 "... success and satisfaction." "History Repeats at CBS; Backe Out as President," *Broadcasting* (May 12, 1980), pp. 25–26.

180 "a battle star." Douglas Bauer, "Why Big Business Is Firing the Boss," *NYT Magazine* (Mar. 8, 1981), p. 25.

180 apartment he kept in Rome. Glenn Fowler, "Maurice R. Valente, 54, Dies; A Former President of RCA," *NYT* (Sept. 10, 1983), p. 21.

181 twenty-six-year-old son. Dennis Kneale, "How Third Generation Came to Take Control at Puritan Fashions," *WSJ* (Sept. 6, 1983), p. 1ff.

182 new cable channel. Sally Bedell, "Fred Silverman Producing, and Smiling Again," *NYT* (Apr. 23, 1983).

182 "an incredible sense of injustice and sorrow." Bauer, op. cit., p. 25.

183 "... *Dallas* and *Dynasty.*" Sandra Salmans, "How a Cable Channel Flopped," *NYT* (Feb. 28, 1983), p. D1.

183 president's job at Tomorrow Entertainment. "Former CBS Chief Settles on New Job," *NYT* (July 26, 1981).

183 TV station in Schenectady. "Ex-CBS President Buys Upstate TV Station," *NYT* (Apr. 27, 1983), p. D2.

183 Tamco Enterprises. Geoffrey Colvin, "The De-Geneening of ITT," *Fortune* (Jan. 11, 1982), p. 36.

184 mine is played out. Information on this gold quarry comes from an interview with Roy Ash and from Walter Guzzardi, Jr., "The Huge Find in Roy Ash's Backyard," *Fortune* (Dec. 27, 1982), pp. 48–65.

185 "... your own imagination." Bauer, op. cit., p. 85.

186 smoothing the way. Gil E. Gordon and Ned Rosen, "Critical Factors in Leadership Succession," *Organizational Behavior and Human Performance*, Vol. 27 (1981), p. 232.

186 "... expect him to function." Ibid., p. 236.

187 running the company. Priscilla S. Meyer, "Araskog Emphasizes He Is ITT's Chief," *WSJ* (Aug. 10, 1979), p. 3.

187 resist new leaders. Gordon and Rosen, op. cit., p. 251.

CHAPTER 9

RAISING LAZARUS: Sanford Sigoloff and the Wickes Bankruptcy

Page

189 buy it for $45. "Where Wickes May Find Synergy," *BW* (Dec. 31, 1979), pp. 40ff.

190 loan payment due April 30. "Wickes: Looking to a Turnaround Expert for a Last-Ditch Rescue," *BW* (Apr. 12, 1982), pp. 119–20.

190 loss of $80 million. Ibid., p. 120.

190 at one point in 1981. Ibid.

190 for the executives concerned. Stephen J. Sansweet, "SEC Probes Charges That Ex-Officials of Wickes Issued False Data before Filing," *WSJ* (June 29, 1982), p. 16.

191 $2 million worth of life insurance. Sansweet, op. cit., and "Wickes Cos. Paid New Chief Sigoloff Nearly $1 Million," *WSJ* (May 4, 1983), p. 10.

192 making the unpopular decisions. Donald B. Bibeault, *Corporate Turnaround* (New York: McGraw-Hill, 1982), pp. 95, 143–44.

193 in possession of their maps. Eugene E. Jennings, *Business Week*-Tratec conference on succession planning, New York City (Sept. 15–16, 1981).

194 thirty-six for every hour. Thomas Petzinger, Jr., "Business Failures Hit Post-Depression High; Tide Expected to Swell," *WSJ* (May 24, 1982), p. 1.

194 pay back their $1.6 billion. Stephen J. Sansweet, "Wickes Conveys Hope, Asks 500 Creditors for Patience in Payment of $340 Million," *WSJ* (June 4, 1982), p. 12.

195 bring to such gatherings. Anthony Ramirez, "Wickes Creditors Told to Expect Rough Going," *Los Angeles Times* (June 4, 1982), Section 4, p. 1.

197 that Wickes was not the culprit. Stephen J. Sansweet, "Management Mistakes Plus Old Problems Led to Collapse of Aldens," *WSJ* (Jan. 6, 1983), p. 1.

197 has taken to the television airwaves. "Move over, Lee," *Forbes* (Nov. 8, 1982), p. 238.

199 "... not afraid to use it." Bibeault, op. cit., p. 168.

200 $1 billion a year. Sansweet, "Wickes Conveys Hope, Asks 500 Creditors for Patience in Payment of $340 Million."

201 MacGregor Golf Company. "Wickes Sells Part of Its Golf Unit," *NYT* (Apr. 6, 1982).

201 to Pillsbury. "Wickes Agrees to Sell Unit for $45 Million to Pillsbury Co.," *WSJ* (May 14, 1982), p. 15.

201 dozens of department stores. "Wickes Talks to Creditors," *NYT* (June 4, 1982), p. D10.

201 until "very late." Peter Drucker, *Management: Tasks, Responsibilities, Practices* (New York: Harper & Row, 1974), pp. 680–81.

202 almost no attention to organizational decline. David A. Whetten, "Organizational Decline: A Neglected Topic in Organizational Science," *Academy of Management Review* (1980), Vol. 5, No. 4, pp. 577–88.

202 ". . . forerunner of future growth." Ibid., p. 580.

203 first quarter under Chapter 11. "Wickes Companies," *NYT* (Oct. 4, 1982), p. D10.

203 could last somewhat longer. Stephen J. Sansweet, "Wickes Aims to Emerge from Chapter 11 by Mid-'84, Swap Stock for Unsecured Debt," *WSJ* (Feb. 9, 1983), p. 4.

CHAPTER 10

CHRYSLER'S LAST STAND: Lee Iacocca's Miracle

Page

206 ". . . of the Detroit carmakers." "Statement by L. A. Iacocca, Chairman of the Board, Chrysler Corporation, before the Subcommittee on Economic Stabilization of the Committee on Banking, Finance, and Urban Affairs," U.S. House of Representatives, Washington, D.C. (Apr. 22, 1982).

206 ". . . will not be able to put the company together again." Lawrence R. Gustin, "The Recession Sinks In," *Nation's Business* (July 1980), p. 28.

206 ". . . never been a viable business that has lacked for financing." Julia Vitullo-Martin, "Chrysler in Chaos: Is the Company Beyond Repair?" *Saturday Review* (Jan. 19, 1980), p. 22.

207 "Let's just say I don't like you." Quoted in Michael Moritz and Barrett Seaman, *Going for Broke: The Chrysler Story* (Garden City, N.Y.: Doubleday, 1981), p. 194.

207 "$56 in '56" went national. Ibid., p. 204.

209 another signal that Chrysler couldn't get its act together. Patricia O'Toole, "Chrysler—Now the Good News," *Savvy* (Sept. 1981), p. 67.

210 Iacocca held out for one. Moritz and Seaman, op. cit., pp. 217–18.

210 what a mess Riccardo had made. Moritz and Seaman, op. cit., p. 219.

210 Iacocca knew what he was getting into. Moritz and Seaman, op. cit., pp. 216–17.

210 And so on. Moritz and Seaman, op. cit., pp. 223–25.

211 "put a Ford in your past." Charles B. Camp, "Iacocca Asks Owners of Fords to Follow His Shift to Chrysler," *WSJ* (Mar. 6, 1979), p. 35.

211 when they wanted to hear it. Moritz and Seaman, op. cit., pp. 228, 238.

211 "... *how the hell* we lost a billion dollars." Moritz and Seaman, p. 228.

211 no less than thirty-nine hundred colors. Moritz and Seaman, op. cit., pp. 231–32 and 241.

211 a way to make smaller cars without reducing passenger space. Kathleen K. Wiegner, "Watch What They Do, Not What They Say," *Forbes* (Mar. 17, 1980), p. 70.

212 lost ... $261 million. "Is Chrysler the Prototype?" *BW* (Aug. 20, 1979), p. 123.

212 going to Washington to ask for help. Moritz and Seaman, op. cit., p. 260.

213 lost an even larger part of the car market. Arthur Burck, "Why Auto Companies Are Too Big," *BW* (Nov. 17, 1980), p. 18.

213 a mere 2 percent ... to almost 20 percent. Wiegner, op. cit., p. 69.

213 "... Everything is 'different.' " "Lee Iacocca's Hard Sell for Help," *Time* (Oct. 8, 1979), p. 74.

213 home state of Wisconsin. Juan Cameron, "Chrysler's Quest for Federal Welfare," *Fortune* (Aug. 27, 1979), p. 31.

214 from the jaws of bankruptcy. Moritz and Seaman, op. cit., p. 274.

214 one out of seven jobs. "Detroit: Hitting the Skids," *Newsweek* (Apr. 28, 1980), p. 58.

214 raising the national unemployment level. Stephen Chapman, "No-Fault Capitalism," *New Republic* (Nov. 17, 1979), p. 12.

214 Michigan's unemployment rate [and Detroit's]. Moritz and Seaman, op. cit., p. 279.

214 $2 billion in unemployment benefits. Quoted in "Would America Be Better Off without Chrysler?" ad by Kenyon & Eckhardt.

215 risk losing his life. Moritz and Seaman, op. cit., p. 282.

217 cutting his salary from $360,000 to $1 a year. Andy Pasztor, "Top Chrysler Officials Give Up Salaries, Except $1 a Year, Until Firm is Profitable," *WSJ* (Aug. 31, 1979), p. 2.

218 UAW workers . . . had to agree to a two-year wage freeze. "The Price of Peace at Chrysler," *BW* (Nov. 12, 1979), p. 93.

218 going to have to wait for their money. "Banks Douse the Fire at Chrysler, for Now," *BW* (July 7, 1980), pp. 21–22.

218 sales dried up altogether. Chrysler Corporation, *Report to Shareholders for the Year Ended December 31, 1980*, p. 3.

219 "It's not like buying a sweater . . ." O'Toole, op. cit., p. 71.

219 probably cost . . . fifty cents in sales for every dollar . . . in loans. "Chrysler Talks Back," *Fortune* (Mar. 23, 1981), p. 146.

219 Chrysler would be bankrupt by February. John Koten, "Chrysler's Directors Clear Survival Plan in Start of Bid to Meet Terms for New Aid," *WSJ* (Jan. 15, 1981).

219 had to accept 30 cents on the dollar. "How Aid Plan Developed," *NYT* (Jan. 17, 1981), p. 31.

219 would sell his children. "Chrysler Talks Back."

219 ". . . an oncoming locomotive." Gustin, op. cit., p. 26.

221 average new car selling for $9,370. John Holusha, "Detroit Bows to Sticker Shock," *NYT* (Aug. 5, 1982), p. D5.

222 twenty-seven hundred car dealerships went out of business. "U.S. Auto Makers Reshape for World Competition," *BW* (June 21, 1982), p. 83.

222 sales of American-made cars dropped. Jerry Flint, "Wipe That Sneer," *Forbes* (June 7, 1982), p. 40, and Holusha, op. cit., p. D5.

222 three of every ten. Ibid.

224 "If you can find a better car, buy it." Kenyon & Eckhardt story board (June 2, 1982).

224 ". . . go out and buy a car." Warren Brown, "Iacocca Dislikes TV Role That Boosted Chrysler Sales," *Washington Post* (June 13, 1982).

225 "Admiration goes up directly . . ." Douglas R. Sease,

"Whom Do Businessmen Admire? After 'Nobody,' They Pick Iacocca," *WSJ* (Jan. 18, 1983), p. 33.

226 the company turned a profit. "Chrysler Has Loss of $96 Million; Despite Results in Quarter, '82 Was Profitable," *NYT* (Feb. 25, 1983), p. D1.

226 Without the $348.5 million. Charles W. Stevens, "Chrysler $348.5 Million Sale of Unit Caps Major Effort to Shed Aura of Desperation," *WSJ* (Feb. 22, 1982), p. 14.

226 all $106.9 million of it. "Chrysler Posts 2nd Quarter Net of $106.9 Million," *WSJ* (July 20, 1982), p. 2.

227 sell only 1.1 million cars to break even. John Koten, "Chrysler Reports Operating Profit of $89.2 Million," *WSJ* (Apr. 22, 1983), p. 2.

229 by such a wide margin. Amanda Bennett, "After Three Bad Years, Many Auto Executives See Permanent Scars," *WSJ* (Aug. 16, 1982), p. 1.

229 Ford has considered similar possibilities. Amal Nag, "U.S. Car Industry Has Full-Sized Problems in Subcompact Market," *WSJ* (Jan. 7, 1983), p. 1.

229 ". . . allows a Toyota to be sold for less in Washington . . . than . . . in Tokyo." Iacocca, op. cit., p. 11.

230 fees on American cars entering Japan. O'Toole, op. cit., p. 71.

230 further reducing the demand for automobiles. "Why Detroit Is Not Selling Cars," *BW* (Aug. 30, 1982), p. 63.

230 could permanently shrink . . . the market. John Schnapp, "America Breaks Off Its Romance with the Car," *WSJ* (Feb. 28, 1983), p. 20.

231 courtesy of tax-loss carry-forwards. Koten, op. cit.

231 salary and bonus of $366,000. "How America's Top Moneymakers Fared in the Recession," *BW* (May 9, 1983), p. 85.

231 another 100,000. "Iacocca's Sweet Rewards," *BW* (Dec. 26, 1983), p. 34.

231 early repayment. John Holusha, "Chrysler to Repay Loan Early," *NYT* (May 6, 1983), p. D1.

231 resulted from closing so many plants. John Koten, "Chrysler to Buy Volkswagen's Michigan Plant," *WSJ* (Apr. 8, 1983), p. 4.

233 "People work hardest when they understand a goal and believe in it." O'Toole, op. cit., pp. 70–71.

233 pension liabilities of $1.5 billion. John Holusha, "Iacocca Rides High in Detroit," *NYT* (Aug. 29, 1982), Section 3, p. 1.

233 agreement with the UAW. "Can Chrysler Keep Its Comback Rolling?" *BW* (Feb. 14, 1983), p. 133.

233 ". . . desperate self-seeking." Eric Hoffer, *The True Believer* (New York: Harper & Row, 1951 [Perennial Library edition, 1966]), p. 68.

234 ". . . individual lives untenable." Ibid., p. 104.

234 results that benefit the group. Gil E. Gordon and Ned Rosen, "Critical Factors in Leadership Succession," *Organizational Behavior and Human Performance* (Apr. 1981), p. 237.

CHAPTER 11

UNHOLY GRAILS: Number Worship, the Japanese Shrine, and Technorapture

Page

235 realizing the vision. Abraham Zaleznik, "Managers and Leaders: Are They Different?" *Harvard Business Review* (May–June 1977), pp. 67–78.

235 leaders should have. Michael Maccoby, *The Leader* (New York: Simon & Schuster, 1981).

236 ". . . exhilaration of victory." Ibid., p. 19.

236 survival in hard times. "Good Leaders Aren't Perfect" (interview with Michael Maccoby), *Inc.* (Jan. 1982), pp. 76–80.

236 "charisma" and "vision." Walter Kiechel III, "Wanted: Corporate Leaders," *Fortune* (May 30, 1983), p. 135.

237 ". . . outstanding successes." Quoted in John Naisbitt, *Megatrends: Ten New Directions Transforming Our Lives* (New York: Warner Books, 1982), p. 83.

238 ". . . temporary tax advantages." Charles Georgeson, "M.B.A., Ideally: M(ore) B(asic) A(nalysis)," *NYT* (Aug. 31, 1982).

240 the right numbers. Richard L. Hudson, "SEC Charges Fudging of Corporate Figures Is a Growing Practice," *WSJ* (June 2, 1983), p. 1.

240 when change is called for. Thomas J. Peters and Robert H. Waterman, Jr., *In Search of Excellence* (New York: Harper & Row, 1982), pp. 44–50.

241 ". . . crisp directives." Robert Reich, "The Next American Frontier," *Atlantic Monthly* (Mar. 1983), p. 51.

241 ". . . look like a nail." Quoted in Daniel B. Moskowitz, "Is Life with Computers Insidious?" (review of David Burnham, *The Rise of the Computer State* [New York: Random House, 1983]), *BW* (July 11, 1983), p. 14.

242 "eternal employment." Terumoto Ozawa, "Japanese Chic," *Across the Board* (Oct. 1982), pp. 6–13.

242 cut stockholder dividends instead of employee payrolls. James N. Ellenberger, "Japanese Management: Myth or Magic," *AFL-CIO American Federationist* (Apr.–June 1982), pp. 10–11.

243 short-term performance, "Japan Inc. Goes International with High Technology," *BW* (Dec. 14, 1981), p. 41.

243 considered expendable. Ozawa, op. cit.

243 ". . . earsplitting noise." From an account by Robert C. Wood, quoted in Ellenberger, op. cit., pp. 6–7.

244 life expectancy. Peter F. Drucker, "Clouds Forming across the Japanese Sun," *WSJ* (July 13, 1982).

244 at lower pay. Ellenberger, op. cit., p. 6.

244 in another organization. Ozawa, op. cit.

244 better jobs elsewhere. B. Bruce-Briggs, "Lifetime Employment: A Non-Lesson from Japan," *WSJ* (Aug. 2, 1982), p. 14.

245 keep factories running smoothly. Robert H. Hayes, "Why Japanese Factories Work," *Harvard Business Review* (July–August 1981), p. 64.

245 could not import . . . or export. "Japan Inc. Goes International with High Technology," p. 40.

245 no longer legally binding. Ibid.

245 subsidized because of political pressures. Steven Ross, "What Is Japan, and What Is Not Japan?" *Business and Society Review* (Spring 1980–81), p. 36.

245 Japanese National Railroad, Drucker, op. cit.

246 ". . . highways and highway construction." Peter F. Drucker, "Behind Japan's Success," *Harvard Business Review* (Jan.–Feb. 1981), pp. 84–85.

246 takes General Motors. Ross, op. cit., p. 35.

246 four times greater. Ellenberger, op. cit., p. 4.

246 increases in Japanese productivity have slowed. Drucker, "Clouds Forming across the Japanese Sun."

246 their Japanese counterparts. John Holusha, "Japan's Leadership among Car Makers Facing Tests Abroad," *NYT* (Apr. 1, 1983), pp. A1ff.

246 "... writing letters or reading novels." Arthur S. Golden, "Group Think in Japan Inc.," *NYT Magazine* (Dec. 5, 1982), p. 137.

246 the standard workweek. Ellenberger, op. cit., p. 6.

246 workweek is getting shorter. Robert C. Christopher, "Changing Face of Japan," *NYT Magazine* (Mar. 27, 1983), p. 87.

247 well below 3 percent. Henry Scott Stokes, "Jobless Rate Reaches a High for Japan," *NYT* (Mar. 9, 1983), p. D9.

247 robots will not lead to layoffs. Steve Lohr, "Labor in Japan Cools to Robots," *NYT* (Mar. 12, 1983), p. 31.

247 Labor Ministry vetoed the idea. Ibid.

247 did not reduce quality. Hayes, op. cit., p. 58.

248 have bothered with them. Robert E. Cole, "A Japanese Management Import Comes Full Circle," *WSJ* (Feb. 22, 1983), p. 30.

248 something for nothing. Cole, "QC Warning Voiced by U.S. Expert on Japanese Circles," *World of Work Report* (July 1981), pp. 49ff.

248 "... Japanese do everything better." Cole, "A Japanese Management Import Comes Full Circle."

248 Sanyo was better. Ellenberger, op. cit., p. 7.

248 labor union magazine. See Ellenberger, op. cit., pp. 3–12.

249 U.S. workers ... more satisfied. "Who's Happy Now?" *Forbes* (Apr. 25, 1983), p. 8.

249 desired patterns. William M. Ringle, "The American Who Remade 'Made in Japan,' " *Nation's Business* (Feb. 1981), pp. 69–70.

250 "... operating as it should." Hayes, op. cit., p. 57.

250 life of factory equipment. Hayes, op. cit., p. 60.

250 routine maintenance. Hayes, op. cit., p. 59.

250 stop the line. Ross, op. cit., p. 35.

250 tailored precisely to their needs. Hayes, op. cit., pp. 64–65.

250 ". . . work it out together." L. Erik Calonius, "In a Plant in Memphis, Japanese Firm Shows How to Attain Quality," *WSJ* (Apr. 29, 1983), pp. 1ff.

251 accountants and lawyers. Hayes, op. cit., p. 65.

251 ". . . between our two countries." "Shinto: Why the U.S. Can't Compete in Japan," *BW* (Dec. 14, 1981), p. 44.

252 loyalty and hard work. Ozawa, op. cit.

253 ". . . worker individuality and judgment." "High Tech May Reduce Job Skills, Stanford Educators Say," Stanford University news release (Mar. 21, 1983).

253 Hong Kong and Taiwan. "What Sent Atari Overseas," *BW* (Mar. 14, 1983), p. 102.

254 factory of the past. Karen Nussbaum, executive director of 9 to 5, speaking at Columbia University conference "Restructuring Work: Alternatives for the 80s" (June 11, 1982).

255 under the electronic whip. "Monitoring Workers by Computer," *BW* (Aug. 9, 1982), p. 62H.

255 "the potential for alienation is enormous." Nussbaum, op. cit.

255 "designer genes." A pun the author owes to her friend Jim O'Brien.

256 ". . . don't have the money to buy it." Danforth W. Austin and J. Ernest Beazley, "Struggling Industries in Nation's Heartland Speed up Automation," *WSJ* (Apr. 4, 1983), pp. 1ff.

256 investment in the future. Carol Hymowitz, "Manufacturers Press Automating to Survive, but Results Are Mixed," *WSJ* (Apr. 11, 1983), pp. 1ff.

256 machines talk to each other. Ibid.

257 ". . . build and maintain the robot ranks." Patricia O'Toole, "Finding Work in Glutted Fields," *Money* (Mar. 1983), pp. 67–72.

257 agree to locate there. "America Rushes to High Tech for Growth," *BW* (Mar. 28, 1983), pp. 84–90.

257 woo high-tech. Hal Lancaster, "Chicago Bids for Piece of the Technology Pie," *WSJ* (Apr. 18, 1983), pp. 1ff.

257 "the premature arrival of the future." Alvin Toffler, *Previews and Premises* (New York: William Morrow, 1983), p. 2.

CHAPTER 12

THE NEXT MESSIAHS

Page

259 Apple stock. "California Bound: A Pepsi Man for Apple," *Fortune* (May 16, 1983), p. 7.

259 worth $10 million. "Philip Morris's Marlboro Man Switches over to Pac-Man," *NYT* (July 24, 1983), pp. F6–F7.

259 one of them. Robert L. Heilbroner, *The Worldly Philosophers* (New York: Touchstone/Simon & Schuster, 1980), pp. 230–31.

260 divestitures rose 31 percent. Jeffrey Madrick, "Cutting Loose: The Drive to Divest," *NYT* (July 3, 1983), p. F1.

260 "... change in the concepts themselves." "Harvard's Search for a Fountain of Youth" (excerpts from William J. Abernathy, Kim B. Clark, and Alan M. Kantrow, *Industrial Renaissance: Producing a Competitive Future for America* [New York: Basic Books, 1983]), *NYT* (June 5, 1983), p. F2.

260 "... almost overnight." Rosemary Brady, "The Wave of the Future," *Forbes* (Dec. 20, 1982), p. 142.

Index